YUGOSLAV
POPULAR BALLADS

T0371415

VUK STEFANOVIĆ KARADŽIĆ

YUGOSLAV POPULAR BALLADS

THEIR ORIGIN AND DEVELOPMENT

BY

DRAGUTIN SUBOTIĆ

Reader in Serbo-Croat in the
University of London

CAMBRIDGE

AT THE UNIVERSITY PRESS

1932

CAMBRIDGE
UNIVERSITY PRESS

University Printing House, Cambridge CB2 8BS, United Kingdom

Cambridge University Press is part of the University of Cambridge.

It furthers the University's mission by disseminating knowledge in the pursuit of education, learning and research at the highest international levels of excellence.

www.cambridge.org
Information on this title: www.cambridge.org/9781107437760

© Cambridge University Press 1932

First published 1932
First paperback edition 2014

A catalogue record for this publication is available from the British Library

ISBN 978-1-107-43776-0 Paperback

Contents

Preface

THE aim of this book is to revive, and possibly widen, the interest of the British people in a subject which, under the name of *Serbian popular ballads*, they thought worthy of their attention throughout the greater part of the nineteenth century, and which, having lost none of its beauty, will, I trust, still prove attractive for them under its new name.

In tracing translations of the Yugoslav popular poetry in Germany, France and England, I have limited myself to the nineteenth century. Several collections of Serbian ballads were published during the War, in both English and French, partly to enlist sympathy for Serbia and partly as a result of the interest which the British and French peoples took in the Serbs, but these have not been included in this book.

Of all the collections that have appeared in the present century, but do not come within the scope of the war and propaganda literature, special attention and praise are merited by the two excellent works, *Heroic Ballads of Serbia*, translated by George Rapall Noyes and Leonard Bacon, Boston, 1913, and *The Ballads of Marko Kraljević*, translated by D. H. Low, published by the Cambridge University Press in 1921. By kind permission of their authors a few ballads have been reprinted here.

Although practically all the works that have been consulted are indicated, either in the text, or at the end of the book, and although my indebtedness to scholars whose opinions I have quoted has been, I hope, acknowledged, I realise that I have not always been able to separate my own views and conclusions from those of others in referring to my numerous notes.

For the second part of this book, in particular the first two chapters of it, I am largely indebted to the works of Dr Milan Ćurčin and Dr Voyslav M. Yovanovitch, mentioned in the list of "Books Consulted", but, in following my own investigation, I have turned to original sources whenever possible and brought out new facts, especially in the last chapter.

In the spelling of Slav names the present Yugoslav spelling has been adhered to, but there are, nevertheless, certain inconsistencies (there is one in the previous paragraph) as I have thought it necessary sometimes to retain the form of spelling adopted by the author himself, or that which, through long usage, has become familiar. The word "Yugoslav" has intentionally been spelt throughout this book with a Y, instead of a J, in order that the reader should not pronounce such curious and comic names as " Jewgoslav," or " Juggoslav," which are heard, unfortunately, too often. It seems futile to expect the average Englishman to pronounce J as Y in any combination of letters. Besides, it should be noted that the Yugoslavs themselves write *Jugoslavija*, not Jugoslavia, and, therefore, if one is to be absolutely consistent in the use of their spelling, what an eyesore the word " Jugoslavija" would be to the English reader, to say nothing of its pronunciation!

This book has been written, as the reader, no doubt, will notice, over a period of several years, and a part of it

was submitted for a degree to the University of Oxford
some time since. While engaged on it, I benefited by the
advice of the late Professor Nevill Forbes, whom I remember with gratitude. I owe sincere thanks also to
several friends for their occasional assistance, and to the
staff of the British Museum for their unfailing courtesy
and efficiency.

Professor R. W. Seton-Watson has very kindly allowed
me to use his translations of three heroic songs, while
Dr W. A. Morison has been good enough to translate for
me four others. My special thanks are due to them.

D. P. S.

LONDON, *St George's Day* 1932

Note on Pronunciation

c like *ts* in *lots*.

ć a sound between the English *t* in *tune* and *ch* in *chalk*.

č like *ch* in *church*.

đ a sound between the English *d* in *dune* and *j* in *John*.

j like *y* in *yes*.

lj like *lli* in *million*.

nj like *gn* in *Boulogne*.

s like *sh* in *ship*.

ž like *s* in *pleasure*.

dž like *j* in *John*.

The vowels are all pronounced 'openly' as in Italian.

Introduction

I T is generally recognised that the term "popular ballads" implies a number of conflicting theories, both as to the meaning of the words themselves and as regards the origin of such poetry. Professor Francis Gummere, in discussing the question of popular ballads, has pointed out that the word "ballad" has always had a loose meaning, having been used to denote "sundry shorter poems, lyrics of whatever purpose, hymns, 'flytings', political satires, mawkish stories in verse, sensational journalism of Elizabethan days and even the translation of Solomon's Song". He admits, however, that in recent times the term "popular ballads" denotes only the poetry that is included under the name of the *English and Scottish Popular Ballads*, as illustrated in the collection of Francis James Child, and the similar poetries of other nations. Therefore, the Spanish *romances*, the German *Volkslieder*, the Danish *Folkeviser*, the Russian *byliny*, the Ukrainian *dumy*, the Yugoslav *narodne pesme*, and all the poetry of "popular origin" that exists among many other peoples, come under this heading.

The word "popular" has been used to mean something created by and belonging to the people, but it is misleading in so far as it reminds one of the old theory that popular ballads were a collective production of the people as a whole. For this reason, and because of the fact that, in spite of a fundamental similarity of all popular ballads, a considerable variety exists between the poetries which this term covers in its wider meaning, some students of this subject have substituted the word "traditional" for the word "popular", taking it to mean "handed on by word of mouth from generation to generation".

The term "traditional poetry" appears to be more suitable and applies most fittingly to the type of poetry we propose to treat here, namely the Yugoslav *narodne pesme*, i.e. the people's songs, their heroic songs, or the *junačke pesme*, in particular. We shall, therefore, use this term whenever referring to these while, however, not rejecting the term "popular ballads".

Whichever term we use, we use it to mean, in the first place, narrative poetry, frequently based upon history or historical events, created mainly by individual members of an unlettered community, which has preserved it by oral tradition through several centuries. Such narrative poems are expressed—either by singing, chanting or reciting—in a particular way, which is characteristic only of traditional poetry, regardless of the language and the place in which it is produced. Its distinctive features are first a simple, disinterested manner in which a report is given of a definite event; secondly, a marked negligence of poetical form, to such an extent that the matter practically overshadows the manner; and lastly a complete freedom from didacticism in any form and an indifference to moral conclusions; events are reported in all their crudeness, and ruthless actions receive no justification.

The traditional poetry of all European countries, and perhaps of most others, possesses many similar themes and common features of style, structure, subject and idea. This likeness is due principally to the fact that the essential characteristics of human nature are alike everywhere, and also because many legends and folk-tales, common in the distant past to most peoples of Europe and Asia, served as sources from which themes for popular ballads were drawn. The late Professor W. P. Ker, in dealing with this subject, so far as the Romance and Germanic peoples are concerned, pointed to the common stock of the popular ballads in France, Languedoc, Piedmont and Catalonia, rightly placing the *romances* of Castile in a class by themselves, these having had a history and growth of their own, different from the popular ballads of other Romance peoples. The Portuguese ballads belong mostly to the French group, while the Italian are, in his opinion, almost pure lyric, except in the north. It might be added here that the remaining Romance ballad poetry, that of the Rumanians, which Professor Ker does not mention, shows a marked likeness to the traditional poetries of the Slavs, by which it is much influenced—by the Ukrainian and the Bulgarian in particular.

In speaking of the ballads of the Germanic peoples, Professor Ker distinguishes between three groups: English, Danish and German; and he mentions, among others, a point which is of special interest to us here. Roughly speaking, he says that, at the time when the Danish ballads came into being, there was nothing in Danish literature to depreciate and overshadow the ballads, as was the case in the Italy of Dante and the England of Chaucer; there were no troubadours or minnesingers. The conditions in Denmark, under which its popular ballads grew and developed, remind us of those which prevailed among the Yugoslavs at the time in which we believe their heroic ballads to have come into existence, in so far as, among them too, there was practically no literature and, to use Professor Ker's words concerning Denmark, "there was room for the ballads and the ballads took up all the room".

Danish and Yugoslav popular ballads differ, however, greatly in their respective "popular features". In the case of the former, they were not derived from the Danish "populace" in the sense in which the Yugoslav ballads originated from the "people". It is now generally agreed that Danish ballads were "originally and for long the pastime of the gentry", that in the sixteenth and seventeenth centuries many ladies of noble stock copied them out, and that it was through the favour of the queen that they were first published. Since, in addition to the gentlefolk, no one else cultivated literature and since, therefore, the imaginative life of Denmark in the Middle Ages was all of the kind which is called "popular", Professor Ker, while admitting the possibility of the argument that the "populace" of Denmark of that period might be identified with the whole nation, gives a warning that the term "populace" or "people" does not mean, either in Denmark or in Castile, the cottagers, the peasants and the wayfaring men. It is in this respect that an essential difference arises between the Danish and the Yugoslav popular ballads, for it is precisely the peasants whom the term people includes on the territory of the Yugoslavs. These peasants did not belong to the rank of ordinary gentlefolk, nor were they boorish: they were an intelligent mountaineer people.

Among the Slavs, the Serbo-Croats, the Bulgarians, the Ukrainians and the Russians are the only peoples who

possess a real national epic, similar, in the first place, to
the Castilian *romances* and also, to a certain extent, to the
French *chansons de geste*, as well as to the type of epics
produced among the Germanic peoples during the Heroic
Age. The Czechoslovaks, the Poles and the Slovenes have
only popular ballads and epic songs of legendary contents,
of the type of the Romance and Teutonic peoples which,
naturally, exist also among all the other Slavs. It is probable that the difference between the traditional poetry of
the two groups of the Slavs is largely due to the historical
and social conditions under which they lived at the time
when their respective poetries were being shaped.

It has been observed that in three different parts of
Europe, where a centuries-long struggle existed between
the Christians and the Moslems, the former created a particular type of traditional poetry, which is included in the
term "popular ballads" but which differs in many respects
from the popular poetry generally defined by this term.
We refer to Spain and the Castilian *romances*, to the Balkan
Peninsula and the Serbo-Croat (and also Bulgarian)
junačke pesme, and to South Russia and the Ukrainian
dumy. The Christians' adversaries in these regions were
the Moslems, the Arabs, the Turks and the Tartars and,
confronted with this fact, one would naturally be inclined
to think that the traditional poetry of the Moslem peoples
is in some way connected with the origin of the heroic
poetry of the Christians. But students of Arab, Turkish
and Persian traditional poetries, on the last of which that
of the Ottoman Turks is founded, have shown that,
although abundant, there is nothing in them that corresponds to the popular heroic poems created by the Chris-

tians. Oriental scholars maintain that the Moslem mind possesses very little imaginative and inventive power and appears to be devoid of originality so far as literary productions are concerned. This applies especially to the Arabs, for in their literature there is nothing of epic character; it is exclusively lyrical and descriptive. Their poetry, like that of the Persians, is intensely *subjective*; their poets describe what they see and feel, but they produce nothing original. The Turks, who blindly imitated Persian poetry, reproduced all the monotony of the everlasting subjects of moon, beauty, roses and nightingales, and all the wearisome repetitions of stock epithets and stock associations. Yet, contrary to the Arabs and the Persians, the Turkish poetry of popular origin shows a certain amount of objectivity which brings it nearer to the popular ballads of Christian peoples. There is, however, nothing in any of these Moslem popular poetries which shows the epic spirit of the Christian heroic songs. The latter stand by themselves and having had a common foe and a common cause—namely, the victory of the Cross over the Crescent—they naturally possess a common likeness in their tone and their spirit, a characteristic rare in the traditional poetries of other peoples.

PART I

Chapter One
Yugoslav Traditional Poetry

I

AT one time the view was held among a number of scholars, and perhaps still is, that the traditional heroic poetry current among the Croats was not created by them, but that it arrived from Serbia with the numerous aristocratic families which had fled towards the north-west, into Croatia and Dalmatia, before the Turkish invasion. Although founded on the fact that the so-called Croat heroic ballads—which were discovered by the prominent Slav scholar, F. Miklosich—glorify not, as one would expect, Croat but Serb national heroes, this statement, as will be shown further on, cannot hold its ground. The existing traditional heroic songs of both the Serbs and the Croats must be regarded as their joint property. The Slovenes, who had been subjugated by the Germans for over a thousand years, and who have never had a chance of fighting for and obtaining their own freedom, have had no material for epic poetry of a national character. The wars with the Turks and the proximity of the Croats and the Serbs caused the fame of their heroes to penetrate right up into the Slovene mountains; hence they glorify the Serbo-Croat national heroes. In quality and

quantity the Slovene popular ballads of epic character do
not approach those of the Serbs and Croats; hardly any of
them consist of more than two hundred lines. On the
other hand, their lyric traditional songs are rich and beautiful; there are many thousands of them, and in quality
they rank with the most beautiful popular ballads.

In comparing the traditional poetry of the Serbo-Croats
with that of the other Slavs, some critics have maintained
that the heroic songs of the former are superior to either
the Russian or the Bulgarian epic poetry. The Russian
literary historian, Alexander Nikolaevitch Pypin, declared
about fifty years ago that no traditional poetry of the
Slavs, or of any other European people, showed so rich a
development as that of the Serbs. The Russians and the
Bulgars possess such poetry, but none shows so great an
abundance of songs, nor so great a living creative power, as
the Serbs—the reason, in his opinion, lying in the specially
energetic character of the Serbs and the nature of their
national history. The Russian *byliny* and the Ukrainian
dumy are similar to the Serbo-Croat *junačke pesme*. The likeness between a number of *byliny* and the *junačke pesme* is
remarkable, to mention only the *pesma* on *Marko and Musa*
and the *duma* on *Prince Vladimir and Ilija Muromec*. In
each case the respective heroes, Marko and Ilija, linger in
prisons for years before they are called upon to fight an
adversary: Prince Vladimir in the case of the Russian
ballad, and the Sultan in that of the Serbian. In each case
the heroes ask for time in which to get into condition for
the fight and, of course, in each case they come out of it
victorious. There is also a great likeness between the Serbian hero Banović Strahinja and the Russian Ivan Godi-

nović, and there is a whole series of motifs common to both, as well as to the traditional poetry of most other European peoples.[1]

Similarity with the Ukrainian *dumy* is especially marked through the fact that their heroes are, like those of the Yugoslav heroic songs, historical persons. The events, too, are historical and in them are related the wars between the Ukrainians on the one side and the Turks, the Tartars and the Poles on the other.

As regards the Bulgarian traditional poetry, although it cannot rank in beauty with the *dumy*, the *byliny*, or the *junačke pesme*, its likeness to the last-named is very great, and is due not only to the sameness of natural surroundings and the similarity of their poetical and social life, but also to a direct influence of the Serbian heroic poetry, with the result that the hero of the Serbs, Marko Kraljević, is glorified also in the Bulgarian heroic song. Many historical persons who figure in the Serbian heroic songs appear also in those of the Bulgars, and the Bulgarian songs of epic character can be understood only if studied comparatively with the heroic songs of the Serbs. Pypin has stated that it is in the Serbian heroic songs that we find in a full light those heroes who figure in Bulgarian epic poetry in a dim light and mostly in distorted memory. The Bulgarian epic songs must, therefore, constantly be completed by those of the Serbs, and although the former, so far as the age and the completeness of historical tradition go, remain behind the latter, in epic motifs as well as in epic forms, the Bulgarian heroic poetry fully matches that of the Serbs. Those who would seek in these the "fruitfulness, abundance, grace,

[1] Maretić, T. (See "Books Consulted".)

tenderness, softness" of the purely Serbian heroic ballads
would find in them only "simplicity, which borders on
coarseness, profundity, vigour and greater brevity".

II

In the Yugoslav traditional poetry we distinguish between
the women's songs, *ženske pesme*, and the men's, or heroic
songs, *muške* or *junačke pesme*. The latter group is subdivided, from the point of view of the verse, into the heroic
songs of the "short verse", the *deseterac*, i.e. the verse of
ten syllables, and the heroic songs of the "long verse",
of fifteen or sixteen syllables. These are called the *bugarštice*, a word probably derived from the verb *bugariti*, to
chant. The women's songs were, and still are, sung chiefly
by women, for the sake of their own distraction, either as
solos, as duets, or in choirs; but they are sometimes sung
also by young men, and in each case the singing is not
accompanied by any instrument. The heroic songs were
chanted, though now rarely, by men, to the accompaniment of a simple instrument called the *gusle*; a one-stringed
fiddle with deeply rounded body, held upright on the
knees when played upon. They were chanted by the *guslari*,
the national bards, not for their own pleasure but for the
pleasure of an audience.

The two groups are distinguished as lyric and epic songs
respectively. All the women's songs are regarded as lyric
songs, but the contents of such songs may sometimes have
an epic touch. All the men's, or heroic, songs, on the
other hand, are invariably epic in character; they glorify
men, heroes and their deeds. In the women's songs it is
the singing that is the end in itself, while in that of the

heroic songs it is a means to an end, namely the description of some event.

As to the theme and subjects treated in this poetry, we have to remember that the *ženske pesme*, being similar to most other popular ballads, speaking generally, deal with all subjects that are common to such poetry, but they are chiefly concerned with all phases and incidents of family and social life, and we know that in this poetry passion, whether expressed in love or hatred, is very prominent. The *ženske pesme* naturally deal with love in the wide sense of the word. Physical passion and courtship in general are, however, almost invariably expressed indirectly, being described delicately, a feature rather remarkable in this type of poetry. The feelings described are, on the whole, pure and chaste and are conveyed discreetly and in a delicate manner; they are expressed sometimes in the form of flirting, but mostly in a desire for marriage; consequently marriage and wedding songs are numerous, while customs practised on such occasions are beautifully described. Among the wedding songs, the best are those in which a maiden's departure from home and her parting from her mother are depicted. Mutual sorrow is intermingled with the girl's joy for her future life.

The feelings of love are very strong and there are songs which describe how even death cannot separate two lovers: plants grow over their graves and their branches twine round each other—a motif common in the popular ballads of many peoples. The feelings of love for members of the family are particularly strong. A mother's love for her children, and then a sister's love for her brothers, figure most prominently: a sister often sacrifices her lover for her brother. Janja, who was married to Paul, far away, not having seen her brothers for three years, was seized with such longing for them that, when they finally came to visit her, she managed only to kiss one, embrace another, and sink dead on the breast of the third.

Yet parallel to the strongest possible love there runs the strongest possible hatred when feelings are aroused. A sister poisons her sister, or her brother, when they stand in the way of her love; two brothers fight to the death to win a girl; a son kills his mother to win his wife's love, takes his mother's heart and carries it to her, but, stumbling on his way, he falls, and, in order to show how boundless a mother's love is, the song tells us that the mother's heart speaks and asks the son: "My boy, did you hurt yourself?". A step-mother is seldom on good terms with her daughter-in-law and is always cruel to her step-daughter, but a brother-in-law and his sister-in-law are invariably the best of friends. The father is rarely mentioned and he is, as a rule, well disposed towards his daughter-in-law. On the whole, sad and tragic motifs prevail in women's songs, which deal with love and family life, over the gay and joy-ful ones. According to a national proverb, "joy drops in ounces, and sorrow in loads" in these songs.[1]

Although the feelings of hatred and revenge run very high, there are also beautiful illustrations of magnanimous sacrifice. Fair Neda, in order to marry her brother-in-law, poisons her own sister and becomes step-mother of her two boys. The elder, in speaking to the younger, expresses his desire that they should grow up and help their aunt

[1] Professor J. Prodanović has made a special study of the *Ženske narodne pesme*. (See "Books Consulted".)

carry water. Nevertheless, she poisons them and buries both in the garden, where they will be trodden upon. But from the boys' graves two basil plants grow and they tell each other that when they have grown the aunt will use their flowers to adorn herself. The aunt, however, picked the plants and threw them on the rubbish heap; but there they grew into two pine trees, and they were anxious to grow big in order to provide shade for their aunt in summer and protect her from the cold winds of winter. The aunt, nevertheless, cut down the young pines and threw them on the fire, whereupon one of the boys spoke to the other: "Burn, my brother, let us burn, so that our aunt may warm herself".[1]

The relation between the *ženske pesme* and the everyday life of the Yugoslavs is so close that practically every possible incident of it finds an appropriate description. The variety of themes in these songs is practically endless. Persons of both sexes and all ages play rôles in them, and their every kind of work, their every action, is reflected in them. Whether people are gathered together at a church festival, or men enjoy their food and drink; whether boys and girls are engaged in gathering corn, or women are spinning round the open fireplaces; whether mothers are journeying to the graves of their children, or youths are dancing a *kolo* on the village green; whether a girl is talking to a nightingale, or a lonely traveller is passing through a forest, these songs accompany every action and event of the people, and it is rightly said that a Yugoslav lives his poetry.

The women's songs are interesting not only for the

[1] J. Prodanović.

variety of the subjects they treat, but also because many of these subjects are described in beautiful, poetical figures and unexpected turns, in a rich language, abundant in poetical phrases. They are remarkable also for their aesthetic sense, expressed as a rule in a brief but surprisingly appropriate reference to natural beauty: to the mountains, the forest and trees, the flowers and birds, the sky and the stars, the sun and the moon. The beauty of young men and girls is described with much taste, and the ideal of a beautiful girl is that she should be tall and slender, have rosy cheeks and dark, big eyes, long, thin and arching eyebrows, long eyelashes, small white teeth and thick, dark hair.

III

The Yugoslav traditional poetry is best known in the collection of Vuk Stefanović Karadžić, who is perhaps the most remarkable man in Yugoslav literature. He was born in a village in Serbia, near the Bosnian frontier, in 1787, when Serbia was still a Turkish province. His parents had five children before him, but all of them died while young. The Serbian peasant people believed, in those days, that, when children die young, witches eat them. To prevent witches eating their sixth child, the parents called him Vuk, which means wolf, because witches are supposed to be afraid of wolves. And indeed, Vuk not only survived his childhood, but even reached the age of 77. When Serbia was being liberated, from 1804 till 1813, he did some clerical work for the Government. On the reconquest of the country by the Turks in 1813, he went to Austria and settled in Vienna. Here were already a number of Serbs, and a young group of them, interested in literary matters.

began publishing in August of the same year a newspaper in Serbian. Its editors were anxious to form a centre of young men round this paper; they therefore sought out Vuk. A young Slovene, Jernej (Bartolomeus) Kopitar, about seven years senior to Vuk, was also in close touch with this group of Serbs, by virtue of the post of Government Censor for Slavonic languages which he held at that time. He had known some Serbian undergraduates and been interested in the Serbian language and the Serbian traditional poetry from his early sojourn in Vienna in 1808. In June of 1813 he expressed the wish that a Serb could be found who would write a Serbian grammar to enable the Germans to listen to the Serbian muse without an interpreter. Towards the end of 1813, an article which Vuk wanted to publish in the Serbian newspaper reached Kopitar in his capacity as Censor. The article was written in the language which the simple, unlettered Serbs spoke and in which they chanted their traditional songs. It should be remembered that this language was despised by most Serbian literary men of those days, as the language of shepherds and swineherds; the language they used was a mixture of Russian Church Slavonic and Old Serbian. On reading Vuk's article, Kopitar knew that he had found his man. He called on Vuk to make his acquaintance. The meeting of Kopitar, who was about thirty-three, and Vuk, who was but twenty-six, was of very great importance to Serbian literature. It has often been said that if it had not been for Kopitar there would have been no Vuk, for Kopitar was the driving power behind him. Vuk, when he came to Vienna, brought with him a keen intelligence, an active mind and a strong desire to learn, but it was Kopitar

who made a scholar out of him. The result of their con-
versations during the winter months was that Vuk wrote
down from memory more than one hundred traditional
songs which he had heard in his native village.

These were published in Vienna at the beginning of
August, 1814, under the title of the *Pesnarica*, lit. "book of
songs".

Having published the first volume of traditional songs
and a small grammar of the Serbian language, Vuk went
to southern Hungary for the purpose of collecting songs
from the lips of Serbian fugitives. He found among them
two remarkable men: a blind *guslar*, Filip Višnjić, and a
former *hajduk*, or guerilla leader, Tešan Podrugović, a
Serb of Bosnia. While the fight for the liberation of Serbia
went on, the latter took part in it, but on Serbia's fall in
1813 he fled to Austria. Vuk found him in a small town,
making his living by selling dried reeds, which he brought
into the town on his back. Having obtained his services,
Vuk wrote down song after song from his verbal dictation.
Contrary to the *guslari*, Podrugović did not chant them,
but recited slowly as if reading from a book. There was an
inexhaustible mine of ballads in this man; he knew more
than one hundred, but Vuk secured only twenty-two,
containing in all 5700 lines, for nothing could prevent
Podrugović returning to Serbia in 1815, the moment he
heard that fighting for liberation had been renewed.

The other man, the *guslar*, Višnjić, came from Bosnia
also and fought in Serbia in 1809, but fled to Austria in
1813, where he died in 1834. Vuk secured from him sixteen
ballads, with a total of 5000 lines. He tells us also that two
old men, Milia and Raško, from Kolašin, and the blind

Dura Milutinović of Montenegro, furnished him with a number of songs and that he obtained from various women a number of women's songs.

IV

Among the many thousands of the *junačke pesme* that were collected in the course of the nineteenth century, those put together by Vuk Stefanović Karadžić, and published by the Serbian Government, stand foremost, and they have always remained the most representative collection of the Yugoslav heroic songs. Their most characteristic feature, the motifs—perhaps not more than one hundred different ones—can be regarded as the nuclei of thousands of stories in which figure innumerable personalities, both historical and legendary. However varied the stories and the personalities which appeared in the collections subsequent to that of Vuk, the motifs that he had brought to light are ever present with but slight variations. They are almost invariably closely connected with history; the historical element makes the Yugoslav *junačke pesme* what they actually are: heroic songs of a higher grade. A closer examination, however, reveals them as true historical poems rather than epic ballads; in many cases they are in all essentials historical documents. They contain, however, too much truth for them to be regarded as popular ballads in the ordinary sense of the word. This applies especially to those that were composed more recently; they had not lived long enough in oral tradition before being collected, and, therefore, they have not acquired all the characteristics of traditional poetry. Nevertheless, there is a considerable number of heroic songs the contents of which, although

not implying an historical background, abounds in anachronisms and in mystic elements of both Christian and
pagan origin.

The brothers Mrnjavčević, for instance, fight in the
battle of Kosovo, although they had actually lost their
lives eighteen years before, in the battle at the Marica.
Marko Kraljević, who was killed in 1394, is made a contemporary of the despot, Vuk Branković, who died in
1486. Constantinople, according to an heroic song, is held
by the Turks during Marko's lifetime, although according
to history the Turks captured it nearly sixty years after his
death. A good chanter is careful not to mention coffee and
tobacco at the time when these were not in use; it nevertheless occurs that someone sips a cup of coffee, or puffs
away at his pipe during the period of Tsar Dušan in the
middle of the fourteenth century. It is also not unusual for
guns to be fired long before gunpowder was invented.
Geographical names, too, are misplaced or confused, and
often new places, like new heroes, entirely unknown to
history, are invented. Side by side with historical personalities, supernatural beings, angels, winged men (*zmajevi*),
flying horses and speaking monsters play a conspicuous
part.

Nevertheless, two groups are clearly to be distinguished:
an historical and a non-historical. The latter deals with
mythological and legendary subjects, as well as with pagan
and Christian themes, while the former comprises personalities and events of Serbian history, from the end of the
twelfth century onwards. The non-historical group is out-
numbered by the historical one; but among the non-historical heroic ballads some equal and perhaps surpass in

quality the most beautiful of the historical heroic songs. The principal subject in all of them, whether of short or long line, is the centuries' long struggle against the Turks; it forms the biggest subject treated in the Yugoslav traditional poetry. Like the Castilian *romances* and the Ukrainian *dumy*, they vividly depict numerous episodes of the struggle between Christianity and Islam. None of these poetries aims at giving a complete story of that long and stubborn contest; they give only a scene, a picture of a story, mostly tragic, which is to be completed by the listener's own imagination. It is in this respect that they are true ballads, for particular attention is paid to selection of tragic motifs, but by no means all of them deal with such motifs only.

Speaking generally, the heroic songs, whether historical or non-historical, which deal with mediaeval history and historical personalities, are of greater beauty than those dealing with modern history. The historical group deals with events from Serbian history from the end of the twelfth century to the modern period and is, as a rule, subdivided into a number of cycles, according to the subjects of which they treat. The first in order describes the founder of the Nemanja dynasty and the ancient rulers, the *župani* and the kings. Among these the *Marriage of Tsar Dušan* (*Ženidba Cara Dušana*) stands foremost. It is historical in so far as one of its personalities is the greatest Serbian ruler of the Middle Ages: otherwise it is a purely legendary heroic epic in which also supernatural beings act and speak. It is a remarkable ballad especially for its composition and for accuracy in detailed description.

The most important and the centre of the whole Yugoslav traditional poetry are the cycle of the battle of Kosovo, fought between the Serbs and the Turks in June, 1389, and the cycle of the national hero Marko Kraljević. The former is invariably tragic; the heroic ballads of Marko, on the other hand, being full of brightness and humour, are, perhaps, the most beautiful of all the Yugoslav heroic songs. Their composer, remaining true to the tradition of ballad-making, that "the bloodier the fray, the better for ballad purposes", brought in a few gruesome scenes, offering no apology for some ruthless actions on the part of the hero.

Marko Kraljević is a typical representative of those heroes who figure as outlaws in the popular ballads of many nations, and for whose character material was drawn from stories of adventure current in the late Middle Ages among almost all European peoples. All these heroes possessed many features in common; in the first instance, almost superhuman strength and indomitable courage, then attractive personal traits, and, finally, they are in revolt against some authority and are the champions of the poor and oppressed. Perhaps the most typical of such heroes was Robin Hood, with whom Marko has a few points in common. But Marko is, above all, an historical person, though history knows very little about him. In the Introduction to his translations of *The Ballads of Marko Kraljević*, D. A. Low gives an account of what history knows about Marko. He was a son of *Kralj* Vukašin of Macedonia, hence his surname Kraljević, "king's son". After the tragic death of his father in 1371, to which we shall refer again presently, Marko established himself at Prilep as King of Western Macedonia, but in a few years' time he became a vassal of the Turks, and as such he fought against the Christians under the Wallachian prince, Mircea, in the battle of Rovine, 1394, where he was killed. A Serbian chronicle records that Marko had wished the Christian arms to be victorious, even were he to be among the first of the killed. His wish was fulfilled, and history does not say anything more about him. It does not tell us whether he was a hero or even a brave man, still less that he was a terror to the Turks, as the traditional poetry represents him. This has not, however, prevented him from becoming famous, not only among the Yugoslavs but also among all the peoples of the Balkan peninsula, with all the usual qualities and drawbacks of mediaeval heroes. Nevertheless, he is essentially the greatest hero of the Yugoslav people, who know and love him dearly.

Physically he dominates his fellows and his terrifying appearance when in full fighting kit is described in detail again and again. His "Samur Kalpak" is pulled low over his dark eyes; his huge black moustache is as large as a lamb of six months' growth; his cloak is a shaggy wolf-pelt; at his girdle swings a damascened blade; on his back is slung a war-spear; at his saddle-bow hangs a mighty mace, with a well-filled wineskin to hold the balance lest the saddle should slip this way or that. The steed he bestrides is a wonder-horse, the piebald Šarac, his inseparable companion and friend. When Marko drinks, he gives Šarac an equal share of wine—"pola pije, pola Šarcu daje"—and the startled observer cries truthfully that this knight is not as other knights nor this horse as other horses.

To obtain a complete picture of this hero, the reader should not fail to read Low's translations of the whole cycle of the ballads of Marko Kraljević.

We should like to draw attention to the ballad *Marko and the Daughter of the Moorish King*, in which one of the three incidents of his cruelty to women is described. Our object, however, is not either to condemn or to justify Marko, but only to let the reader compare this with the beautiful Scottish ballad *Young Bicham*, in order to see the marked contrast in the attitudes of the respective heroes, which are so characteristic of the conditions under which these ballads were created. The Moorish king and his daughter in the Yugoslav ballad are representatives of what was most hateful to the Serbs, namely the oppressive rule of the Turks, and, by the existing code of those days, "that deed was virtuous which did scathe to the enemy, to his children and to his children's children". The Scottish minstrel who composed *Young Bicham*—such ballads exist in the traditional poetries of most European peoples—must needs have looked differently upon a Moor and his daughter. If no cruelty was committed to Shusy Pye, or Lady Jane, as she was called on becoming Young Bicham's wife, it does not mean that cruelty to women, perhaps equally gruesome, was not committed in some other Scottish ballad.

The periods of Serbia's vassalage to the Sultan, and Montenegro's life under the last national dynasty, are well illustrated in the cycle of the Branković, the last *despoti* of Serbia, and the cycle of the Crnojevići, Ivan and Maksim respectively. In the former there are a few ballads which count among the most beautiful Yugoslav heroic songs, such as the *Death of Despotović-Jovo*, the *Death of Vojvoda Priezda* and *Kajica Radonja*, while in the latter the *Marriage of Maksim Crnojević* stands foremost. Its principal motif of wooing the bride through a friend is reminiscent of the *Nibelungenlied*.

The heroic songs of the historical cycle deal further with the period of subjugation to the Turks, their oppression and individual reprisals carried out by the *hajduci* and *uskoci*, the memory of whom is preserved in the two cycles thus named, both of which contain many beautiful songs. The *hajduci* were a kind of guerilla warriors who fought the Turks while they kept Serbia subdued; while the *uskoci* were the Yugoslavs who had fled to Dalmatia and the Croatian littoral after the fall of Herzegovina in 1482, where, as mercenaries of the emperors, they defended the borders from the Turks, often raiding and pouncing upon them.

The liberation of Montenegro and Serbia at the beginning of the eighteenth and nineteenth centuries respectively has been described in the two cycles thus named, both of which—and the former especially—relate true historical events, with very little poetry. They differ greatly in this respect from the earlier heroic songs. These are, perhaps, the least interesting and the least beautiful.

In a very large number of these songs, an outstanding feature is a strong sense of right and justice. "What is right is dear to God", and justice must be dispensed impartially.

> Ni po babu, ni po stričevima,
> Već po pravdi Boga istinoga.[1]

Injustice is hateful and great sinners are they who violate right and justice. Wrongdoers are, as a rule, cruelly

[1] Neither by sire nor by grandsire,
But by the truth of the living God.

punished, but, if they often receive no chastisement from the mouth of the chanter, it is because he believes that God's justice will reach them in due course, wherever it be—in this world or in the next.

V

Besides the traditional poetry composed by the Christian Yugoslavs, there is a very large number of popular ballads, of both lyric and epic character, composed in the same language, by Bosnian and Herzegovinian Moslems. Their traditional poetry stands apart and in some respects differs from that of the Christian Serbo-Croats. In order to obtain a clear idea of the Moslem traditional poetry it should be remembered that Bosnia had been, from the earliest days of its history, a meeting-ground of the West and East, and that before the Turkish conquest there throve, apart from the Roman Catholic and the Greek Orthodox Churches, a powerful sect known as the Bogomil sect, hostile to both. Having originated in Bulgaria under the influence of the Manichaean teaching, it found its way to Serbia, but, owing to her well-organised church under Prince Nemanja, it settled in Bosnia, where the ground was most favourable, owing to the friction of the Western and the Eastern Churches. From Bosnia the Bogomils spread to Italy and France, under the names of the Paterenes and the Albigenses. Opposed to the Roman Catholic Church, the Bogomils facilitated the Turkish conquest of Bosnia in 1463, and Herzegovina in 1482, for the greater part of the nobles of these lands were ardent adherents of the Bogomil sect. Immediately Bosnia was conquered they were the first to accept Islam, in order to preserve their properties and positions. They came under the new regime as a privileged class, as the Begs of large landed properties, and thus mediaeval feudalism continued to exist there long after it had died out in the rest of Europe, and it survived, indeed, until the end of the Great War. The Moslem feudal lords of Bosnia preserved, however, the consciousness of their origin, and their mother language has always remained Serbo-Croat, though Islam has, naturally, left its mark upon their characters. It is, therefore, no wonder that the Bosnian and Herzegovinian Moslems should have cultivated, and still cultivate more than anyone else, a traditional poetry of the same type as the Christian Serbo-Croats.

In language, verse and style, the Moslem popular ballads are very much like those of the Serbs and Croats, except that they possess a much larger vocabulary of Turkish and Arabic origin. They differ greatly, however, in their spirit and character. While lovers and sweethearts are practically excluded from the former, everything centres round women in the latter. Women are the cause of fights and duels, and sometimes they take an active part in them. Marriage, raping, dispersing of wedding parties, redemption of captives, revenge, falsehood and fraud, when bravery is lacking, are their most common subjects. Many songs begin with drinking and end with the shedding of blood, but there is a large number of them in which various sports are described: wrestling, riding, throwing the lance, putting the weight and jumping. In a number of songs, girls dance the *kolo* at festivals, and men pay court to them, flatter them and admire their beauty in terms reminiscent of Oriental courtship.

The Moslem songs deal also with historical events, but mostly of a date more recent than those described in the Serbo-Croat heroic songs; hardly any events earlier than the sixteenth century take place in them and most of them occur in the district of Lika, with Mustaj Beg as the central figure and Moslem national hero. Fights and battles with the oppressed Christians are the most common subjects, and the Moslems in them are invariably victorious. They are described as superior to Christian heroes in every respect: in beauty, strength, valour, wisdom and honesty. It is seldom that due respect is paid to the Christian adversaries, but friendships between Moslems and Christians are sometimes established.

Although historical events form the background of a large number of these songs, they are seldom described as they actually happened. There is, however, no event among them so great as Kosovo, although there is much talk of great armies, great battles and great leaders, without any particulars of who they actually were. The Turkish Empire and the Moslem world stand against the Emperor of Vienna and the Christian world. Among the seven kingdoms and the seven kings that are under the emperor, Poland and Russia, in addition to Hungary, are sometimes mentioned.

Unlike the Serbian *junačke pesme*, in which a patriotic idea is common to most of them, prominence is given in the Moslem heroic songs to the idea of the Islamic religion, to which the peoples of every other creed must be sacrificed at all times and at all costs. A Christian chief, when taken prisoner, is not treated with the courtesy with which the Spanish *hidalgos* treat the Moorish chiefs; he is but a slave to be exchanged or sold for a large ransom.

It is considered that the Moslem heroic songs were composed, towards the end of the seventeenth century, by
unlettered, intelligent men of humble origin, either from
their own experience, or from a story which they had
heard, or which had been read to them from a chronicle by
a literate man. In composing them, the chanters often
made them unnecessarily long because they were anxious
either to please their Moslem patrons for whom they
chanted them, by giving an elaborate description of the
bravery of their ancestors, or to amuse the Moslem ladies
of high birth by describing before them elaborate women's
dresses and their appearance. They would often devote a
hundred lines to such a description. Moslem women especially were a grateful and patient audience, and no song
was long enough for them; no story, however fanciful and
untrue, was unbelievable to them.

Contrary to the practice of the Christian *guslari*, the
Moslem chanters, the *pevači*, when reciting, accompany
themselves on an instrument of two metal strings, called
the *tambura*. While this instrument is never used by Christian *guslari*, the *gusle* has replaced the *tambura* with a large
number of Moslem chanters.

VI

The *guslari* and the *pevači* were both creators and spreaders
of heroic songs, and to a certain extent they correspond to
the Greek rhapsodes; but it stands to reason that they never
enjoyed the same reputation, nor could all of them have
been true creators, like those God-favoured poets. The
status of the Yugoslav chanters was never so high even
as that of the Celtic bards or Anglo-Saxon scôps, or
Scandinavian skalds; they had more the reputation of the

mediaeval Scottish minstrels and of the itinerant French *trouvères* and *jongleurs*. They were not minstrels in the sense of the "royal minstrels" of Edward III, but rather minstrels of the people of that period, though we know that it was difficult in the fourteenth century to make a clear distinction between the two classes of minstrels: the singer of the court was often seized with a desire to wander among the people, while the singer of the people not infrequently visited the cloister, to cheer the hearts of the pious brotherhood. It is to this class of mediaeval minstrels that the *guslari* and the *pevači* correspond.

Almost without exception they were poor men and many of them had no other occupation than that of chanting heroic songs for a modest remuneration, either in kind or in money, at church gatherings or coffee houses. They were not organised, nor were they formed into guilds like the French or the English minstrels; the earliest of such guilds among the former goes back to the first decade of the twelfth century—the Parisian guild was formed in 1321—while the latter were granted a royal charter in 1469 to form a guild, and another in 1604. Such organisations are unknown among the Yugoslav professional chanters, nor were they trained in proper schools, like the French and the English minstrels.

At one time or another, blind men as chanters of popular poetry existed among practically all peoples, ancient or modern. In Germanic countries they were already known in such capacity in the ninth century; in England they were mentioned by the author of *Piers Plowman*; in Scotland they were favoured by nobles and even kings in the fifteenth century; nor were they rare in the century following. During these centuries they were common in Switzerland and France. They existed also in Spain and Portugal, as well as in Russia, Armenia and Georgia.

Among the Serbs, as we have seen, many a blind man, and also blind women, supplied the great collector, Vuk Karadžić, with heroic songs, and we have proofs that some of these songs were their own composition. Yet, on the ground that blind men as chanters of heroic songs are at present extremely rare among those Serbs and Croats who still cultivate such songs, they have lately been denied the importance which is due to them in creating and spreading heroic songs among the Yugoslavs a hundred and more years ago. Nevertheless, the fact remains that the origin of many an heroic song is due to blind *guslari*. If they did not form guilds and if they were not trained in proper schools, we know that the trade as such existed, that they lived by chanting heroic songs—and consequently endeavoured to keep them alive—and that blind men were taught by other blind men, both to play the *gusle* and to compose and to chant.

The political conditions under which the Serbs lived at the time when the heroic poetry was being created and collected were very different from those in England under which the mediaeval minstrels practised their profession. If, therefore, the *guslari* had no opportunity of chanting for royalties and nobles, they did so for the leaders of the First Rising of the Serbs, during the first two decades of the last century. Filip Višnjić, for instance, spent four years in the district of Mačva, and almost all his songs, which he recited for Vuk Karadžić a few years later, describe the fighting between the Serbs and the Turks, which took place in that district while he was there, and glorify the deeds of the contemporary Serbian leaders. There are several instances which prove that many Serbian leaders of that period had their own *guslari*, and these very often composed songs in which the heroic deeds of their masters were glorified. This, perhaps, explains the fact that heroic songs which deal with the liberation of the Serbs, and those which chant the achievements of the *hajduci* and *uskoci*, are far more numerous than those dealing with the events and personalities of mediaeval Serbian history.

There are indications also that the *hajduci*, like the *guslari*, participated in both the creation and the spreading of the heroic poetry, though there is no positive proof as in the case of the *guslari*. Vuk Karadžić, for instance, tells us that the *hajduci* were chiefly responsible for spreading knowledge of the heroic songs; that in winter time they indulged in drinking and in chanting such songs, which dealt mainly with the exploits of their own class. In enumerating the men who had supplied him with heroic songs, Vuk says that first the *guslari* and then the *hajduci* were the most numerous. One has, however, to bear in mind that, at the time when Vuk collected the heroic songs, the activities of the *hajduci* had practically come to an end, and that he met only those who were on the territory freed from the Turks, while he had no means of coming into touch with any of those who were still fighting the Turks in Serbia proper, which at that time was in their occupation.

A young Serb, S. Matić, who has recently made a special study of the rôle played by the *guslari* and *hajduci*—and some of the results of his investigations we have mentioned in connection with this question—believes that the cruelty which is so marked in the Yugoslav heroic songs is due to the fact that the *hajduci*, merciless and ruthless fellows, either composed many of such songs or indirectly gave tone to them. Their ideology and moral conceptions are reflected in the larger portion of the Yugoslav heroic poetry, just as Christian and religious thoughts of the blind *guslari* were reflected in the smaller portion composed by them.

There can be no doubt that the character of the chanters of heroic songs, as well as the character of his audience— for the chanter must please his audience—find their expression in such songs, but let us not forget that the Yugoslav traditional poetry is not any poorer in "moral and humane feelings"—of which it is sometimes accused— than the popular ballads of any other people. The selection of tragic and cruel motifs is one of the chief objects of such poetry, and "no one feels the necessity of apology either for ruthless aggression or for useless blood-letting; the bloodier the fray, the better for ballad purposes".[1] Hence Marko's cruelty to the daughter of the Moorish king, hence his cruelty to Captain Leka's sister, and hence all other cruelties.

VII

According to Vuk the ordinary metre of the Yugoslav traditional songs varies with the three groups, viz. the women's songs, the heroic poems of the short line, and the heroic poems of the long line. The typical metre, however, is that of the heroic poems of the short line. It consists of ten syllables or five trochaic feet, the charac-

[1] H. W. Mabie, Introduction to *A Book of Old English Ballads*, by G. W. Edwards.

teristic feature of which is a pause, a caesura, after the fourth syllable, i.e. the second foot, marked here ||, e.g.

$$\acute{}\smile \mid \acute{}\smile \parallel \acute{}\smile \mid \acute{}\smile \mid \acute{}\smile$$

Podi|že se || Crno|jević | Ivo.

Very often the quantity of a syllable is altered to suit the exigencies of the verse-metre; syllables which in ordinary speech are long become short and *vice versa*,[1] e.g.

Ĭ pó|něsě || trí tó|vără | blágă
Jă kád | tákŏ || svádbŭ | ŭré|dĭšě,

but when chanting, all are trochaic:

Í pŏ|nésě || trí tŏ|vára | blágă.

The verse of most of the women's songs is exactly the same, but many of them show a great variety of the number of syllables in each line; they vary from four to fourteen syllables, but the most frequent lines consist of eight or ten syllables.

(I) A line of *eight* syllables consists of either (1) four trochaic feet and the caesura in the middle:

Bógă | mólĭ || mládŏ | mómčě,

or (2) three feet, dactyls in the beginning and at the end, but a trochee in the middle; as to the caesura, it comes either (*a*) after the second or (*b*) after the first foot:

(*a*) Pórănĭ | ránŏ || ná vŏdŭ;
(*b*) Póglĕdăj || vójnŏ | póglĕdăj.

(II) Consisting of *seven* syllables, or three feet, of which two are trochees at the beginning and a dactyl at the end; the caesura coming after the second foot:

Ój tĭ | źrnŏ || šénĭčnŏ.

---

[1] The acute accents represent the accented syllables.

A dactyl can, however, take the first place:

Kálŏpĕr || Pérŏ | ljéljŏ.

(III) Consisting of *ten* syllables, but four feet, two dactyls and two trochees:

Óblăk sĕ | víjĕ || pó vĕdrŏm | nébŭ;

or

Mílă | májčĭcĕ || bélă | cŕkvĭcĕ;

or

Srétnŏ tĭ | bílŏ || rúŏ | vénčănŏ.

(IV) Consisting of *eleven* syllables, or five feet, the first four of which are trochees and the last a dactyl:

Próđŏ | górŭ | próđŏ | drúgŭ || í trĕćŭ.

(V) Consisting of *twelve* syllables with either four dactyls or six trochaic feet:

Ránĭlă | dévŏjkă || lávă ĭ | lábŭdă,
Slávŭj | ptícă | málă || svákŏm | pókŏj | dálă.

Dactyls and trochees are often found in one and the same line:

Ájdĕmŏ | tám' dŏlĕ || ú tŏ | zlátnŏ | póljĕ.

(VI) Consisting of *thirteen* syllables, but six feet, the caesura falling after the fourth, always preceded by four trochees and followed either by a trochee and a dactyl or *vice versa*:

Dá s' vă|támŏ | tánkĕ | slámkĕ || tánkĕ | tánănĕ,
Dá glĕ|dámŏ | kó ćĕ | kómĕ || ú srĕćĭ | pástĭ.

(VII) Consisting of *fourteen* syllables or of seven trochaic feet:

Dévŏj|čĭcă | vódŭ | gázĭ || nógĕ | jój sĕ | bélĕ.

(VIII) Consisting of *six* syllables of either three trochees or two dactyls:

Krá|ljŭ || svétlĭ | králjŭ,
Králjĭcĕ || bánĭcĕ!

(IX) Consisting of *five* syllables; one dactyl and one trochee in each line:

Áh štŏ ćŭ || štó ćŭ,
Né spăvăm || nóćŭ.

The heroic songs of the long line differ from both the women's songs and the heroic songs of the short line, in the length of the line, the place of the caesura, the accent and the distribution of syllables; in this respect they show a considerable variety amongst themselves. The chief metre is, however, a line of fifteen or sixteen syllables, or of seven or eight feet, with the caesura after the seventh, all the feet being trochees except the one preceding the caesura in the line of fifteen syllables, which is a dactyl:

Pódĕ | králjŭ | búdĭm|skómĕ || séstră | svójă | góvŏ|rítĭ.

Many of these songs have a refrain, consisting of six syllables or three trochees. It is placed after the first line and then after each two subsequent lines, but the last line has no refrain at all, and probably never had. This is in contradistinction to the song of ten syllables, where no such strophes are to be found. The *bugarštice* look, there-fore, as follows:

/ ∪ / ∪ / ∪ ∪ || / ∪ / ∪ / ∪ ∪
                       / ∪ / ∪ / ∪
/ ∪ / ∪ / ∪ ∪ || / ∪ / ∪ / ∪ ∪
/ ∪ / ∪ / ∪ ∪ || / ∪ / ∪ / ∪ ∪
                       / ∪ / ∪ / ∪
/ ∪ / ∪ / ∪ ∪ || / ∪ / ∪ / ∪ ∪
/ ∪ / ∪ / ∪ ∪ || / ∪ / ∪ / ∪ ∪
                       / ∪ / ∪ / ∪

As records have not been left of the actual accentuation of these songs it is not possible to indicate accents accurately. The following are examples of the long line with and without a refrain:

Trí tǐ glásǎ dópǎnúlǐ || hrábrě Márkǔ Králjěvíčǔ,
                           Králjěvíčǔ Márkǔ,
Prvǐ glás mǔ dópǎdě || ód krǎljǎ ód ǔgǎrskógǎ:
Dá gǎ póđě vjénčǎtǐ || králjǐcǒm slávnǒm góspǒđǒm,
                           Králjǎ úgǎrskógǎ;
Drúgǐ glás mǔ dópǎdě || ód Jǎnkǎ ód vǒjévǒdě:
Dá mǔ ídě krstǐtǐ || ód srdáčcǎ mládǒ čédǒ,
                           Úgrǐn vójěvódǎ;

Kádǎ nó mǐ sě žénjǎšě || ód Bǔdímǎ sv'jétlǐ králjǔ,
Ón sě králjǔ žénjǎšě || ód Krǔšévǎ líjěpógǎ,
Svátǒvé jě skúpǐǒ || úgǎrskú svǒjú gǒspódǔ
Jánkǒ mú jě vójvǒdǎ || zá kǔmá, zǎ vjénčǎnógǎ,
Stárǎc Đúrǎđ déspǒtě || zá svǎtóvǐm ú zǎstávǐ,
Á Sěkúlǒ séstrǐčíč || zá đěvérǎ úz něvjéstǔ;
Í ǒní sě vésělě || ú krǎljévǔ b'jélǔ dvórǔ,
Sámǒ mí sě né věsélǐ || Úgrǐn Jánkǒ vójěvódǎ.

The line of fifteen or sixteen syllables has been accepted as the typical line of the heroic songs of the long line, but considerable variety as regards the length of line is met with in these songs. Nevertheless, the lines of less than fifteen and more than sixteen syllables are regarded as irregular. The number of syllables in a line may even be twenty, but it must be noticed that, however numerous the syllables may be, the second part of each line must consist of *eight* syllables; the irregularity, therefore, is to be found in the first part of the line only, i.e. in the part which pre-

cedes the caesura. From the point of view of the variety
of syllables, the *bugarštice* stand nearer to the Russian
byliny than to the heroic songs of the short line, for both
have an elastic verse.

As to the actual length of these songs, they are, on an
average, shorter than the songs of the short line. Again,
the *bugarštice* with a refrain are shorter than those without.
The *bugarštice* with and without refrains do not appear ever
to have been two different groups of songs. Those with a
refrain undoubtedly must be older, for a refrain in popular
ballads is, in general, a sign of an early origin. It is reported
that the *bugarštice* were chanted by one person for the
others to listen to, but it is not improbable that the refrains
were repeated at an early stage by the audience. When the
listeners ceased to take part in the recitation, the refrain
was dropped.

Like the decasyllabic heroic songs, the *bugarštice* have
no rhyme, except that now and then the endings of two
lines, or more frequently words at the end of each part of
the same line, rhyme. Sometimes two words in the second
part alone rhyme, e.g.

> Ognjen Vuka pri*stignuo*, Ali-bega do*stignuo*;

or

> Sve se sk*ita*, a za Musu p*ita*;

or

> Sedam paša, bi*še* i ubi*še*.

VIII

The following few women's songs, in the versions of the
first English translators of Yugoslav traditional poetry—
John Gibson Lockhart, John Bowring and Lord Lytton

(Owen Meredith)—may serve as illustrations of this type
of songs:

> O lovely was the sight I saw
> By moonlight o'er the still Danaw,
> When heroes lay on tented ground,
> And the golden wine went round and round.
>
> A beautiful and gentle maid
> From hand to hand the cup conveyed,
> And ever as she poured the wine
> She heard the whispered prayer, "Be mine!"
>
> "Ah, noble lords!" the damsel said,
> "Take lowly service, gladly paid;
> But know the heart of love is frozen
> For all but one, the dear, the chosen".
>
> J. G. LOCKHART

THE LOVER'S BLESSING

> The wild hawk sat the dark night long
>   Beside the window of Melan,
> And ever and anon her song
>   Thus sharp and clear began:—
>
> "Rise up, it is a noble feast,
>   Thine own true-love to-night doth wed;
> Rise, taste the cup, or send at least
>   Thy blessing to the bed".
>
> Melan made answer: "By my word,
>   To drink her wine I will not go;
> But thou shalt bear my blessing, bird,
>   Since thou wilt have it so.
>
> May for each drop this night she drains
>   Ten thousand tears hereafter flow!
> Be child-birth pains the only pains
>   That bed shall ever know!"   J. G. LOCKHART

THE KNITTER

The maiden sat upon the hill,
Upon the hill and far away,
Her fingers wove a silken cord,
And thus I heard the maiden say:
"O with what joy, what ready will,
If some fond youth, some youth adored,
Might wear thee, should I weave thee now!
The finest gold I'd interblend,
The richest pearls as white as snow.
But if I knew, my silken friend,
That an old man should wear thee, I
The coarsest worsted would inweave,
Thy finest silk for dog-grass leave,
And all thy knots with nettles tie".

J. BOWRING

PARTING OF THE BRIDE

Sweetest of maidens! O be still,
Be silent—prithee weep not now,
Thy mother she will weep—wilt fill
Her sorrowing eyes with tears, for thou
Wilt leave thy cherish'd home ere long:
And when thy young companions go
To the fresh stream, amidst the throng
She'll seek thee—will she find thee? No!

J. BOWRING

CURSE

The maiden cursed her raven eyes,
She cursed them for their treacheries.
"Be blinded now, to you if heaven
All that is visible has given!

If ye see all, ye traitors, say
Why saw ye not my love to-day:—
He pass'd my door,—but, truants, ye
Gave not the gentlest hint to me.
He had a nosegay in his hand,—
He wore a gold embroider'd band,—
'Twas made by other hands than mine!
Upon it wreathing branches twine:
May every branch embroidered there,
A miserable heart-wound bear;—
Upon each branch, may every leaf
Bring and betoken toil and grief."

J. BOWRING

SECRETS DIVULGED

Two lovers kiss each other in the meadows;
They think that no one sees the fond betrayal,
But the green meadows see them, and are faithless;
To the white flocks incontinent they say all;
And the white flocks proclaim it to the shepherd,
The shepherd to a high-road traveller brings it;
He to a sailor on the restless ocean tells it,
The sailor to his spice-ship thoughtless sings it;
The spice-ship whispers it upon the waters,
The waters rush to tell the maiden's mother.

And thus impassioned spoke the lovely maiden—
"Meadows! of spring-days never see another!
Flocks! may the cruel ravenous wolves destroy ye.
Thee, shepherd! may the cruel Moslem slaughter.
Wanderer! may oft thy slippery footsteps stumble.
Thee, sailor! may the ocean billows smother.
Ship! may a fire unquenchable consume thee;
And sink into the earth, thou treacherous water!"

J. BOWRING

EMANCIPATION

The Day of Saint George! and a girl pray'd thus:
"O Day of Saint George, when again to us
Thou returnest, and they carouse
Here in my mother's house,
May'st thou find me either a corpse or a bride,
Either buried or wed;
Rather married than dead;
But however that may betide,
And whether a corpse or a spouse,
No more in my mother's house".

OWEN MEREDITH

The following two were translated by Talvj, a German authoress, of whom we shall say more presently.

A TRISTFUL GIRL

Rain fell in the evening
And a frosty night came,
I rose to look for my sweetheart
And I found the green meadow,
And on the meadow my sweetheart's cloak,
And on the cloak his silk handkerchief,
And on the handkerchief his guitar,
By the guitar an apple.
I thought all thoughts.
If I should take his cloak,
He is young, inexperienced, and I am afraid
He might catch cold—
If I should take his handkerchief.
I gave it to him as a sign of my love.
If I took his guitar,
His guitar was given him by my brothers.

I thought of everything and I decided
To bite his apple.
So that he may know I had come
To see my sweetheart.

HOUSEHOLD MATTERS

Come, companion, let us hurry,
That we may be early home,
For my mother-in-law is cross.
Only yesterday she accused me,
Said that I had beat my husband;
When, poor soul, I had not touched him.
Only bid him wash the dishes,
And he would not wash the dishes;
Threw then at his head the pitcher;
Knocked a hole in head and pitcher;
For the head I do not care much,
But I care much for the pitcher,
As I paid for it right dearly;
Paid for it with one wild apple,
Yes, and half a one besides.

IX

As an illustration of the type of *junačke pesme* relating to
non-historical themes, we shall quote here the *Sister and
Brothers* (*Braća i sestra*) in the translation of G. R. Noyes
and L. Bacon. The subject of this ballad is treated also in
modern Greek, Bulgarian and Albanian traditional poetry;
also by Bürger in his *Lenore*, and by Goethe in *Der un-
treue Knabe*.

Professor Noyes, bearing in mind that the beauty of
Serbian traditional songs consists, above all, in the simple

way in which the narrative proceeds, says that in translating them the most important point is not that each line
should be rendered in decasyllabic trochees, but that the
spirit of the narrative should be rendered as faithfully as
possible; the metre and the number of syllables in each
line being of secondary importance. Since most of the
English translations have closely followed the Serbian
metre, which in his opinion is "essentially foreign to the
genius of the English language", he has adopted for his
translations "a verse modelled on that which, in *Sigurd
the Volsung*, William Morris has made classic by his hand-
ling of a subject that is spiritually akin to the Kosovo
ballads".

Nine dear sons and a daughter, a mother bore and bred;
She reared them up till they were grown and the sons were
    ready to wed,
And the maiden ripe for marriage. And straightway asked for
    her
Three suitors, a ban, and a marshal, and a neighbor villager.
To the neighbor the mother would give her, but her brethren
    to the man
From over sea would give her. They said to her: "Marry the
    ban,
The great lord from beyond the sea. In every month of the
    year
We will come, and every week in the month, to see thee, sister
    dear".
  The sister obeyed them, and the ban from over sea she wed.
But behold a marvel! God's pestilence struck her nine
    brethren dead,
And the solitary mother was left. So passed three years.

In her grief little Yélitsa the sister mourned with tears:
"Dear God, a mighty marvel! What great sin have I done
To my brethren, that of all of them cometh to me not one?"
The wives of her lord's brethren reviled her sharp enow:
"O wife of our lord's brother, a wanton one art thou.
Hateful unto thy brethren now hast thou come to be,
That not one of thy brethren comes here to visit thee".
And little sister Yélitsa wept much both day and night;
But the dear God, in mercy, took pity on her plight,
And sent forthwith two angels:
      "Go down, ye angels of mine,
To the white tomb of Yovan, the youngest of the nine;
Breathe light upon him with your breath; from the tomb
  frame him a steed;
From the earth make cakes for the festival all ready to his
  need;
Of his shroud make gifts, and get him in readiness to appear
Upon his wedding visit at the house of his sister dear".
 To the white tomb of Yovan the angels of God made
  speed;
They breathed upon him with their breath; from the tomb they
  framed him a steed,
And cakes from the earth for the festival all ready to his
  need;
Of his shroud they made gifts, and got him in readiness to
  appear
Upon his wedding visit at the house of his sister dear.
Swiftly went Yovan the feeble. When the house before him
  lay
His sister saw, and to meet him came forth a little way;
And O her tears fell bitter, all for her sorrow's sake!
They spread their arms, and each other kissed, and sister to
  brother spake:

"Did ye not promise, brother, when ye gave me in marriage
    here,
That ye would come to see me every month in the year,
And every week in every month, to visit your sister dear?
But ye never came to see me, though three full years have
    fled".
    And little Yélitsa further unto her brother said:
"Why hast thou grown so dark, brother? 'Tis as though
    beneath the sod
Thou hadst been". Said Yovan the feeble: "Be still, as thou
    lovest God.
A hard constraint is on me. I have wedded eight brothers well,
And served eight sisters by marriage; and, sister, it befell
That, when my brothers were married, we made nine houses
    white.
Therefore, my little sister, am I grown as black as night".
    And little sister Yélitsa got ready. She fashioned then
Gifts for her brethren and sisters; silken shirts for the men
She made, and, for her sisters, fair rings and bracelets fair.
And ever Yovan her brother besought her strongly there:
    "Dear little sister Yélitsa, I prithee go not home,
Till on their wedding visit thy brethren to thee come".
    But Yélitsa would not turn back; her fair gifts she prepared.
Thence Yovan started homeward, and his sister with him fared.
When they were come to their home again, a white church
    stood thereby.
Said Yovan the feeble:
                            "Sister, I prithee tarry nigh,
Until I go behind the church; for here at the marrying
Of the fourth of our eight brethren, I lost my golden ring.
Let me go to seek it, sister".
                            To his tomb went Yovan straight,
And little sister Yélitsa for Yovan there did wait.

She waited and sought him. Nigh the church a fresh grave she
    espied;
Suddenly she knew in sorrow that Yovan the weak had died.
Quickly she went to the white house. When she was come to
    the hall,
In the hollow rooms of the white house she heard a cuckoo
    call.
Nay, it was not a cuckoo blue, but her mother crying sore.
Yélitsa lifted up her voice as she came unto the door:
"Open the door, poor mother". Said the mother thereunto:
    "Get hence, thou pestilence of God, nine sons of mine that
    slew!
Their ancient mother, also, wilt thou smite stark and dead?"
    And little sister Yélitsa lifted her voice and said:
    "Poor mother, open now the door! No pestilence is here;
It is only little Yélitsa, and she is thy daughter dear".
    She opened the door. Each other they clasped their arms
    around,
Wailing like cuckoos. Mother and child fell dead upon the
    ground.

To illustrate the type of the *junačke pesme*, which is legendary by its theme and historical inasmuch as historical
persons figure in it, we might quote *The Building of Scutari*
(*Zidanje Skádra*) in the translation of Dr W. A. Morison.
Its subject, the immuring of a human being, exists in the
traditional poetries of all Balkan peoples, as well as in
those of most other European races. It no doubt goes
back to the heathen times when primitive people believed
that the Gods in their jealousy allowed men to build
strongholds only in return for the sacrifice of human
beings.

Three full brothers built a town together,
Three full brothers, three Mrnjavčevići,
And the first of them was King Vukašin,
And the second Uglješa the Voivode,
And the third was Mrnjavčević Gojko;
Skadar built they, on Bojana river,
Three long years the royal brothers laboured,
Three long years, and with three hundred workmen,
And they could not lay the town's foundations,
Much less could the brothers raise the city;
What the workmen in the day constructed
In the night a fairy's hand demolished.

When at length the fourth year was beginning,
Loudly called the fairy from the mountain:
"King Vukašin, do not waste thy labour,
Waste thy labour, nor expend thy treasure.
For thou canst not lay the town's foundations,
King Vukašin, much less build the city,
Till thou findest names that bear a likeness,
Till thou findest Stoja and Stojane,
Takest them, the brother with his sister,
To immure them in the town's foundations:
When 'tis done, the building will hold firmly,
And thou wilt construct the town of Skadar".
When King Vukašin had heard the fairy,
Then his servant Desimir he summoned:
"Desimir," quoth he, "my child beloved,
Thou hast been a faithful servant to me,
Henceforth thou shalt be my child beloved:
Harness now the horses to the wagons,
Take with thee six loads of precious treasure,
Go, my son, the whole wide world traversing,

Seeking for two names that bear a likeness;
Seek, my son, for Stoja and Stojane,
Search for them, the brother with his sister;
Seize the two, or purchase them with treasure,
Bring them back to Skadar on Bojana,
That we may immure them in the building,
So that the foundations may hold firmly,
And we may construct the town of Skadar".
When the servant Desimir heard this,
Then he harnessed horses to the wagons,
Took with him six loads of precious treasure,
Then went forth, the whole wide world traversing,
Seeking for two names that bore a likeness,
Went to seek for Stoja and Stojane;
For the space of three long years he sought them,
Could not find two names that bore a likeness,
Ne'er encountered Stoja and Stojane;
So returned to Skadar on Bojana,
Gave the King his horses and his wagons,
Gave him back the loads of precious treasure:
"Take, O King, thy horses and thy wagons,
Here are thy six loads of precious treasure;
Far and wide I sought but could not find them,
Ne'er encountered Stoja and Stojane".

And when King Vukašin heard his servant,
Rade summoned he, the master-builder,
Rade called for his three hundred workmen;
King Vukašin laboured at his building,
What he built the fairy's hand demolished,
Would not let him lay the town's foundations,
Much less let him raise the town of Skadar.
Loudly called the fairy from the mountain:

"King Vukašin, list to what I tell thee,
Do not waste thy labour and thy treasure,
For thou canst not lay the town's foundations,
Much less, King Vukašin, build the city.
Three of you are there, three royal brothers,
Each one of you has his faithful lady;
Which one goes to-morrow to the river,
Bearing to the labourers their dinner,
Take her, and immure her in the building,
Firmly will ye lay the town's foundations,
And ye will construct the town of Skadar".
And when King Vukašin heard the fairy,
Then he called to him his royal brothers:
"Listen to my words, my dearest brothers;
From the mountain top the fairy tells me
'Tis in vain that we expend our treasure,
She'll not let us lay the town's foundations,
Much less will she let us build the city,
Listen now to what the fairy tells me,
There are three of us, three royal brothers,
Each one of us has his faithful lady;
Which one goes to-morrow to the river,
Bearing to the labourers their dinner,
Must we take and wall her in the building,
When 'tis done the building will hold firmly,
And we must construct the town of Skadar.
We must swear a solemn oath, my brothers,
None of us shall tell his faithful lady,
In the hands of fortune must we leave it,
Which one goes to-morrow to the river".
So they swore a solemn oath together,
None of them should tell his faithful lady.

As they thus discussed the night had fallen,
To their white-walled dwelling they departed,
Sat them down before a lordly supper.
Listen now to what befell thereafter:
King Vukašin broke the oath he plighted,
He was first to tell his faithful lady:
"Thou must now beware, my faithful lady;
Do not go to-morrow to the river,
Neither take the labourers their dinner;
If thou dost so, thou wilt surely perish,
For they will immure thee in the building!"
And Uglješa broke the oath he plighted,
Thus he spoke unto his faithful lady:
"Do not be deceived, my faithful lady;
Do not go to-morrow to the river,
Neither take the labourers their dinner;
Surely, young and blooming, wilt thou perish,
For they will immure thee in the building!"
But young Gojko to his oath was faithful,
He said nothing to his faithful lady.

When the morning dawned upon the morrow,
Early rose the three Mrnjavčevići,
Went out to the building by the river.
Came the time to take the men their dinner,
And it was the Queen's turn next to bear it.
To her sister[1] then the Queen proceeded,
To her sister, to Uglješa's lady:
"Listen now," quoth she, "my dearest sister!
Since the morning has my head been aching,
Now God grant thee health! I cannot bear it;
Do thou take the labourers their dinner".

[1] I.e. sister-in-law.

Then replied Uglješa's faithful lady:
"O my sister dear, and royal lady!
Since the morning has my hand been paining,
Now God grant thee health! I cannot bear it;
Go thou now and ask our younger sister".
Off went she, and thus addressed their sister:
"Dearest sister, youthful wife of Gojko!
Since the morning has my head been aching,
Now God grant thee health! I cannot bear it;
Do thou take the labourers their dinner".
Then replied the youthful wife of Gojko:
"Hear me, sister mine and royal lady!
Gladly, sister mine, would I obey thee,
But I have not bathed my feckless infant,
And I have not washed my snow-white linen".
Then replied to her the royal lady:
"Do thou as I say, my dearest sister,
Carry to the labourers their dinner;
I will bathe thy feckless infant for thee,
And our sister wash thy snow-white linen".
All that Gojko's lady said was useless,
So she bore the labourers their dinner.

When the lady came unto the river,
Then perceived her Mrnjavčević Gojko,
And the hero's heart was wrung with anguish,
Filled with sorrow for his faithful lady,
For the feckless infant in its cradle—
Scarce a month had passed since it was born them;
Down his cheeks the heavy tear-drops trickled.
When the slender bride perceived her husband,
Modestly she walked till she was by him,
Modestly she walked and thus addressed him:

"What afflicts thee, my good lord and master,
That thou sheddest heavy tears of sorrow?"
Then responded Mrnjavčević Gojko:
"Great is my distress, my faithful lady!
For I did possess a golden apple,
And it now has fallen in the river:
Great my sorrow, I cannot endure it".
But the lady did not understand him,
And she said unto her lord and master:
"Pray to God that he with health may bless thee;
Thou wilt yet a fairer apple fashion".

Then his heart was wrung with greater anguish,
And he turned his head aside in sorrow,
Could not bear to gaze upon his lady;
Then approached the two Mrnjavčevići,
By her snow-white hands they took the lady,
Took her to immure her in the building,
Summoned Rade, who was master-builder,
Rade called for his three hundred workmen;
Gaily laughed the slender bride of Gojko,
For she thought that they were only joking.
In the wall they thrust the youthful lady,
And the workmen set about their labours,
All three hundred, piling stones and woodwork,
To her knees the lady soon was covered.
Still laughed gaily Gojko's youthful lady,
Still she thought that they were only joking.
Still the workmen carried on their labours,
All three hundred, piling stones and woodwork,
To her waist the lady soon was covered:
Then the weight pressed heavily upon her,
Then she saw that she was doomed to perish;

Piercingly she cried, as cries the serpent,
Thus besought she her beloved brothers:
"By great God in Heaven, do not let them
Wall me, young and blooming, in the building!"
Thus she begged, but all in vain her pleading,
For the brothers turned their glances from her.
Then she lost her wifely shame and shyness,
And she thus besought her lord and master:
"My good lord and master, do not let them
Wall me, young and blooming, in the building!
Send a message to my aged mother,
For my mother dear has wealth in plenty,
Let her buy a man-slave or a maiden,
And let them immure her in the building".

When the slender lady saw full clearly
That her prayers and pleading nought availed her,
Rade then she begged, the master-builder:
"Master-builder Rade, dearest brother,
Do thou leave a window for my bosom,
Pass my snowy bosom through the window,
When my infant Jovo comes unto me,
When he comes, that I may feed my infant".
Rade listened to the lady's pleading,
And he left a window for her bosom,
Passed her snowy bosom through the window,
When her infant Jovo came unto her,
When he came, that she might feed her infant.
Once again the lady called to Rade:
"Master-builder Rade, dearest brother,
Leave thou for my eyes a little window,
Let me gaze towards my white-walled dwelling
When they bear my infant Jovo to me,

When they bear him back into the dwelling".
Rade listened to the lady's pleading,
For her eyes he left a little window,
So that she might gaze towards her dwelling
When they bore her infant Jovo to her,
When they bore him back into the dwelling.
Then the men immured her in the building,
And they brought the infant in its cradle,
For a week she fed her feckless infant;
When the week was up, her voice had failed her,
But the milk still issued from her bosom:
For a year she fed her feckless infant.

As 'twas then, so it remains unchanging,
Still, the liquid trickles from the window,
As a wonder, as a cure for women
Lacking milk with which to feed their infants.

X

The following heroic song, *The Death of Ivo* (*Smrt Senja-nina Iva*), is one of the most remarkable songs of the cycle on the *uskoci*. In translating it, Professor Seton-Watson has marked the caesura with a distinct space between the fourth and fifth syllables.

A dream has dreamt   the mother of Ivo.
Darkness she saw   fall upon Senj,
The clear heavens   burst asunder,
The shimmering moon   fell down to earth,
On the Church of St Rose,   in the midst of Senj.

And the stars were swept   across the sky,
And the dawn rose up   all red with blood,
And the cuckoo bird   she heard a-calling,
In the midst of Senj,   on Senj's white church.

When from her dream   the dame awakened,
Her staff she took   in her right hand,
And went forthwith   to St Rose's Church;
And there she told   the Archpriest Nedeljko,
Told him all   that she had dreamed.

And when the old man   had heard her out,
'Twas thus he did   expound the dream:
"Hear me, O hear me,   aged mother!
'Twas an evil dream,   and worse shall befall.
That darkness fell   on the town of Senj,
It is that desolate   it shall remain.

That the clear heavens   burst asunder
And the shimmering moon   fell down to earth,
It is that thine Ivo   is to die.
That the stars were swept   across the sky,
It is that many   a widow shall be.

That the dawn rose up   all red with blood,
It is that thou   shalt be left to weep.
That the cuckoo bird   by St Rose sang,
It is that the Turks   shall plunder it,
And me in my old age   they shall slay".

While that the old man   still was speaking,
Lo, Ivo of Senj   stood there before them.
His coal black steed   was bathed in blood,
Seventeen   were the wounds of Ivo.
His right hand   in his left he bore.
He pressed his steed   to the white church door,
Then to his aged   mother he cried:
"Help me, mother,   from my steed,
Bathe me my wounds   with water cold,
And give the chalice   to my hand".

Swiftly then   did his mother obey,
Helped him down   from his foaming steed,

And bathed his wounds   with water cold,
And poured him out   the red, red wine.
Then did his aged   mother ask him:
"Son, how didst thou fare   in Italy?"

And thus made answer   Ivo her son:
"Well did we fare   in Italy.
Captives enough   did we take, my mother,
And yet more treasure   we did find:
Then hale and blithe   we homeward turned.
So when our first   night's stage we reached,
A foremost band   upon us fell.
Black were the horses,   black the heroes,
Black were the turbans   on their heads.
Forthwith upon them   we gave fire.
Of *them* not one   was left, my mother:
Of *us* not one   did fall, my mother.

So when our second   stage was reached,
A second band   upon us fell.
White were the horses,   whiter the heroes.
White were the turbans   on their heads.
Forthwith upon them   we gave fire.
Of *us* not one   did fall, my mother:
Of *them* not one   was left, my mother.

So when our third   night's stage was reached,
Another band   upon us fell.
Black were their mantles,   long their muskets,
Forthwith upon them   we gave fire,
Scorched were their legs   to the very knees.
And fiercely then   the fight began.
Of them, my mother,   not one did fall:

Of us, my mother,   not one was left—
Not one, save only   Ivo thy son,
And him thou seest   stricken of wounds,
Bearing his right hand   in his left!"

Thus spake he,   as his spirit struggled,
Thus said his say   and softly passed.
He died, and left   his grieving mother,
God grant to him   in Heaven his dwelling,
To us, my brothers,   health and joy.

Chapter Two

The Heroic Songs on Kosovo

I

THE CYCLE on the battle of Kosovo represents the classical centre of the Yugoslav heroic poetry; it describes a battle between the Serbs and the Turks which took place on the plain of Kosovo in Serbia, nearly five and a half centuries ago. The Serbs were defeated, and the Turks, having lost their ruler in the battle and having sustained heavy losses, withdrew to Adrianople. It was one of the most important battles of the Middle Ages, and it has left a deeper impression on the minds of the Yugoslav people than on those of the historians. We propose to give both a brief historical account of it and a survey of the events as they are recorded by the people themselves in their heroic poetry.

In the second part of the twelfth century, the Serbs succeeded in establishing a solid state, after about five centuries of struggle both among themselves and with their many neighbours. The founder of this state, Nemanja (ruled from 1168 till 1195), was at the same time the founder of the Nemanja dynasty, which ruled the Serbs, in an unbroken line of many able and successful rulers, for nearly two hundred years. During this period, Serbia was the centre of the Slavonic literature in the Balkans, a place held previously by the Bulgarians up till 1018. As everywhere else in the Middle Ages, so too in Serbia it was the Church that was the means of attaining to such a rank. The youngest son of the founder of the Nemanja dynasty, known in the history of the Serbs as Saint Sava, succeeded in establishing an independent Serbian Church and in placing himself at the head of it as the first Serbian Archbishop. He established the first schools, became the first known writer, "the father of Serbian mediaeval literature", and prepared and organised the Church in such a way that it could play among the Serbs the same rôle as that played by the Church in the west of Europe, among the Western peoples. The mediaeval literature of the Serbs was, therefore, mainly ecclesiastical in character and, having been closely in touch with, and influenced by, Byzantium, it represents at the same time Byzantine literature in miniature.

By the middle of the fourteenth century, under Tsar Dušan—a contemporary of Edward III of England—the Serbs reached the culminating point in their political as well as in their cultural activities. The Serbian Empire was then at its zenith and Tsar Dušan held sway in the Balkans. His empire was, however, an unconsolidated conglomeration of rapidly conquered states and nations. Like that of many mediaeval empires, the power of Serbia consisted in the individual power and authority of its ruler. After Dušan's sudden death in 1356, nine months before Edward, the Black Prince, won the battle of Poitiers, his empire fell to pieces. He was succeeded by his only son, Uroš, known in the heroic songs as "a child", but nineteen years of age at his succession. Uroš had neither the power nor the authority of his father and disruption soon set in. Dušan's lands were seized and divided by many nobles of the country, among whom the most prominent were two brothers, Vukašin and Uglješa. These renounced the authority of Uroš in 1366 and ruled independently in their provinces. The elder brother, Vukašin, practically dethroned Uroš and assumed the title of king. He made his seat at Skoplje and extended his authority over North-Western Macedonia and Old Serbia, while his younger brother, Uglješa, ruled in the district round the Struma. Like the many other petty rulers who hurried to establish themselves as independent monarchs, they possessed no sense of a common cause and communal defence; they too were utterly absorbed in local and personal interests. Under such conditions and ten years after Dušan's death, the Serbs were confronted with the Turks, who had by that time subjugated Bulgaria and firmly established themselves in Thrace. Under their able leader, Murad, they had gone from one victory to another. Murad himself was a great hero. He ascended the throne in 1359 and in the very next year he crossed the Hellespont. In 1365 he established his seat at Adrianople, thus planting his foot firmly in the Balkans.

Realising the coming danger, Vukašin and Uglješa determined to throw the Turks out of Europe. Gathering a strong army, they met the Ottoman forces in September, 1371, in Eastern Thrace, on the Marica, now the boundary between Greece and Turkey. They met with practically no resistance at first, because the main Turkish forces were in Asia Minor with Sultan Murad; but his marshal, Evrenos, utterly defeated the Serbs in a night of battle at Černomen. The bodies of the two brothers were not found and it is supposed that they were drowned in the river, like most of their army. According to stories recorded by Laonicus Chalcocondylas and by some Serbian and Turkish chronicles, the Turkish victory is represented as an extremely easy one, although there were not more than 4000 (or 800 according to Chalcocondylas) of the Turks. The Turks have marked the day as the *sirfsindughi*, i.e. the defeat of the Serbs. The whole of Eastern Macedonia was now lost to the Serbs and the Turkish cavalry roamed afterwards as far as Thessaly and Albania. The defeat was a direct blow to all the Balkan States and a great encouragement to the victorious Osmanlis. The Byzantine Emperor, alarmed at the rapid progress of the Turks, went personally to Italy and France to implore help. The Pope, Gregory XI, then seated at Avignon, wrote in May of the following year to the Hungarian king, Lewis, asking him to stem the tide of this cruel people who were threatening the Adriatic ports. A renewed, and wider, appeal was made by the Pope in November of the same year. France, however, was at war with England, and Venice at war with Genoa, and no help was to be expected from those quarters or from Hungary.

Soon after the battle of the Marica, Tsar Uroš died, in December, 1371, at the age of thirty-five and left no heir. The Serbian throne was claimed by three men: by King Vukašin's son, Marko, by a nobleman named Lazar, and by the King of Bosnia, Tvrtko. King Marko claimed the throne because it had been held by his father. He established himself at Prilep, in Southern Macedonia, and shared the authority with his younger brother, Andriaš. Like other rulers in the Vardar valley, the two brothers were forced to acknowledge Murad's suzerainty. Lazar and Tvrtko claimed descent from the Nemanja dynasty and

both aimed at the re-establishment of the Serbia of the
Nemanići. Lazar's wife, Milica, was a daughter of Prince
Vlatko, a descendant of Nemanja, through his son Vukan.
Lazar was born about 1329, in a family of nobles, and as a
young man he was a courtier at the palace of Tsar Dušan.
In the heroic songs he is represented as one of Dušan's
servants and a man of humble origin; while his wife is said
to have been the only daughter of a certain Jug Bogdan
and the sister of nine brothers, Jugovići. Although Lazar
had secured the greatest amount and the most central
portion of the Serbian lands, he modestly assumed the
title of *knez*, i.e. prince, leaving to Marko and Tvrtko the
name of king. There are no records of enmity between
Prince Lazar and Tvrtko; it seems probable that they
divided the Serbian lands by mutual agreement. Tvrtko
claimed to be a direct descendant of Nemanja in the female
line. Having conquered many lands, previously under
the sway of the Nemanja dynasty, he considered himself
doubly entitled to crown himself "rex Rasciae, Bosniae,
maritimarumque partium". This was in the summer of
1377, Rascia being the original name for Serbia. Unlike
King Marko and Prince Lazar, he was not yet forced to
recognise the Sultan's suzerainty.

During the nine years that followed the battle of the
Marica, Prince Lazar succeeded in consolidating the lands
in his possession and in this work he was much assisted by
his son-in-law, Vuk Branković, a man of high birth and
one of the most prominent state dignitaries of the period.
His wife, Mara, was the eldest of the five daughters of
Prince Lazar. Although he had lands of his own and ruled
more or less independently, he acknowledged Lazar as his

supreme lord and sincerely helped him in all his work. We shall see presently, however, that in the traditional heroic poetry he is described as a traitor, without any historical foundation whatsoever.

Having enforced his suzerainty upon the neighbouring rulers, Sultan Murad meanwhile proceeded slowly and cautiously in consolidating and colonising the conquered lands, and at the same time prepared for the final conquest of the Balkan Peninsula. His plan was to push forward in two directions, towards the Adriatic and towards the Danube, in order to separate the Serbs and the Bulgarians and thus prevent any possible co-operation of the two countries against himself. He therefore forced his way towards the Danube in 1382 and aimed at conquering Niš, the key of the gateway to the valley of the Morava, and led his army personally against Lazar. Prince Lazar, realising the danger, undertook to stem the Turkish tide. In 1386, fierce fighting took place in the valley of the Nišava and finally, after a twenty-five days' siege, the fortress of Niš surrendered to Murad. Lazar withdrew to the valley of the Toplica, towards Kruševac, his capital, and in 1387 he defeated a Turkish army near Pločnik. This set-back caused Murad to bring fresh forces and prepare for a decisive battle with the Serbs.

Accompanied by his two sons, Bayezid and Yakub, the Sultan headed a strong army against the Serbs in the summer of 1389, commanded by his experienced marshals, Evrenos, Saridze and Balaban. A number of Christian vassals reinforced him with their own contingents. Prince Lazar had secured the assistance of his son-in-law, Vuk Branković, and of the Bosnian king, Tvrtko. A number of Croats also came to help him. The two forces met on the plain of Kosovo, in the territory ruled by Vuk, on Tuesday, the 15th June (28th June, New Style), 1389. A short but fierce battle followed. Sultan Murad was killed by a Serbian knight at the end of the battle, while Knez Lazar was taken prisoner and beheaded by the Turks after the battle.

II

In the heroic songs, there is not much reference to the events that preceded the conflict. It is simply stated that Sultan Murad, having "fallen" upon Kosovo with his army, sent to Prince Lazar the following message:

> O Prince Lazar,   Head of the land,
> It never was known,   and it never can be,
> That in one Empire,   two should rule,
> And that the lieges   should doubly be taxed.
> We cannot both of us   bear the sceptre.
> Send to *me* then   the keys and the taxes.
> The golden keys   of each strong place
> And the taxes   for seven years
> And shouldst thou decline   to send them me
> Then let us meet   on the Field of Blackbirds
> And with our sabres   divide the Empire.[1]

Tsar Lazar, as he is often called in the traditional heroic songs, having been asked by St Elias to choose between the earthly and the heavenly kingdom, decided for the latter, and at once issued a writ calling upon all his men to join him in a fight to the death against the Turks. The willingness and enthusiasm with which they responded is

[1] Translated by Professor R. W. Seton-Watson.

described in the heroic songs *Musić Stevan* and *Car Lazar i Carica Milica* (Dr W. A. Morison's translations). The first hundred lines of the former run as follows:

MUSIĆ STEVAN

Musić Stevan cooling wine was drinking
At the Majdan, rich in purest silver,
In his beautiful and lordly dwelling;
And his servant Vaistina poured it.
When of cooling wine he had drunk deeply,
Then said Musić Stevan to his servant:
"Vaistina, thou my child beloved,
I will lay me down a while to slumber;
Drink some wine, and take a bite of supper,
Then walk before my lordly dwelling,
Look upon the clear blue sky, and tell me
If the silver moon is sinking westward,
If the morning star is shining eastward,
If the time has come for us to travel
To the fair and level Plain of Blackbirds
To our meeting with the Prince of Serbia.
For thou knowest well, my child beloved,
When we swore our solemn oath before him,
Then the Prince of Serbia adjured us,
He adjured us, threatened us with curses:
'He who is a Serb, with Serbian forebears,
And of Serbian blood and Serbian nurture,
And comes not to battle at Kosovo,
He shall ne'er be blessed with descendants,
With descendants, either male or female,
And beneath his hand shall nothing flourish,
Neither yellow wine nor waving cornfield:
Let him rot, together with his children!'"

Stevan lay upon his downy cushions,
Vaistina took a bite of supper,
Ate some supper, and some wine he swallowed,
Then walked out before the lordly dwelling,
Gazed upon the sky, and saw full clearly
That the silver moon was sinking westward,
That the morning star was shining eastward,
That the time was come for them to travel
To the fair and level Plain of Blackbirds
To their meeting with the Prince of Serbia.
Then he viewed the horses in their stables,
Viewed them, and led out two noble horses,
Saddled them and put their harness on them,
One for him, the other for his master;
Then, returning to the lordly dwelling,
Out he brought the cross-emblazoned banner;
There were crosses twelve upon the banner,
And each cross of purest gold was fashioned;
And the image of Saint John was on it,
(Patron Saint was he of Musić Stevan:)
Stood it up against the lordly dwelling,
Then he mounted to the upper storey
To arouse his sleeping lord and master.

And when he had mounted to the doorway,
He encountered Stevan's faithful lady,
She embraced him and she kissed him warmly:
"My blood-brother, servant Vaistina,
By Saint John and God above I beg thee:
Thou hast ever been my faithful servant
Since we swore blood-brotherhood together;
Do not wake my sleeping lord and master,
For I have been dreaming, woe upon me!

In my dream a flight of doves was winging,
And in front of them were two grey falcons,
And they flew over our lordly dwelling,
Flew away to Kosovo the level,
And they fell amid the camp of Murad,
Stayed where they descended, never moving.
That, my brother, is an omen for you,
Ye must now be careful lest ye perish".

Then responded servant Vaistina:
"Dearest sister, Stevan's faithful lady,
Never will I, sister, be unfaithful
To the man who is our lord and master;
For thou didst not see the Prince of Serbia
When we swore our solemn oath before him,
How the Prince of Serbia then adjured us,
Then adjured us, threatened us with curses:
'He who is a Serb, with Serbian forebears,
And of Serbian blood and Serbian nurture,
And comes not to battle at Kosovo,
Nothing beneath his hand shall flourish,
Neither yellow wine nor waving cornfield;
May the fields ne'er shower their gifts upon him,
May he ne'er be blessed with descendants;
Let him rot, together with his children!'
I should never dare to be unfaithful
To the man who is our lord and master".
Then he went into the upper storey,
And awoke his sleeping lord and master:
"Now rise up, my dearest lord and master,
For the time has come for us to travel".
To his feet the hero then rose swiftly,
And he laved his face with cooling water,

Then did Stevan don his lordly raiment,
Girded on his sword of tempered metal,
Took a jug of yellow wine and quaffed it,
Drinking to the patron of his forebears,
Luck in travel, and the cross of glory,
In his dwelling, at his lordly table;
'Twas the last time he was e'er to do it.
Forth he went then from his lordly dwelling,
And they mounted on their noble horses....

According to the traditional poetry, Princess Milica was
the only daughter of an old noble, Jug Bogdan, and the
sister of nine Jugovići. On the eve of the battle she im-
plored Prince Lazar to leave her at least one of them:

..."Thou, Tsar Lazar, golden crown of Serbia,
Goest out to-morrow to Kosovo,
Taking with thee serving-men and voivodes,
Leaving no one at thy white-walled dwelling,
Yea, Tsar Lazar, not a single servant,
Not a man to carry thee a letter
To Kosovo, and bring back an answer;
Thou art taking with thee my nine brothers,
My nine brothers, the nine Jugovići;
Leave to me at least a single brother,
Just one brother, that I may swear by him."

Then responded Lazar, Tsar of Serbia:
"Milica, my Queen and dearest lady,
Which of thy brothers art desirous
That I leave thee in my white-walled dwelling?"
—"Do thou leave me Boško Jugoviću."

Then responded Lazar, Prince of Serbia:
"Milica, my Queen and dearest lady,

When the white day dawns upon the morrow,
When the white day dawns, and the sun is shining,
And the gates are opened in the castle,
Go thou out unto the castle gateway,
There in serried ranks will pass my army,
All on horseback, with their gleaming lances,
And before them Boško Jugoviću,
Carrying a cross-emblazoned banner;
Tell him that I give the lad my blessing,
Let him give the banner to another
And remain with thee about the dwelling".

When the day had dawned upon the morrow,
And the gates were opened in the castle,
Forth went Milica the Queen of Serbia,
And she waited by the castle gateway
Till in serried ranks there passed the army,
All on horseback, with their gleaming lances,
And before them Boško Jugoviću,
On a chestnut, all in golden armour,
Covered by the banner which he carried
(My blood-brother!) to his chestnut warhorse.
On the flagstaff was a golden apple,
On the golden sphere were golden crosses,
From each golden cross hung yellow tassels,
And they dangled around the young man's shoulders,
Then the Empress Milica approached him,
And she seized the chestnut by the bridle,
Threw her arms about her brother's shoulders,
Quietly the lady addressed him:
"O my brother, Boško Jugoviću,
Now the Tsar my master gives thee to me,
Says that thou must not go forth to battle,

And he sends his blessing to thee, Boško,
Thou must give the banner to another,
Stay behind in Kruševac to guard me,
That I have a brother I may swear by".

Then responded Boško Jugoviću:
"Go, my sister, to thy white-walled tower;
I should not remain behind to guard thee,
Shouldst thou not give the banner to another,
If the King should offer me Kruševac;
For my scornful comrades would cry loudly:
'See the coward, Boško Jugoviću!
Him who durst not venture out to battle,
Shed his life-blood for the cross of glory,
Durst not give his life, his faith defending!'"
Then he spurred his chestnut through the gateway.

Then rode by the aged Jug Bogdan,
After him came seven Jugovići;
In their turn she strove to stop the seven,
But not one would even look upon her.

For awhile she waited by the gateway,
Then came riding Jugoviću-Vojine,
Leading all the sovereign's noble horses,
And of purest gold were all their trappings;
Then she seized his warhorse by the bridle,
Threw her arms around her brother's shoulders,
Pleadingly the lady thus addressed him:
"O my brother, Jugoviću Vojine,
Now the Tsar my master gives thee to me,
And he sends his blessing to thee, brother,
Thou must give the horses to another,
Stay behind to guard me in Kruševac,
That I may have a brother to swear by".

Then responded Jugovićư Vojine:
"Go, my sister, to thy white-walled tower;
I would not remain behind from battle,
Give the Emperor's horses to another,
If I knew that I must surely perish;
I must go to battle at Kosovo,
Shed my life-blood for the cross of glory,
Perish for my faith with all my brothers".
Then he spurred his warhorse through the gateway.

And when Milica the Queen had seen this,
Down she fell upon the chilly cobbles,
Swooning down she fell, and lay unconscious.
Lazar then rode by, the Prince of Serbia;
When he saw her lying on the cobbles,
From his eyes the heavy tear-drops started,
And from right to left he looked around him,
And he called his servant Golubane:
"Golubane, thou my faithful servant,
Do thou now dismount from thy white warhorse,
In thy arms take Milica my lady,
Bear her gently to her slender tower;
I will give to thee my royal blessing,
Do not go to battle at Kosovo,
But remain within the white-walled dwelling".

When the servant Golubane heard this,
Down his cheeks the heavy tear-drops trickled,
From his snow-white warhorse he dismounted,
In his arms he took the royal lady,
Bore her gently to her slender tower;
Then his stout heart's promptings overcame him,
Then he felt he must go forth to battle;
To his snow-white warhorse he betook him,
Mounted it, and rode out to Kosovo.

On the eve of the battle, Prince Lazar gave a feast to his noblemen. In Professor Seton-Watson's translation, the scene is described as follows:

> The Tsar Lazar kept his nameday
> In the silent fortress of Kruševac.
> At his rich table he seated his guests,
> All his lords and noble courtiers.
> On the right sat the old Jug Bogdan,
> At his side the nine Jugović brothers;
> Vuk Branković on his left,
> And the other lords in their due order.
> But facing him was Miloš seated,
> And beside him two Serbian Voivodes—
> Ivan Kosančić was the one,
> And the other was Milan Toplica.
> The Tsar lifted the brimming goblet,
> And thus he spake to his noble guests:—
> "To whom shall I quaff the brimming beaker?
> If it be age that should decide,
> Then I must pledge the old Jug Bogdan.
> If it be rank that should decide it,
> Then I must drink to Vuk Branković.
> If I may follow the voice of feeling,
> Then the cup falls to my wife's dear brothers,
> To my wife's brothers, the nine Jugović.
> Should manly beauty prescribe my choice,
> Then the cup is the prize of Kosančić,
> And if height is to decide,
> Then the cup is Milan Toplica's.
> But if hero's prowess decides my choice,
> Then I drain it to Miloš the Voivode:
> To no other may it be pledged.
> To the health of Miloš Obilić!

Thy health, O Miloš, loyal and false—
First loyal to me—and at last to me false.
To-morrow thou wilt in battle betray me,
Wilt pass over to Murad's army.
Thy health, O Miloš, and drain the beaker:
Drink, and keep it as a gift".

Up to his feet sprang Miloš Obilić,
Then to the black earth down he bowed.
"Thanks to thee, most gracious Tsar Lazar,
My heartfelt thanks to thee for thy toast;
For thy toast and for thy present;
But no thanks for such a speech!
For—else may my faith undo me—
Never unfaithful have I been,
Ne'er have I been, and ne'er shall be.
But I am resolved on the field to-morrow
For the faith of Christ to give my life.
But faithless sits at thy very knee
And drinks the wine from his silk-draped glass,
He the accursed, the traitor Branković.
On the sacred Vitus-Day to-morrow
We shall see on the Field of Blackbirds,
Who is faithful and who is faithless.
But by God the Almighty I swear it—
To-morrow I'll go to the Field of Blackbirds,
And there I shall kill the Sultan Murad,
And plant my foot upon his throat.
Should God and fortune grant to me
My safe return to Kruševac,
Vuk Branković shall be my captive,
And to my war-lance I shall bind him,
As a woman the flax to her apron,
And shall drag him thus to the Field of Blackbirds."

While of the actual battle a brief and unimpressive account is given in a ballad of about fifty lines, some of the events that followed immediately are described in several very beautiful songs. Of these we shall quote Professor Seton-Watson's translation of *The Mother of the Jugović*. Some of the others can be found in English translations by Helen Rootham, in the little book entitled *Kossovo* published at Oxford in 1920, or in those of Madame Elodie Lawton Mijatovich, published in her book *Kossovo* in London in 1881. Most of the Kosovo heroic songs have been translated also by George Rapall Noyes and Leonard Bacon, in their book *Heroic Ballads of Servia*, published at Boston in 1913. Professor Seton-Watson's translation of the *Smrt Majke Jugovića* runs as follows:

> Dear God, how great a marvel!
> When the army camped on the field of Kosovo,
> And in that army nine Jugović brothers,
> And the tenth, the old Jug Bogdan.
> The mother of the Jugović prays to God,
> That He may give her the eyes of a falcon
> And the white wings of a swan,
> That she may fly to the Plain of Kosovo
> And may see the nine Jugović brothers,
> And the tenth, the old Jug Bogdan.
>
> As she prayed, her prayer was granted,
> God gave her the eyes of a falcon
> And the white wings of a swan.
> Then she flies to the Plain of Kosovo.
> Dead she found the nine Jugović brothers,
> And the tenth, the old Jug Bogdan.
> And above them, nine spears of battle;
> Perched on the spears, falcons nine;

Around the spears, nine good steeds;
And beside them nine grim lions.
Then did they winny, the nine good steeds;
Then did they roar, the nine grim lions;
Then did they scream, the nine falcons.
E'en then the mother was hard of heart,
And from her heart no tear did rise.

But she takes the nine good steeds,
And she takes the nine grim lions,
And she takes the nine falcons.
Back she turns to her castle white.
From afar her sons' wives saw her;
A little nearer they came to meet her.
There was clamour of nine widows:
There was weeping of nine orphans:
There was neighing of nine good steeds:
There was roaring of nine grim lions:
There was screaming of nine falcons.
E'en then the mother was hard of heart,
And from her heart no tear did rise.

When night was come, and the midnight was there,
Then the grey horse of Damjan groaned.
And Damjan's mother asked his wife:
"Daughter of mine and wife of Damjan,
What sets the horse of Damjan groaning?
Can it be hunger for pure white corn?
Can it be thirst for water of Zvečan?"
Then answered the wife of Damjan:
"It is not hunger for pure white corn:
It is not thirst for water of Zvečan.
It is, that Damjan had taught him,

Till midnight, to feast on hay,
And after midnight, to take the road.
Now 'tis his master he is mourning,
For he will never bear him more".
E'en then the mother was hard of heart,
And from her heart no tear did rise.

When morning came and break of dawn,
There came flying two coal-black ravens.
Bloody were their wings up to the shoulders.
Round their beaks there clung white foam.
And they carried the hand of a hero,
And on the hand a wedding-ring of gold.
They threw it into the mother's lap.

The mother of the Jugović took the hand,
She turned it round, she fondled it,
And then she called the wife of Damjan.
"Daughter of mine and wife of Damjan,
Could'st thou tell whose hand is this?"
Then answered the wife of Damjan:
"Mother of mine, O mother of Damjan,
This is the hand of our own Damjan,
For I do know the ring, my mother;
At the betrothal I did have it".
The mother took the hand of Damjan,
She turned it round, she fondled it.
Then to the hand she softly spake:
"O my hand, my fresh green apple,
Where did'st thou grow, where wert thou plucked?
'Twas on my bosom thou did'st grow.
The plucking, 'twas on Kosovo's plain".
Speaking, she breathed her soul away.

It has been mentioned that love and love-making are almost excluded from the Yugoslav heroic poetry. The song *The Maiden of Kosovo* (*Kosovka devojka*), which we quote here in Dr W. A. Morison's translation, illustrates in what form and to what extent women are allowed to express their feelings for men.

> Early rose the maiden of Kosovo,
> Early rose she on the Sunday morning,
> On the Sunday, ere the sun was shining,
> Up she rolled her snow-white sleeves, the maiden,
> Up she rolled them, to her snowy elbows:
> On her shoulders two white loaves she loaded,
> In her hands she took two golden pitchers,
> And the one was filled with cooling water,
> And the other with red wine was brimming;
> She went out upon the Plain of Blackbirds,
> Over the field of battle walked the maiden,
> Turning every blood-stained hero over;
> Every hero whom she found still breathing,
> Gently laved she with the cooling water,
> Gave him wine to drink from out her pitcher,
> Offered him white bread to stay his hunger.
> As she walked the field, she chanced to stumble
> On the hero Orlović Pavle,
> On the Prince's standard-bearer,
> And she found the hero was still breathing:
> At his wrist his right hand had been severed,
> And his left leg severed at the knee-cap;
> All the hero's curving ribs were broken,
> And his lungs were showing through the gashes;
> Gently from the pool of blood she moved him,
> Gently laved his wounds with cooling water,

Gave him wine to drink from out her pitcher,
Offered him white bread to stay his hunger.

When the hero's heart commenced to flutter,
Spake the hero Orlović Pavle:
"Dearest sister, maiden of Kosovo,
Tell me of the great distress that drives thee,
That thou turnest o'er the blood-stained heroes;
Whom thou dost seek upon the field of battle?
Is't perhaps a brother or a cousin,
Or is it perchance thy aged parent?"

Then replied the maiden of Kosovo:
"Dearest brother mine, thou unknown hero,
'Tis not for a kinsman I am searching,
Neither for a brother nor a cousin
Seek I now, nor for my aged parent;
Listen to my words, thou unknown hero:
When the Prince administered communion
At the lovely church of Samodreža,
Thirty monks for three long weeks were busy,
All the Serbian army took communion;
Last of all there came three noble Voivodes:
And the first was Milošu the Voivode,
And the second Kosančić Ivane,
And the third was Toplica Milane;
As it chanced, I stood within the gateway
When the Voivode Milošu was walking,
Tall and handsome was the noble hero,
With his sabre dragging on the cobbles,
And his silken cap bedecked with feathers;
From his shoulders hung a coloured mantle,
Round his neck a silken scarf was knotted;

Looking round, he cast his eyes upon me,
From his shoulders took the coloured mantle,
Took his mantle off, and gave it to me:
'Take, O maiden fair, this coloured mantle,
That the mantle may remind thee of me,
And recall my name to thee hereafter;
I go forth perchance to fall in battle
In the forces of the Prince of Serbia;
Pray to God above, my dearest sister,
That unharmed I may return from battle,
And that happy fortune may befall thee:
I will take thee as a bride for Milan,
For my Milan, for my own blood-brother,
For we swore blood-brotherhood together,
By Saint John and God above we swore it;
I will be thy sponsor at the wedding'.

"After him came Kosančić Ivane,
Tall and handsome was the noble hero,
With his sabre dragging on the cobbles,
And his silken cap bedecked with feathers;
From his shoulders hung a coloured mantle,
Round his neck a silken scarf was knotted,
And a golden ring was on his finger;
Looking round, he cast his eyes upon me,
Took the golden trinket from his finger,
Took it from his finger, gave it to me:
'Take this golden ring, O fairest maiden,
That the trinket may remind thee of me,
And recall my name to thee hereafter:
I go forth perchance to fall in battle
In the forces of the Prince of Serbia;
Pray to God above, my dearest sister,

That unharmed I may return from the battle,
And that happy fortune may befall thee:
I will take thee as a bride for Milan,
For my Milan, for my own blood-brother,
For we swore blood-brotherhood together,
By Saint John and God above we swore it;
I will be thy best man at the wedding'.

"After him came Toplica Milane,
Tall and handsome was the noble hero,
With his sabre dragging on the cobbles,
And his silken cap bedecked with feathers;
From his shoulders hung a coloured mantle,
Round his neck a silken scarf was knotted,
In his hand a handkerchief he carried;
Looking round, he cast his eyes upon me,
From his hand he took the golden kerchief,
Took it from his hand, and gave it to me:
'Take, O maiden fair, this golden kerchief,
That the kerchief may remind thee of me,
And recall my name to thee hereafter:
I go forth perchance to fall in battle
In the forces of the Prince of Serbia;
Pray to God above, my dearest sister,
That unharmed I may return from battle,
And that happy fortune may befall thee:
I will take thee for my faithful lady'.

"Then the three departed, all three voivodes:
Them I seek upon the field of battle".

Then responded Orlović Pavle:
"Dearest sister, maiden of Kosovo,
Dost thou see, my sister, those bright lances,

Where they stand the tallest and the thickest?
There was shed the blood of the noble heroes,
Till it flowed about their horses' stirrups,
Round about their saddle-girths and stirrups,
Round the silken waistbands of the horsemen;
There it was that all three voivodes perished!
Now betake thee to thy white-walled dwelling,
Do not smear thy skirt and sleeves with bloodstains".

When the maiden heard the words he uttered,
Down her cheeks the heavy tear-drops trickled,
Back she wandered to her white-walled dwelling,
Loud laments the beauteous maiden uttered:
"Woe upon me, miserable maiden!
If I laid my hand upon a fir-tree,
Young and green, it would dry up and shrivel!"

III

The earliest known reference to the battle of Kosovo is
that of the Russian deacon Ignatius of Smolensk, who in
the year and the month of the battle accompanied Pimen,
the Moscow Metropolitan, to the seat of the Byzantine
Emperor. They were on Turkish territory a few days after
the battle, and having passed the towns of Dafrusia and
Karfia they reached the town of Astravia (?), where they
stopped to enquire about the Sultan Murad, because they
were told that he had gone to fight the Serbian Tsar Lazar
and that the rumour was afloat that both rulers had been
killed on the Suima (?). Being on Turkish territory and
fearing disorders they left the town on Sunday, the 27th
June, the day of their arrival, and went to Constantinople,

which they reached with "indescribable joy". Ignatius says nothing further about the event, nor does he mention Kosovo and Miloš, as has been maintained by some Yugoslav writers.

In the firman of the Sultan Bayezid, issued in the middle of the month of Shaaban, year 791 (July, 1389), to the Kadi of Brusa, where Murad's body had been transferred for burial, the statement is made that the Turks had won the battle at the field of Kosovo, but that one Miloš Kobilić, by means of a ruse, entered the Sultan's tent and stabbed him with a poisoned dagger; that he then tried to run away, but was caught and cut down by Turkish soldiers. The fresh detail in this document is Miloš's surname, Kobilić.

The conclusions which we derive from these two records are practically identical and they express the belief that was current in the Turkish Empire immediately after the battle. We shall turn now to see what was known of it abroad at that time. In the instructions which the Council of Venice gave to its ambassador, Andrea Bembo, on the 23rd July, 1389, in sending him both to the Byzantine Emperors (John VII and Emanuel II) at Constantinople and to the Sultan at Adrianople, the battle between Murad and Lazar and the death of the former are mentioned, but not the place or the date of the battle. The Council, although considering the news of the Sultan's death as not quite reliable, expressed its sorrow for Murad's death. On the 1st August, 1389, the Bosnian king, Tvrtko, sent a letter to the town of Trogir (or Trau) in Dalmatia, in which he informs the inhabitants that the Bosnian kingdom had fought a battle with the Turkish Sultan Murad on the 15th June, that he had defeated him and practically annihilated his army, while he himself had suffered but few losses. That Tvrtko had sent similar letters to other towns is seen from the answer which Florence sent to him on the 20th October of the same year. Florence, however, had received the news also from other sources, both written and oral, which showed that Murad, with many thousands of his soldiers and his two sons, fell at Kosovo on the 15th June, St Vitus's day, in a fierce and bloody battle. Florence rejoiced over this news and the victory of the Bosnian kingdom. As regards Murad's death, the current rumour in Florence was that twelve Christian nobles, having sworn to kill the Sultan, had penetrated into his tent, and that one of them had killed him with a dagger, while the rest of them were cut down on the Sultan's body. There is no mention of either Prince Lazar or the knight Miloš. The explanation of the Bosnian king's taking all the credit is to be found in the fact that Tvrtko considered himself, and was also considered by the Venetian Republic after 1377, as "rex Rasciae[1] Bosniae, maritimarumque partium". In Venice, however, it was well known that it was Lazar who faced Murad at Kosovo and not Tvrtko. It is probable that King Tvrtko did not intend to spread a false account of the battle, but that, on receiving the news of Murad's death and the withdrawal of the Turkish armies from Kosovo, he no doubt regarded the Turks as having been defeated and hastened to announce the good news to the Christian world of the West.

Of the five records of the fourteenth century, the earliest dates from twelve or thirteen days after the battle of Kosovo; the latest, that of Florence, is dated about four months after the battle. Among the records of the fol-

[1] See p. 55.

lowing century, that of the Spanish ambassador, Ruy Gonzalez de Clavijo, should be mentioned as the earliest. He was among the personalities selected to represent the King of Castile at Samarkand, the seat of Timur. The embassy sailed from the port of Seville on the 22nd May, 1400. Clavijo decided to give a description of the countries through which they passed. The result was a curious chronicle, the oldest Spanish narrative of travels of any value, written at the time when hardly any prose literature in Spanish existed. While passing through Constantinople in 1404, fifteen years after the battle of Kosovo, Clavijo heard that Bayezid's father, Murad, an excellent knight, was killed on the battlefield by a Christian count, called Lazaro, who thrust his lance into Murad's breast twice, till it came out at his back, and that Ilderim (the "Lightning") Bayezid avenged the death of his father by killing Count Lazaro in the battle with his own hand. Clavijo adds also that the son of Lazaro joined Bayezid, and that he then lived with Muzulman Chalabi, the son of Ilderim Bayezid. It is obvious that the way in which the two rulers lost their lives is pictured as Spanish *hidalgos* would have acted under similar conditions. Clavijo returned to Spain in March, 1406, after an absence of nearly three years and died in Madrid in April, 1412. His itinerary was published first at Seville in 1582 and then at Madrid in 1782.

Next in order should be mentioned a number of Yugo-slav chronicles, genealogies and lives of various personalities of the fifteenth century. What is said in them about Kosovo mostly amounts to the statement that a battle was fought between Sultan Murad and Prince Lazar on Tuesday, the 15th June, 1389, at Kosovo, and that Miloš killed

Murad, while the Turks killed Lazar. In the life of Stephen Lazarević, Lazar's son, written in 1431–2 by Constantine the "Philosopher", Miloš's name is not mentioned, but it is said that a faithful follower, accused of disloyalty to his master, in order to justify himself, went over to the Turks and killed Murad with a dagger. It is mentioned also that a Turk called Sarash caught Lazar alive. It is important to add that in one of these short records it is asserted that the Serbs defeated the Turks at first, but that then some of the Serbian troops *left the battlefield*, whereupon the Turks turned back, and defeated the Serbs.

This first suggestion of treason was followed by a definite statement to the same effect. At the end of the century a Serb, Konstant, son of Mikhail Konstantinović of Ostrovica, who had been captured by the Turks in 1455 and recaptured by the Hungarians in 1463, wrote[1] that the battle was lost "through faithlessness, discord and envy of evil and unrighteous men", who refused to help Lazar and stood looking on at the battle. The Turks, however, captured them all and they were put to death by order of the Sultan, who said that since they were traitors to their own master so they would be to him.

An anonymous Ragusan chronicle of about the same time says that the "Bosnian King Lazar", supported by Vuk Branković and Vlako Vuković, fought the Turks on the above-mentioned date, but that neither the Bosnians nor the Turks were victorious because "it was a great slaughter".[2] A little later, a Ragusan, Lj. Crievič Tubero,

---

[1] *Pamiętniki Janczara Polaka, przed rokiem* 1500 *napisane. Zbiór pisarzow polskich*, tom v. W. Warszawje, 1828.
[2] *Monumenta spectantia historiam Slavorum Meridionalium*, XIV. Zagrabiae, 1868.

wrote an account of the battle of Kosovo and of the events which led up to it, based on popular stories. He states that Prince Lazar had summoned his nobles on the eve of the battle to reprimand Miloš for alleged treason. Warmed by wine, he told Miloš this, but Miloš gaily answered that he would justify himself on the morrow. He killed Murad early on the next day. The Turks, infuriated, attacked the Serbs, who, led by Lazar, resisted bravely. During the battle, Prince Lazar dismounted to change his tired horse for a fresh one, and the Serbs, having lost sight of him, thought he had fallen, and lost confidence. The Turks pressed on again and defeated the Serbian army. Lazar, in trying to get away, fell into a trap set for beasts and was captured by the Turks.[1]

But, of all the foreign documents, the most important are the Byzantine and the Turkish. Three Greek historians, Georgios Phrantzes, Laonicus Chalcocondylas and Michael Ducas, wrote about the event of Kosovo a few generations after: some time about the middle of the fifteenth century. Of these, the account of Phrantzes, given in the first volume of his *Chronicle*, which goes down to 1476, is the least important; it is short and nebulous. He drew his information from Turkish sources and, from fear of the Turks, was anxious to say nothing that would hurt them. The Turks were loath to admit that their great Sultan was killed in his own tent by an enemy who had penetrated into it, sacrificing his own life. They always endeavoured to prove that Murad was killed by unfair means after the battle was over. Chalcocondylas and Ducas, on the other hand, based their statements on the tradition that was

---

[1] *Ludovici Tuberonis Commentariorum de rebus, etc.* Francfurti, 1603.

current among the Serbs and transmitted to them in all probability through the Serbian monks of Mount Athos. From all their writings it may be summarised: that Lazar, having heard that Murad was marching against him, collected an army from all parts of his kingdom; that he also expected help from Hungary, and from the Bulgarian king, Šišman, his son-in-law; that Lazar was joined, however, only by his other son-in-law, Vuk, and moved with his army to Kosovo. Murad, having heard of this, led his army thither also. With him were both his sons, Bayezid and Yakub. The fighting was fierce and undecided at first, but the death of Murad turned it in favour of the Turks. The Turks tried to keep Murad's death a secret, but the higher officers acclaimed Bayezid the Sultan. Bayezid at once ordered that his brother Yakub, who had commanded the right wing of the Turkish army, should be killed. The Serbs knew nothing of either Murad's or Miloš's death and were losing confidence. The Turks, eager to avenge Murad and stimulated by Bayezid, pressed on the Serbs and drove them to flight. Lazar and many of his nobles were taken prisoners, brought into the tent where the dead Murad was lying, and all beheaded. The Turkish losses were so heavy that Bayezid gave up the idea of going further into Serbia and returned to Adrianople, having come to terms with Stephen, Lazar's son.

Chalcocondylas, who was, apparently, a more thorough historian than his two contemporaries, investigated both the Greek and the Turkish records, with a view to making it clear when and how Murad was killed at Kosovo. According to the Turkish records, Prince Lazar was about to run away from the battlefield in the midst of the fight,

when Sultan Murad saw him and gave chase, during which
an ordinary Serbian infantryman intercepted the Sultan
and pierced him with his spear. The Greek records, on the
other hand, say that before the battle began a certain Milo,
a brave and enterprising man, offered himself to Lazar to go
and kill Murad, and that he immediately rode towards the
front line of the Turkish army, which was drawn up for
the attack, and, pretending to be the bearer of an important
message, asked for an immediate audience of the Sultan.
Having been admitted to him, he killed him in front of
his janissaries, before they could do anything to prevent
him.

It is important to know that both Chalcocondylas and
Ducas speak of Sultan Murad as a tyrant and hence, as in
the contemporary opinion of the Greeks any means used
against a tyrant were justified, Miloš's deed was hailed by
them as a great and heroic one; they wrote about him with
as much love and admiration as if he had been a Greek: a
very unusual attitude on the part of Byzantine historians
of that time when speaking of Slavs, whom they had considered from the earliest times as barbarians. Through the
Latin and Greek translations of Chalcocondylas's work,
published in 1556 and 1615 respectively, as well as through
that of Ducas, published in Paris in 1649, the event of
Kosovo and Miloš's heroic deed became widely known in
Europe.

Ducas wrote about the battle of Kosovo after 1463. His
account was translated into Italian, probably by a Dalmatian, towards the end of the fifteenth or at the beginning
of the sixteenth century. In this translation, the battle of
Kosovo is described with greater detail than is the case

with Ducas's original. It seems certain, therefore, that the translator introduced into it some popular stories and details about Kosovo, such as were current among the people at that time. He says, for instance, that the Sultan had made overtures to Miloš, in order to detach him from Lazar; that Miloš, however, had shown the Sultan's letters to Prince Lazar and that the prince instructed Miloš to act as if he were going to accept the Sultan's offers. Lastly, he states that Lazar began to suspect Miloš and, at a feast given on the eve of the battle, called him a traitor, whilst drinking his health; whereupon Miloš answered that on the following day he would show who was a traitor and who was not.

Ducas's translator also states that the Bosnian king, Tvrtko, sent 20,000 brave Bosnians under the command of Marshal Vlatko Vuković (Vlatco Vlagevico) to help Lazar; that Lazar, ignorant of Miloš's act, had ordered Vlatko to attack the Turks, the result being the defeat of the opposite wing of the Turkish army. When, however, he pressed on with the attack, a rumour, cleverly spread by the Turks, went about that Lazar's marshal, Dragoslav Pribišić had turned against his prince. Thereupon the Bosnian marshal, Vuković, left the battlefield and the Turks won the victory. We have seen that the first mention of treason was made in a document written forty-two years after the battle, but that no statement was made as to who was the traitor. In the Italian translation of Ducas, the traitor is named as Pribiscio, a name completely unknown to history. It will presently be shown how and why this name was replaced in sixteenth-century documents by that of Lazar's son-in-law, Vuk Branković.

According to the Turkish historian, Muhamed Ibn Mus-
tafa Mautana, called Neshry, a native of Brusa, who wrote
early in the fifteenth century, the Serbian army consisted of
500,000 infantry, commanded by 500 princes, composed of
troops sent from Rumania, Hungary, Bohemia, Germany,
Albania and Bulgaria, supported by 300,000 (*sic*) armoured
knights on good horses. On his estimate, the Serbian army
was eighteen times larger than the Turkish. The whole
narrative abounds in details of popular character and it
implies that oral tradition must have been Neshry's principal source of information. He says that the Turkish army
was about to suffer a complete defeat, when a rumour
spread about that the Serbs were in flight, whereupon
Bayezid delivered an attack and inflicted a defeat on the
enemy. At the end of his narrative he speaks of Murad's
death. When the battle was over, he and some of his staff
went to see the battlefield. Among the fallen was one
Miloš Kobilović, a brave man, who in Lazar's presence
had said: "I am going to kill the Turkish Tsar". Having
encountered the Turks in the battle he was wounded but
he hid among the dead. When Murad approached he rose
and walked towards him, falling and rising on the way.
Murad's suite wanted to prevent him from approaching
the Sultan, but Murad ordered them to let him come.
Miloš came up to him and, pretending to kiss the stirrups,
stabbed him with a knife, which he had concealed, whereupon Murad's followers cut him to pieces. Neshry concludes by saying that Prince Lazar and his son were
accidentally caught and both beheaded.

An English historian of the late sixteenth century,
Richard Knolles, Fellow of Lincoln College, Oxford, in

his *General History of the Turks*, published in London in 1603, gives the same description of Murad's death and adds that

ever since that time the manner of the Turks has been and yet is, that when any ambassador or stranger is to come to kiss the Sultan his hand, or otherwise to approach his person, he is as it were for honour's sake, led by the arms into his presence, between two of the great courtiers; but indeed by so entangling him, to be sure that he shall not offer him the like violence, that did this Cobelitz unto Amurath.

Some of the new details introduced by Neshry are accurate, but others are without foundation. This applies especially to his statement concerning Prince Lazar's allies at Kosovo and the number of the Serbian army. So far as can be proved, Lazar's only allies were the Bosnians, accompanied by a contingent of Croats, under I. Horvat, both commanded by V. Vuković, and perhaps the Serbs of Zeta (i.e. Montenegro), commanded by Đ. Sracimirović, one of Lazar's sons-in-law. These commanders, with Prince Lazar and Vuk Branković, were the chief marshals of the Serbian army. How large that army was, it is difficult to say, but it is certain that Serbia, Bosnia and Zeta of those days could not possibly have produced an army half a million strong. The alliance with Bulgarians, Albanians, Wallachians and Hungarians was a sheer invention of the Turkish historian, designed to show with what formidable forces they had to contend and thus to emphasise their own valour and the importance of their victory.

It will have been seen that history and the heroic poetry agree in all the main facts, except the one concerning the alleged treason of Vuk Branković. It has been proved beyond doubt that he was no traitor, yet the people have branded him as such. Why should one of the greatest officers in Lazar's state, his son-in-law, his faithful supporter and loyal ally at Kosovo, be given such a name? An explanation may perhaps be found in the historical events that took place after the battle. Lazar's son, Stephen Lazarević, hastened to come to terms with Bayezid, because the Hungarians had invaded his lands from the north. Having given his sister Mara into Bayezid's harem, he assumed the title of his father, viz. *knez*, but called himself also *despot*. He shared the power first with his mother, Milica, and then with his brother, Vuk Lazarević, their mother having taken the veil. Vuk Branković ruled over his domain from his capital, Priština, but without recognising Stephen as his supreme lord. He, like Stephen, styled himself Lord of the Serbs and of the Danubian Lands. Contrary to that of Stephen, his policy was to continue fighting the Turks, relying upon the Western Powers. When, however, the Turks occupied the fortress of Golubac (1390), in Northern Serbia, on the Danube, and forced the Wallachian prince, Mircea, into vassalage, and when the death of the Bosnian king, Tvrtko, in 1391 made an alliance between the Serbs, the Hungarians and the Bulgarians impossible, Vuk Branković had also to recognise Bayezid's suzerainty in November, 1392. But, before this happened, he had quarrelled with Lazar's son. The story of the quarrel must have been generally known, and it is perhaps due to this fact that the people, who sympathised with Lazar's family, came to conclude that Vuk Branković was an enemy of the country. As to the alleged retreat from the field of battle, there seems to be some confusion in names. It is known to history that the commander of the Bosnian army, Vlatko Vuković, did retreat from the battlefield directly Lazar was taken prisoner. The surname Vuković seems to have been confused with Branković's Christian name, Vuk. Indeed, some heroic songs confirm this, inasmuch as they say that Vuk Branković came from Herzegovina. He may also have been confused with Lazar's second son, Vuk Lazarević. We know from history that Vuk Lazarević, as a vassal of the Turks, had inflicted many evils on Serbia, and that he died at Plovdiv in Bulgaria (1398) where, according to some, he was imprisoned with Vuk Branković, although it is not known for certain what actually happened to Branković after 1394, when Venice gave him the freedom of that city. The Turks appear to have deprived him of his lands and to have given them to Stephen, who throughout practically the whole of his reign of thirty-five years remained their faithful vassal.

It is the irony of fate that the historical facts about Vuk Branković should so unfortunately have been turned against him in the heroic songs. Such irony appears more conspicuous still when one compares the rôles assigned to him and to Marko Kraljević by the national poets. Before, during, and after Kosovo, Vuk was a sworn foe of the Turks and even when forced to become their vassal it is not recorded that he ever helped them. Marko, on the other hand, did not fight at Kosovo, or at least not on the side of the Serbs. There are historians who believe— though this cannot be proved—that he fought as an ally of the Turks. He had submitted to them about fourteen years after the death of his father, some four years before the battle of Kosovo. We have already mentioned that, five years after Kosovo, Marko, Lazar's son Stephen, and Constantine Dejanović, the Lord of Küstendil, joined Bayezid as his vassals against the Wallachian prince, Mircea, in 1394 (p. 14 f.). It remains a mystery why the Yugoslav heroic poetry should have made him out to be the greatest national hero, while converting Vuk Branković into a traitor.

Mavro Orbini (d. 1614), who wrote more than two centuries after the battle of Kosovo, was the first to accuse Vuk Branković of treachery, though with a certain reserve: "as some people say". He was also the first to speak of a quarrel between Vuk and Miloš, caused by a quarrel between their wives. Orbini's story is obviously connected with the popular belief. We find it repeated, but with changes and fresh details, in a Serbian chronicle (*Tronoški letopis*) written towards the end of the eighteenth century (1791). Its unknown author mentions Orbini and seems to have used a Ragusan translation (of 1722) of his book *Il Regno de gli slavi*, 1601.

There is no doubt that Miloš killed the Sultan at Kosovo, and that he did it by means of a ruse, but whether it happened in the Sultan's tent or on the field cannot be proved. Beyond the fact of his deed, history knows nothing about him. It is quite probable that he was one of the lesser nobles, but in the heroic songs it was thought necessary to make him a rival of Vuk Branković, of equal status, and to represent Miloš also as a son-in-law of Lazar. On this hypothesis, it was natural to explain their quarrel as the result of an earlier quarrel between their two wives over the respective merits of their two husbands. Finally, the loyalty of one son-in-law was to be emphasised in contrast with the treason of the other.

Miloš's true name seems to have been Kobilović or Kobilić; this is attested by all the historical documents up to the middle of the eighteenth century. According to popular belief he was nursed by a mare, and this is suggested by his surname Kobilić (*kobila* means "mare"). Two Serbian historians of the eighteenth century (V. Petrović and P. Julinać) were the first to call him Obiljević and Obilić, a name which suggests a man who abounds in many qualities (*obilje* means "abundance"). They evidently thought it undignified that a man who became a national hero should be said to have been nursed by a mare. On the other hand, Andreja Kačić Miošić always wrote Kobilić, while asserting that Miloš's original name was Obilić.

We ought not, perhaps, to leave the subject of Miloš's deed without referring to the comments of two modern historians. While Knolles, writing in the seventeenth century, said that the name of Miloš was "worthy of eternal memory", because of his courage, H. A. Gibbons, in his excellent *Foundation of the Ottoman Empire*, published in 1916, writes as follows: "It is a commentary on the Serbian character that this questionable act has been held up to posterity as the most saintly and heroic deed of national history". Professor Temperley, commenting upon these words in his *History of Serbia*, published in 1917, says that generalisations of this sort are dangerous and he adds that

the murder of the Red Comyn did not prevent Bruce from becoming the idol of Scotland, and the assassination of tyrants by Harmodius and Aristogeiton and by Brutus was much admired at both Athens and Rome. Yet these facts do not establish the Scot, the Greek, or the Roman as a nation of barbarians.

In this connection it may be of interest to quote the concluding words of Junius Brutus's *Vindiciae Contra Tyrannos*:

Justice requires that tyrants and destroyers of the commonwealth be compelled to reason. Charity challenges the right of relieving and restoring the oppressed. Those who make no account of these things, do as much as in them lies to drive piety, justice, and charity out of this world, that they may never more be heard of. (W. Walker's translation.)

The student of Homeric poetry will be interested in Professor Chadwick's statement, that for the story of the *Iliad* a fairly close parallel, "perhaps the closest of all, is to be found in those Serbian poems which deal with the battle of Kosovo". This parallelism, he says, has long been noticed, but it has unfortunately given rise to an unnecessary controversy.

It is clear enough that Serbian heroic poetry bears little resemblance to the Homeric poems as we have them. But we may strongly suspect that at an earlier stage in the history of Homeric poetry the resemblance would be much closer, although the art of heroic poetry in Greece had doubtless been elaborated for centuries to a far higher degree than was ever attained by Serbian poets.

It is to the treatment of the story, however, and not to the qualities of the poetry, that Professor Chadwick wishes to draw attention.

NOTE

Two different currents existed in the traditional poetry about Kosovo: one literary, the other oral. Both currents flowed into each other: the heroic songs chanted by the *guslari* found their way into literature, while written stories reached the *guslari*, who turned them into decasyllabic lines. In addition to these a fresh current appears towards the end of the eighteenth and the beginning of the nineteenth centuries, when attempts began to be made to describe the whole battle of Kosovo and the tragedy of Lazar in a single epic, entitled the *Lazarica*, the material having been drawn from the written material on Kosovo. As soon as literary activities were awakened among the Serbs, with the opening of the nineteenth century, some men of letters began to group together the heroic songs about Kosovo (Gavrilo Kovačević, *Kosovo*, 1805). When the traditional poetry, including the Kosovo cycle, was collected and edited by Vuk Stefanović Karadžić, many people thought that there must have existed an unfinished epic on the battle of Kosovo, similar to the *Iliad*. Among the first to take up the study of this subject was the great Polish poet, A. Mickiewicz. In 1840–1 he delivered a series of seven lectures in the Collège de France on the subject of Serbian traditional poetry. The lectures were published in 1849. Mickiewicz held the view that there was never, and could never have been, a complete epic about Kosovo, but that it was possible to arrange the existing heroic songs in a special order, so as to make an apparent whole. He himself suggested the order in which they should be put. Following Mickiewicz's suggestion, a Ragusan, Medo Pucić, tried in 1860 to give, in an Italian translation, a complete epic on Kosovo (Orsato Pucić, *Mickiewicz dei canti popolari illirici*. Zara, 1860). A patriotic Serb, Joksim Ilić

Nović, was the first to attempt to represent the events of Kosovo in a single epic of 2156 lines, aiming thus at composing a Serbian *Iliad*. His work, the *Lazarica, or the Battle of Kosovo between the Serbs and the Turks*, 1847, was, however, a feeble imitation of the decasyllabic lines of the heroic songs. A Jewish writer, born in Bohemia, Siegfried Kapper, of whom we shall speak later, published first in 1851 *Lazar, der Serben Zar*, and then in 1853 *Fürst Lazar, epische Dichtung nach serbischen Sagen und Heldengesangen*, an extensive epic about Kosovo; a free composition of his own imagining. A few years later, in 1857, a Russian scholar, P. Bezsonov, produced a prose epic on Kosovo in Russian.

Twenty years after Mickiewicz's lectures had been published a Frenchman, Baron A. d'Avril, published his *La Bataille de Kossovo: Rhapsodie Serbe, Tirée des chants populaires et traduites en français*. He took all the heroic songs that Mickiewicz had chosen and adopted his order of arranging them, but he added three more songs—in all, twelve heroic songs. His idea was not to make one poem of the extant heroic songs, but to collect and put them together in a logical sequence, a plan more sound than some of the former attempts. He was sure that the heroic songs of Kosovo were detached from each other, and that they had never constituted parts of one single epic. Following this plan, he translated twelve such songs. A. d'Avril also drew a parallel between the heroic songs of Kosovo and the *Chanson de Roland*, not only so far as the characters are concerned but also as to the plot. Lazar, for instance, is the Serbian Charlemagne, while Miloš has many similarities to Roland himself. The "traitor", Vuk, corresponds to the traitor *Gane* of the *chanson de geste*. The dispute between the two rivals, Miloš and Vuk, was settled on the banks of the Sitnica, recalling the dispute in the *chanson de geste*, settled in the deep passes of the Pyrenees. Prince Lazar, in his opinion, reminds us more of Indian, French and Spanish heroes than of the Greek and German, because of his fanatical sense of duty, submission to God and absolute devotion. Like the songs about the Cid Campeador, or about Guillaume the "short-nosed", the heroes of Southern France, so the Serbian heroic songs about Kosovo are a legend idealised and popularised, a chronicle both national and religious. Like the French heroes, Lazar also is officially placed among the saints. In giving practically a verbal translation, line for line, d'Avril used the line of the *chanson de geste*, and of the *Chanson de Roland* in particular.

A Serbian scholar, S. Novaković, impressed by d'Avril's work, published in 1871, in Belgrade, and in the following year at Zagreb, his *Kosovo: Serbian National Songs on the Battle of Kosovo*. He used d'Avril's collection, aiming at combining them in logical sequence. When two new collections of Serbian traditional songs were published (by Petranović in 1867 and by Miklosich in 1870), a Croat, A. Pavić, published his *National Poems about the Battle of Kosovo*, at Zagreb, 1877. The work consists of nine heroic songs, running into one whole. He believed that a single epic on Kosovo had at one time existed, of which only a few poems and some fragments have been preserved from the fifteenth century onwards.

In the same year, another Frenchman, C. Courrière, considering that the heroic songs on Kosovo, although translated into French several times, had never been rendered as a whole, published in the *Revue britannique* twelve of these songs. In basing his translation, of nearly one thousand lines, on Novaković's collection, he endeavoured to give as faithful a translation of the original poems as possible. Unlike d'Avril he did not give any titles to his songs.

In the following year, S. Novaković criticised Pavić (*Godišnjak N. Čupića*, 11), and stated that a single epic on

Kosovo neither existed nor could have existed; only isolated songs existed but all dealt with the same subject, and thus formed a cycle which, however, underwent changes between the seventeenth and the beginning of the nineteenth centuries. Another Croatian scholar, T. Maretić, when writing the *Kosovo Heroes and Events in the National Epics* in 1889, on the occasion of the fifth centenary of the battle of Kosovo, entirely agreed with Novaković and fully endorsed his statement. He thought that the first of the heroic songs of the Kosovo cycle to be created was the one dealing with the best-known incident, that of Miloš killing the Sultan. Once this ballad had been created, from the stories that existed among the people, the others followed, dealing with the other events of the story of Kosovo.

The most recent attempts to form a single epic on the battle of Kosovo are the *Lazarica* by S. J. Stojković (Beograd, 1908), containing twenty-five songs, and the *Kosovo* by Dr Laza Dimitrijević (Sarajevo, 1924), consisting of fifteen heroic songs.

Chapter Three

Relationship to English and Scottish Popular Ballads

BEFORE we show in what way the Serbo-Croat and the English-Scottish popular ballads can be compared, it will be of interest to sketch briefly the relationship of the former to the Germanic heroic poetry, the *chansons de geste* and the Spanish *romances*.

I

The word "heroic" is an appropriate equivalent to what is meant in Serbo-Croat by *junački*, and the Yugoslavs invariably use this word when speaking of their *muške pesme*. In dealing with heroic poetry in his book *The Heroic Age*, Professor H. Munro Chadwick refers also to the heroic songs of the Serbs, and in order to give a clearer idea of what they actually are like he compares them with the epic or heroic poems which belong to the so-called Heroic Age—a period of history "extending over about two or probably three hundred years and coming to an end in the latter half of the sixth century"—and which, therefore, in time precede the popular ballads. The heroic poems were cultivated by a society distinctly aristocratic, but different in civilisation from the aristocracy of the later Age of Chivalry. In his opinion, the Serbian heroic songs have many features that are common to the heroic poetry, such as the *Hildebrandslied, Sigurd and Brynhild* and also the *Nibelungenlied* in the Germanic world, and the *chansons de geste*, especially the *Chanson de Roland*, in the Romance world. In English literature the closest analogy to the Serbian heroic songs of the non-historical group is the poetry, mainly of a religious character, which existed before the Norman Conquest. The songs of the historical group seem, on the other hand, to correspond to heroic poems such as *Beowulf*, *Waldere* or *Deor*, or the historical narrative poems inserted in the text of the Saxon chronicle, but the Serbian heroic songs are far more national in character than is the case with *Beowulf*.

Although the Serbian heroic songs of the historic group possess many features that are common to the poetry of the Heroic Age, they also show distinct traits that are common to popular ballads. Professor Chadwick specifies them as the "short heroic poems", in which he includes the Castilian *romances* also, and to which, no doubt, could be added the Ukrainian *dumy* and the Russian *byliny*.

A few years after the publication of Professor Chadwick's work, a treatise appeared in the *Archiv für Slavische Philologie*, in which a Serbian author[1] discussed the similarity between the common motifs of German mediaeval epics, the *Hildebrandslied*, *Waltharius*, *Nibelungenlied* and *Gudrun*, on the one hand, and a number of Serbian heroic songs on the other. Quarrels and fights between father and son before they recognise one another; the freeing of a hero from prison by a girl, and their flight; a quarrel between the wives of two rival heroes, and the coming of a hero disguised as a merchant, in a ship full of merchandise, to win his girl—these constitute the principal subjects in the four German epics and also of several Serbian heroic

[1] Dr Mirko Simonović. (See "Books Consulted".)

songs. The first of these subjects is, however, common to both the East and the West, but it is probable that the Serbs had borrowed it from the German epic. The likeness between the story of the Latin epic about Walther and Hildegunde is very great, in practically all details, with the story in the Serbian heroic song about Stojan Janković and his Moslem sweetheart, Hajkuna. The motif of the quarrel of wives may have come to both the Germans and the Serbs from the ancient Greek sagas about Jason and Medea, and about Melanion and Atalanta. It is perhaps to these sagas that is due the motif that a hero, because of his illness, woos his bride through a friend, who then falls in love with her; a motif which appears in both the *Nibelungenlied* and the beautiful Serbian poems *Maksim Crnojević* and the *Marriage of Tsar Dušan*.

In the same treatise mention is made of the *Oedipus Saga* and *Wolfdietrichsage*. The subject of the former—a marriage between mother and son—was drawn by Hartman von Aue from a French epic for his *Gregorius*. The beginning of this epic tallies so much with the opening lines of the Serbian ballad *Nahod Simeon*, that one is led to believe that the French epic may have been their common source. The French epic was, no doubt, derived from mediaeval Latin literature, which in its turn borrowed this subject from that of Byzantium. The likeness with the Serbian ballad was first noticed by the German poet Wieland, when it was published in a German translation. Since that time, reference to this subject has frequently been made by several scholars, particularly by Herman Paul, and it was he who pointed out that both the French epic and the Serbian ballad must have originated from a Byzantine version of the old Greek story about the Theban king, Oedipus. This conclusion seems to be most probable.

As to the *Wolfdietrichsage*, its subject—a hero's wife carried off in his absence and her rescue by him—appears in a few Serbian heroic songs about the national hero Marko Kraljević, and bears a considerable likeness to Drasian's adventure when rescuing his wife, Sigmine. There is also a number of details common to both the Serbian heroic songs on the one hand and the Saga of Wolfdietrich and of the heathen Belian on the other. The carrying off and rescuing of a faithless and cruel wife is also a subject common to the German as well as to the Yugoslav heroic epic. A comparison of *Salman and Morolf*, with the faithless wives of Gruica—in the heroic song *Nevjera ljube Gruičine*—and of Stojan, in the song *Janković Stojan*, reveals details of remarkable likeness. The same subject is treated in the Russian traditional epic, and it appears probable that it was drawn originally from a Byzantine source, though some scholars believe it to have come from a northern saga.

Professor Chadwick distinguishes in the history of heroic poetry four stages, ascribing to the first the court poems of the Heroic Age itself; to the second the epic and the narrative poems based on these, such as the *Hildebrandslied* and *Beowulf*; to the third the popular poetry of the eighth and following centuries, such as the *Seyfridslied*; and, finally, to the fourth stage the German poems of the twelfth and following centuries, composed at the time when heroic subjects again found favour among the members of higher society. In pointing out parallel characteristics between stage III in the history of Germanic poetry and that of the

Serbo-Croats, he limits himself as regards the latter to the poetry composed by Bosnian Moslems, believing it to be the nearest modern analogy in Europe to the heroic poetry which "makes its appearance in various nations and in various periods of history". This is an important fact to be remembered and we shall refer to it again. The analogy between the poetry of the Heroic Age and that of the Bosnian Moslems exists, in his opinion, not only because the latter deals with similar themes, "but also since the events with which they are concerned and the conditions they reflect belong to a well-marked historical period, which we may regard as a kind of Heroic Age". He means the seventeenth century in particular, when the Turkish Empire was at its zenith and when its armies fought those of Austria. Personalities that figure in the heroic poetry of the Bosnian Moslems were well-known historical people; therefore, this poetry was a living, heroic poetry, and the minstrels who composed and chanted it correspond in some respects to the Frisian minstrel Bernlef or the English minstrels mentioned by Alcuin. The features which distinguish these heroic songs are those which are associated with the heroic poetry of stage III, but Professor Chadwick is a little in doubt whether he was really justified in including them in this category, because there was no evidence that they had passed through anything corresponding to stages I and II, i.e. that they had ever been connected with a proper court.

We have no proofs that they ever were. Although a frequent mention is made in them of the court of the Sultan and that of the Austrian Emperor, their knowledge of these is vague and remote and we are not justified in attributing to the songs the characteristics of a court poetry. If they are to be included in the category of heroic poetry of stage III, it could be done only on the ground that they deal with similar themes: "heroism in battle, single combats, love and revenge". On this ground the heroic songs of the Christian Serbo-Croats could equally well be included in the same category, but there are no proofs for these either that, at the time when the earliest of them was composed, conditions were any more similar to the Heroic Age than in the case of those of the Bosnian Moslems. Many of them show obvious traces of a feudalism not very far distant. This is to be seen especially in the heroic songs of the long line, in a certain dignity of style, even a modest aristocratic tone, reminding us of some of the simplest of the Germanic heroic poems. Whether these songs were the last offspring of a courtly and aristocratic poetry that may have existed and faded away, we have no means of proving.

The chanters of the earliest Serbo-Croat heroic songs may have been in the permanent service of various rulers. We know that at each court a scribe had existed and it is not unlikely that in addition to his ordinary clerical duties he chanted for his master and the guests. But this is only a mere conjecture. What we know for certain is that in the sixteenth century servants, while riding in front of their masters, chanted songs in their honour, and that at feasts noblemen and military leaders were entertained by chanters who glorified in their songs important personages of the land. This fact leads us to believe that professional chanters, in a relation similar to that of a vassal to his lord, may have existed at some early stage. It does not matter if that

stage was much later than the corresponding one in the
Heroic Age, the main point being that heroic poetry
"makes its appearance in various nations and in various
periods of history". The Yugoslav heroic songs, the
Russian *byliny*, the Ukrainian *dumy* and the Spanish
romances may, therefore, be regarded as comparatively
modern equivalents of the heroic poetry that flourished
during the Heroic Age.

However close the similarity of the heroic ballads of
popular origin is to the Germanic heroic poems, the former
do not possess either the weight or the dignity of style of
the latter, for the ballads were composed for an audience
of simple people, while the heroic poems were made for
kings and noblemen. Ambitious rhyme and solemn language were essential to the success of the court poets as
much as simplicity of style and lack of high poetical form
were necessary to the chanters of the ballads in order to
ensure the sympathy of the simple crowd. The dignity of
heroic poetry has often been surpassed but the poetic
beauty of some of the heroic songs of popular origin has
rarely been reached by the great poets of any nation.

II

The *chansons de geste* and the *junačke pesme* have several
points in common. Both deal with historical as well as
romantic subjects and both are the work of gifted individuals who, in composing them, allowed their imaginations
great liberty. The *ménestrels*, like the *guslari*, chanted or
recited their poems accompanied by an instrument, *la
vielle* in the case of the former, the *gusle* in the case of the
latter. They chanted before a gathering, either at a court

or at church festivals. It has not been possible to prove
for either of the groups that they originated, like the
Castilian *romances*, from earlier epics, but it is generally
considered that the *chansons de geste* were preceded by
another epic poetry in which heroes and their deeds figure,
and certain critics have maintained, as we have seen, a similar
view for the *junačke pesme*. The usual view, however, that
the "popular ballad" follows the "popular epic" as a kind
of aftermath, and that the former almost reproduces the
qualities and characteristics of the latter within a narrower
compass and on a smaller scale, cannot hold good so far as
the Yugoslav heroic songs are concerned. They are not,
as we have already pointed out, popular ballads in the
ordinary sense of the word; they are popular or, rather,
heroic epics—whether preceded or not by any other epic
poetry we have no means of saying—but certainly not
followed by any kind of "popular ballads". Although,
therefore, of a different stage, they are more closely connected with the Western heroic poetry of popular origin
than is generally supposed.

The tendency to look towards this poetry as a source of
inspiration for the Serbo-Croat *junačke pesme* goes back
some fifty years. The Russian scholar A. N. Veselovsky
(or Wesseloffsky) pointed out, in 1881, that the Roland
saga and the Carolingian epics reached Dalmatia from
Italy, and, according to Pio Rajna's investigations, the
Carolingian and Arthurian heroes were made popular in
Italy from the first half of the twelfth century by the pil-
grims going from France to Italy, almost invariably accompanied by *jongleurs*. According to a note on the last page of
a manuscript, at present in Milan, of a *chanson de geste*,

belonging to the cycle of "Williame au court nez", Veselovsky revealed that the same MS. was at a nunnery at Ragusa from the early part of the fourteenth century for nearly a hundred years. Khalansky and some other Russian scholars pointed to an analogy between the episodes of Roland's death and that of Marko Kraljević, while Veselovsky himself, after a close study of the Serbo-Croat heroic poetry, believed that the *junačka pesma* on the *Marriage of King Vukašin* had borrowed its principal motif from the Italian novel *Bovo d'Antona*, which in turn had originated from the *chanson de geste*, *Bueves d'Hantone*.

In building on Veselovsky's and Khalansky's statements, and on P. Rajna's investigations, a Serbian student of the Yugoslav traditional poetry, N. Banašević, aimed recently at discovering a still closer analogy between the Serbo-Croat heroic poetry on Kosovo and the *chanson de geste*. According to him, in addition to the MS. of the *Chançun de Williame*, which was written in England, several others must have existed in the Middle Ages, and perhaps one of them had found its way to Italy and from there to Dalmatia. A professional Yugoslav chanter would thus have acquainted himself with the Western epic and would have been inspired to compose similar songs in his own language, about historical persons and events of his own land. Moreover, bearing in mind the close relations between Dalmatia and Italy, he rightly believes that Italian chanters must have found their way to Dalmatia and there spread the French popular poetry. Since the MS. of the *Chançun de Williame* had been in Ragusa for nearly a century, the Serbian fugitives, including the members of the ruling houses, who settled within the walls of the Republic after the catastrophe of Kosovo, may have read in it the story of the glorious defeat of d'Aliscan or of d'Archamp. In the hero, Vivian, and the traitor, Tribaut, Banašević recognises the Serbian heroes Miloš and Vuk respectively, and he finds a number of motifs and episodes common to both the *Chançun de Williame* and the cycle of Kosovo. He is anxious to assure us that the MS. of this *chanson de geste* had caused an unknown author in Ragusa to compose heroic songs out of the Kosovo material, modelled in form on the heroic songs on other subjects which had already existed there. We shall express our opinion on N. Banašević's views in the next chapter.

III

Like the *chansons de geste* and the *junačke pesme*, the Castilian *romances* possess many characteristic features of the *popular ballads*, but, at the same time, they are more narrative, and practically free from the fairy superstition. The opinion that they are imitations of the narrative and lyric poetry of the Arabs should be ruled out definitely. There was nothing in Arabic poetry that could have served as a model to the *romances*, just as there was nothing in the Turkish poetry to inspire the *guslari* to compose their *junačke pesme*. In each case, the strong Christian tone, devotion to the Cross and freedom, and loyalty to their native land, indicate only too clearly a different creative spirit from that of the soft and effeminate Eastern poetry. After the Arab conquest of Spain, Arabic and Spanish literature followed their own independent developments, and each possessed its own distinctive ideas: essentially Moslem on the one side; essentially Christian on the other.

The word *romance* meant at first the vernacular as opposed to Latin, which was used by Spanish authors for eight centuries after the Roman rule in Spain came to an end. At a later period this word came to be used to denote short heroic poems of a period not later than the fifteenth century: poems of a particular form, a *stanza* of four lines of either eight syllables, with a rhyme only between the second and fourth lines, and with a prevailing trochaic movement, or of sixteen syllables, with a caesura after the eighth and a continuous rhyme. In each case the rhyme was merely assonant, such as existed in the old French *chansons*, before a full rhyme took its place in the thirteenth century. Like the *junačke pesme* and the *chansons de geste*, they were chanted before a public gathering by the *juglares*. Of these, two classes existed: the *juglares de péñola*, who composed or wrote these *romances*, and the *juglares de boca*, who only recited them. They were the predecessors of the *ciegos*, the blind men who, like the blind *guslari*, took the rôle in modern times of the original chanters.

Among the Castilian *romances* an historical group is to be distinguished from a non-historical, which is partly legendary in character, and partly romantic and fantastic. The principal subject treated in them is the traditional struggle against the Arabs, but quarrels and fights between the Christian states or their chiefs, and their frequent frontier wars, constitute the themes of numerous *romances*. Like the *junačke pesme*, they are essentially national, and three principal motives guide the action of their heroes: loyalty to the king, devotion to Christianity, and personal honour; the warriors being always courteous and gallant *hidalgos* on every occasion, especially when capturing a defeated Arab chieftain. Among the personages who play parts in them, those of the upper classes are most prominent, and in character the *romances* are more aristocratic than the *junačke pesme*.

Like the *junačke pesme*, the *romances* of an early date are of greater interest and beauty than those of the more modern period, which have lost much of their original simplicity. Of greatest poetic value are those related to national history and the national heroes, and among these the *Romances del rey D. Rodrigo, de Bernardo del Carpio, de los siete Infantes de Lara*, and *del Cid* stand foremost. The best are, perhaps, the ballads of the seven princes of Lara, but those of King Rodrigo are the most popular in their inspiration. It is very doubtful whether Bernardo was an historical person, but the actions attributed to him in the popular poetry are, in any case, fabulous. The Cid of the *romances* is very different from the person described in the *Poema de Myo Cid*, the earliest literary work in Spanish. Like the Yugoslav national hero, Marko Kraljević, so is the Cid of Spain an historical personality, but, while history knows very little about King Marko and of Ruy Diaz de Bivar, which is the Cid's real name, in the traditional poetry of the two countries they are described in the usual manner in which most national heroes are described in popular ballads, and are given all the virtues and charged with all the vices of the times in which the ballads about them were composed. In each case they were chosen by the popular imagination as champions of religion and patriotism. Each man must have been conspicuous in real life for some unusual achievement which appealed to the popular taste, and once they had become the people's idols it was easy to build up fantastic stories about their names.

The relation between the Castilian *romances*, and indeed of popular ballads in general, and the epics of the Middle Ages, has been a subject of discussion among many students. So far, with the exception of the *romances*, nothing definite has been proved, though it is believed that "many Danish ballads are a kind of revival in a new form of the old heroic lays", and it is stated in respect of the *junačke pesme* that they originated from an earlier epic poetry no longer in existence. The popular ballads in general, when compared with the mediaeval epic poems, show the same common scale and often the same type of story, but they differ greatly in spirit and taste. Professor Ker says that the plain fact is that the relation between the epics of the Middle Ages and the popular ballads is "different in different cases, both generally as between one country and another, and particularly as between several ballads". And if we look at the Castilian *romances*, where the relation to an earlier epic appears to be certain, we are given definite proofs that, for instance, the ballads of the Infantes de Lara are traced through the chronicles to something like their original epic form. The Spanish scholars Mila y Fontanals, Menéndez Pidal and Menéndez y Pelayo hold the view that the best of the Castilian *romances* are remnants of the *cantares de gesta*, which are lost, but the fragments of which, preserved in the memory of the people, were used by the courtly poets of the fourteenth and fifteenth centuries, who added to the subjects they treated new ones, either foreign or of contemporary events, such as *fronterizos* and *moriscos*, thus composing the existing *romances*. The historical *romances* were, in their opinion, derived either directly from the *gestas* or indirectly from the chronicles, while the knightly *romances* and the *fronterizos*, since their subjects are treated in the manner of historical ballads, must have originated in the fifteenth century. All Spanish scholars rule out the theory of collective authorship and the oral transmission of the *gestas*, but Menéndez Pidal's theory is that the Spanish epic, having been aristocratic in the beginning, fell from the hands of the courtly poets into those of wandering minstrels, who recited or chanted them in public squares and market-places, changing their contents, however, so as to suit the taste of the popular audience. The people who listened to them naturally remembered parts of the ballads and on the basis of these they spontaneously created the old *romances*. Thus the bulk of a poetry which was originally composed by troubadours for the noblemen became the property of the populace and their *juglares*.

Some students[1] of the Castilian *romances* find it difficult to believe in this spontaneous and collective authorship of a whole series of poems, but we shall be able to prove, when discussing the origin of the Serbo-Croat *junačke pesme*, that this theory is sound.

When we turn to the question of the origin of the Serbo-Croat heroic poetry of traditional character we shall endeavour to show that the Spanish *romances*, like the French *chansons de geste*, were, in all probability, not unknown to the Yugoslav composers and chanters of the *junačke pesme*. Since, however, we do not hold the view

[1] Kelly, Fitzmaurice. (See "Books Consulted".)

that any particular Castilian *romance* or *chanson de geste* served as a model for any particular Serbo-Croat heroic poem, we believe it useless to look for imitations pure and simple among the *junačke pesme* of any Western traditional poetry. What we can look for and find are similar phrases and even whole lines: Conde Arnaldos, *la caza iba cazar*, "with a falcon on his arm", and Marko Kraljević, *lov lovio*, "with his falcon". The two phrases are identical. So are the following lines:

and
> Quien es aquel caballero
>
> Koji ono dobar junak beše.

Very similar are:

or

and
> Bien oireis lo que dira (i.e. el moro)
>
> Bien oireis lo que hablo
>
> Da je kome poslušati bilo.

The lines of the romance *Bernardo y el rey Alfonso*:

> Por las riberas de Arlanza
> Bernardo de Carpio cabalga,

remind us of the following lines:

> Poranio Kraljeviću Marko
> Pokraj mora urvinom planinom.

What is far more similar than the isolated phrases and lines is the manner in which an event is described; it is approached straightway and told simply and clearly in each poetry. The tone and the spirit, and to a certain extent the atmosphere, are remarkably similar. The similarity exists especially between the historic ballads of the two poetries, but the *romances* of miscellaneous character possess certain common points with the Yugoslav traditional poetry of both the lyric and the epic group. Such points are, however, common to popular ballads of other nations, so that, for instance, in the *Romance de Rico Franco*, elements of Scottish and Danish as well as of Yugoslav popular ballads are to be found.

An analogy to the heroic poetry composed by Serbo-Croat Moslem chanters is to be found in the Spanish *romances fronterizos*, in which the innumerable frontier wars and skirmishes, between the Caliphate of Granada and the Christian kings, are described.

IV

In comparing the Serbo-Croat with the English and Scottish traditional poetry, one might wonder whether there really is any similarity between them. Yet it is possible to find similarities between these two groups of popular ballads, just as it is possible to see the likeness between the Scottish bagpipes and those of the Serbs, or between the Scottish tartans of the Highlands and the Serbian woollen cloth in coloured stripes, crossed at right angles, of the district of Rudnik. There is, however, a considerable difference between the latter in the manner in which they are used: in Scotland men's kilts are made of the tartan; in Serbia, women's skirts of the cloth. So it is with their popular ballads; they are very different from each other, yet they are similar in some points, and all we can do is to mention common and similar features and also different methods of treating similar subjects. In speaking of the two groups of popular ballads, we shall use the words Serbian and English, when we mean Serbo-

Croat and English-Scottish; for the English and the Scots, like the Serbs and the Croats, have combined in traditional poetry so long that it is impossible to separate one from the other.

In the Serbian, as well as in the English ballads, the very first few lines of a ballad tell us its subject. No time is wasted on any sort of preliminary. There is, however, a large number of Serbian ballads which begin with practically the same line or lines that, strictly speaking, have nothing to do with the contents of the ballad. They are there either for the sake of poetical beauty or to attract the attention of an audience. Thus, among the women's songs we find opening lines as follows:

> Against white Buda's walls, a vine
> Doth its white branches fondly twine:
> O, no! it was no vine-tree there;
> It was a fond, a faithful pair,
> Bound each to each in earliest vow.

Or

> Lo! upon the mountain green
> Stands a fir-tree tall and thin—
> 'Tis no fir-tree—none at all—
> 'Tis a maiden thin and tall.[1]

The opening lines of many heroic songs run as follows:

> God of mercy! what a wondrous marvel!
> Is it thunder, or is it earthquake?
> Is it sea that beats waves against the rock?
> No thunder is it, nor yet earthquake;
> No sea beats its waves against the rock.
>   They are firing guns in the castle.

[1] Translated by John Bowring.

Nothing corresponding to any of these opening lines is to be found in the English ballads.

If we leave aside the actual form and turn to the contents, which the opening line indicates, we shall find in the Serbian heroic songs that someone rises, or walks, or rides out early, or begins to hunt, or drinks wine, or writes a letter, or prays to God for something, or has dreamt of something, or has sat down to eat his dinner, or that someone has fallen ill, or is lamenting in prison, or that the dawn has not yet broken. Each of these items is clearly indicated in a single line, with which the song begins.

It stands to reason that corresponding instances are to be found among the English popular ballads. Several of them begin by saying that someone was "walking in the garden green", or in the woods, or "over yon gravelled green"; also that

> The King he sits in Dunferling,
> Drinking the blude red wine.

Or that
> Fair Isabell of Rochroyall,
>   She dreamed where she lay,
> She dreamed a dream of her love Gregory,
>   A little before the day.

Or that
> Childe Maurice hunted i' the siluer wood.

Or that
> There was a knight, in a summer's night, was
>   riding o'er the lee.

Or that
> Johnny he has risen up i' the morn.

But more frequent ways of opening a ballad are those where it is said that a lady "sits in her bower" or in her "bower-window", "mending her midnight coif", or at her "bower-door", "sewing her silken seam".

If we consider the line "Dear God, what a wondrous marvel" as the most typical first line with which a large number of Serbian heroic songs begin, the corresponding typical first line of the English ballads would be that which begins with the words "There was a..." (or, "there were...") and which leads immediately to the subject of the ballad in question, e.g.

> There was a rich lord, and he lived in Forfar.
> There was a knight and a lady bright.
> There was a youth, and a well-belov'd youth.
> There was a shepherd's daughter.
> There was a knight and he had a daughter.

The following stanzas will show how directly and quickly the subject is approached already in the first stanza:

> Willie was a widow's son,
>   And he wore a milk-white weed,
> And weel could Willie read and write,
>   Far better ride on steed.

Or
> Lord Thomas and Fair Annet
>   Sate a' day on a hill;
> When night was cum and sun was sett,
>   They had not talkt their fill.

We often find that an English ballad begins with an introduction: i.e. by referring first to something that is not in close connection with its subject. This kind of digression occurs especially among the Robin Hood

ballads. More than ten of them begin with an address to
the audience in the following manners:

> Lythe and listin, gentilmen,
>> That be of frebore blode;
> I shall you tel of a gode yeman,
>> His name was Robyn Hode.

Or

> Come, all you brave gallants, and listen a while,
>> With hey down, down, an a down
>> That are in the bowers within;
> For of Robin Hood, that archer good,
>> A song I intend for to sing.

Similar beginnings occur in the Serbian heroic songs,
though such an address to the audience is expressed by a
single line, e.g.

> Čujte ljudi i počujte,

which means   Hear, people, and hearken.

This is one of the very few instances in which the
chanter brings his own person into the song and addresses
his audience personally. This occurs also in Homer and
in many Castilian *romances*.

Another characteristic feature of the way in which the
Robin Hood ballads begin is that one or two stanzas contain a description of Nature, usually the greenwood, e.g.

> In summer time, when leaves grow green,
>> Down a down a down
> And birds sing on every tree,
>> Hey down a down a down

> Robin Hood went to Nottingham, etc.

In the Serbian ballads, not much homage is paid to

Nature's beauty, but when such references occur they are brief and of an impressionistic kind, e.g.

> A mother's darling was walking in the green garden;

or

> Under the high forested mountain a *kolo* was being danced;

or

> A bright moon was shining in the evening, over the green meadow, where two lordly horses were grazing.

There is, however, in Serbian traditional poetry a kind of comradeship and friendship between persons and Nature. This is expressed particularly in the women's songs. We find in them, for instance, that the trees bow their branches when a girl tries to hang herself and thus make it impossible for her to do so. A girl speaks to a mountain over which her sweetheart is journeying, begging it to see him safely through. A hero gives to the forest through which he is travelling confidences about his love. Further, all Nature mourns for a fallen hero, and not only does it mourn with those that are in sorrow, but it rejoices with them in their happiness. Girls speak to flowers and trees, e.g.

> O thou brotherly maple-tree!
> Wilt thou be a friend to me?
> Be a brother, and be a friend!
> To the green grass thy branches bend,
> That I may climb to their highest tip!
> Look o'er the sea, and see the ship,
> Where my lover sits smiling now;
> He binds the turban round his brow,

And over his shoulders the shawl he flings,
Which is full of mine own embroiderings.
For three long years my hands inwove
Those golden flowers to deck my love:
The richest silk of the brightest dyes
I work'd for him, and now my eyes
Would fain my absent lover see:
Assist me, brotherly maple-tree!
And tell me, if he thinks of me![1]

We find also that one star gossips with another: the moon chats with the morning star:

"Morning star, say where hast thou been wandering?
Where hast thou been wandering and where lingering?
Where hast thou three full white days been lingering?"
To the moon the morning star has answered:
"I've been wandering, I've three days been lingering,
O'er the white walls of the fortress Belgrade,
Gazing there on strange events and wonders".

In another song, the morning star *danica* is boasting that she will get her brother, the bright moon, married to the lightning from the cloud.

Serbian traditional poetry abounds in such, and similar, apostrophes and personifications. This does not seem to be the case with English and Scottish popular ballads.

These appear to take Nature for granted and say little or nothing about it. When "romantic" scenes are mentioned, they are shorn of all romance. Moonlight is as little regarded as daylight for imaginative purposes. With a slight allowance, it may be said that the seasons pass unnoticed.

[1] Translated by John Bowring.

In epithets and standing phrases, the Serbian traditional poetry seems more abundant than the poetry of many other peoples, but such epithets and phrases are rather primitive and by no means so artistic as they are with Homer. Homer's epithets are often composed and invented words which did not exist in the common speech; in the Serbian traditional poetry all the epithets are to be found in the common, everyday, language. We constantly meet with a "clear sky", "brilliant sun", "bright moon", "dark night", "green forest on the mountain", "green garden", "green meadow", "ice-cold water", "slender fir-tree", "small pearls and precious stones". But the most frequent epithet, and one common to both the Serbian and the Scottish ballads, is *white*. Thus, in the Serbian songs heroes go to "white towers", mothers to "white churches", men kiss each other's "white faces", girls hold each other's "white hands", call from their "white throats", wait for their sweethearts for "three white days", and so on.

The same epithet is frequent, though much less so, in English and Scottish popular ballads. Young Andrew takes his lady's "lillye-white hand", a gallant squire holds the "milk-white hand" of a fair maid; Willie, a widow's son, wears a "milk-white weed" and Lady Margerie's feet are "as white as sleet", while sweet Margaret stretches out her "lily-white hand", and Gill Morice's groom dresses "a milk-white steed" and so on. Among the most common phrases in Serbian songs are these: to sup a lordly supper; to drink wine over three days, till the wine gets into one's face; to eat sugar and to drink plum brandy; to shed tears down a white face, or down a lordly face; to

take off a cap and bow down to the black earth; to go right
across an even field like a star across a blue sky; to take
three loads of treasure, i.e. about seven hundredweights,
before starting on a journey; to rise early to hunt; to call
one's own manservant.

It is interesting to observe the attitude of peoples towards animals. In the traditional songs of all the Slavonic
nations, one of the very common features is not only
talking to animals, but also of animals that talk. It becomes natural to talk to animals with whom one is in
constant touch, but in the ballads of the Slavonic peoples
it seems to be equally natural for the animals to talk. In
the Russian *byliny*, a horse often speaks to his master. In a
Serbian heroic song, Marko's horse weeps when he feels
that the death of his master approaches. But we have an
example that the same horse not only understands and
follows the instructions of his master, but that he also
talks. Marko went to fight Philip the Magyar, but not
finding him at his home went to the new tavern past the
market-place, dismounted from Šarac and tied him before
the tavern, while he went in to drink red wine. Philip,
hearing from his wife that Marko had called:

> He turned his grey Arab mare about,
> And forthwith went down through the market-place
> Until he came before the new tavern.
> But Sharatz was tethered by the door.
> Philip urged his grey Arab mare,
> For he would have her enter into the new tavern,
> But the war-horse Sharatz suffered it not,
> But with his hoofs smote her in the ribs.
> Philip the Magyar waxed wroth,

He seized his studded mace
And made to smite Sharatz before the tavern;
But Sharatz lift up his voice in lamentation before the
    tavern:

"By the merciful God—woe is me!
That I should perish this morn before the tavern,
At the hands of mighty Philip the Magyar,
With my illustrious master nigh at hand!"
But from within Marko spake to him:
"Suffer him to pass, Sharatz!"
When Sharatz heard Marko,
He suffered him to pass into the new tavern.
And when Philip entered into the tavern,
He gave no "God aid thee",
But grasped his heavy mace
And smote Kraljević Marko,
Smote him on his hero's shoulders.
Little enough recked Marko,
And to Philip the Magyar he said:
"Sit thee down in peace, thou Magyar bastard!
Wake not the fleas on my skin,
But light down from thy horse that we may drink wine.
There will still be time for fighting".[1]

There are numerous examples in which man's love and
tenderness for a good horse are described. Thus we find
that a certain Bogdan serves a knight Dragija for nine
years, not because of want of money but because of his
good steed, to approach which one had to open ten locked
doors. In the end, by a ruse, Bogdan obtains Dragija's
horse from his wife, and runs away. A horse's beauty is

[1] Translated by D. H. Low.

often described: that a sun is shining from his forehead, and a bright moon from underneath his throat, while two morning stars are sparkling from his flanks. Sparks fly from his hooves and blue flame comes from his nostrils. He jumps aside the length of three lances and for as far in height, while no one can calculate the length of the many lances that he can jump forward.

In the popular ballads of the Germanic peoples, there are not many such instances. Examples of talking to animals and especially of animals themselves talking are not numerous. In the English and Scottish ballads, the horse stands in high esteem; and in the ballad, *Tam Lin*, we find a stanza as follows:

> The steed that my true-love rides on
>   Is lighter than the wind;
> Wi siller he is shod before,
>   Wi burning gowd behind.

In another ballad, *The Lass of Roch Royal*, we find that a horse is similarly shod:

> They shoed him with the beat silver,
> They grind him with the gold.

In Serbian heroic songs also, a hero's steed is shod, sometimes, with silver and burning gold.

In both Serbian and English popular ballads cases are more frequent in which birds speak and are addressed. While in the *ženske pesme* a nightingale is most frequently to be met with, in the *junačke pesme* a "grey falcon" and a "black raven" play a prominent part. The falcon, besides being a synonym for a brave man, appears as the protector of warriors. When Marko fell ill by the roadside and was longing for water and shade, a falcon brought him water in his beak and, by spreading his wings, protected him from the sun's rays. When Marko asked the bird why he did this, the falcon replied:

> Jest not, Kraljević Marko!
> When we were in Kossovo battle,
> And endured fierce onslaught of the Turks,
> The Turks took me,
> And clipped both my wings,
> Then thou tookest me in, Marko,
> And didst set me on a green fir-tree,
> That the Turkish horses might not destroy me.
> Thou gavest me the flesh of heroes to eat,
> And red blood thou gavest me to drink,
> 'Twas then, O Marko, that thou didest me service![1]

The raven, as a rule, is a messenger of unhappy tidings. When the battle of Kosovo was over, two ravens came flying to the palace of Princess Milica, who, having seen them on the turret wall, spoke to them:

> "In God's great name, black ravens, say,
> Whence came ye on the wind to-day?
> Is it from the plain of Kossovo?
> Hath the bloody battle broke?
> Saw ye the two armies there?
> Have they met? And, friend or foe,
> Who hath vanquisht? How do they fare?"

And the two black fowls replied:
> "In God's great name, Militza, dame,
> From Kossovo at dawn we came.
> A bloody battle we espied:

[1] Translated by D. H. Low.

We saw the two great armies there,
They have met, and ill they fare.
Fallen, fallen, fallen are
The Turkish and the Christian Tzar."[1]

Speaking hawks and ravens appear in many English ballads, to mention only *The Gay Goshawk*, *The Three Ravens*, *The Carnal and the Crane* and *The Twa Corbies*. The last of these runs as follows:

1. As I was walking all alone,
   I heard twa corbies making a mane;
   The tane unto the t'other say,
   'Where shall we gang and dine to-day?'

2. 'In behint yon auld fail dyke,
   I wot there lies a new slain knight;
   And naebody kens that he lies there,
   But his hawk, his hound, and lady fair.

3. 'His hound is to the hunting gane,
   His hawk to fetch the wild-fowl hame,
   His lady's ta'en another mate,
   So we may mak our dinner sweet.

4. 'Ye'll sit on his white hause-bane,
   And I'll pick out his bonny blue een;
   Wi ae lock o his gowden hair
   We'll theek our nest when it grows bare.

5. 'Mony a one for him makes mane,
   But nane sall ken where he is gane;
   Oer his white banes, when they are bare,
   The wind sall blaw for evermair.'

Next to the falcon and raven, a cuckoo often figures in Serbian ballads. According to a legend, the cuckoo was

[1] Translated by O. Meredith.

originally a woman who had lost her only brother and
who mourned for him constantly. In all Slavonic traditional poetry, a mourning woman is represented in the
image of a cuckoo; a mother mourns for her son, or a
sister for her brother, like "a black cuckoo". Like the
falcon and the raven, this bird also speaks, or listens to
talk: e.g.

> I heard a sprightly swallow say
> To a gray cuckoo t'other day,—
>   "Thou art a happy bird indeed;
>   Thou dost not in the chimney breed,
>   Thou dost not hear the eternal jarring,
>   Of sisters and step-sisters warring;
>   Their woes and grievances rehearsing,
>   Cursing themselves, and others cursing.
>   A young step-sister once I saw,
>   Foul language at the elder throw,
>   'Perdition's daughter! hence depart;
>   Thou hast no fruit beneath thy heart'".[1]

Though most other birds are frequently mentioned, the
lark, which figures so much in English popular ballads,
does not seem to be at home in Serbian traditional poetry,
although it is seen everywhere in the country.

In examining the feelings that are expressed among
members of a family, a mother, who plays so prominent
a rôle in Yugoslav traditional poetry, does not appear
nearly so often in English popular ballads. In the former
she is invariably deeply respected by her sons, and all the
brave and intrepid Serbian heroes, particularly Marko
Kraljević, ask their mothers for advice before undertaking

[1] Translated by John Bowring.

anything; they carefully follow her instructions and report
to her on the results of their actions. The friendly talk
between them takes place usually at table, during an
evening meal.

> Marko sat at supper with his mother,
> And she began to speak with Marko:
> "O my son, Kraljević Marko,
> Thy mother is now well stricken in years,
> She cannot prepare thy supper,
> She cannot serve the dark wine,
> She cannot make light with the pine splinter.
> Take thee a wife, therefore, my dearest son,
> That so I may have a successor afore I die".
> Marko said to his aged mother:
> "God be my witness, dear old mother!
> Through nine kingdoms have I been,
> Yea, through ten, and the tenth was the Turkish
>   Empire;
> When I found a maiden for myself,
> There was no friend for thee,
> And when I found friends for thee,
> For me there was no maiden there.
> Yet stay, one maid there was,
> At the court of King Šišman,
> Mother mine, on Bulgarian soil,
> I found her by the waters of the cistern,
> And when I saw her, mother,
> Meseemed the ground turned about me.
> Behold, mother, the maid for me,
> And for thee also worthy friends.
> Make ready of slender meal-cakes,
> That I may go and ask the maid in marriage".[1]

[1] Translated by D. H. Low.

There is nothing of a corresponding kind to be found in English and Scottish popular ballads; sons do not ask their mothers' advice, nor does her influence bear any weight upon their actions. However, in the ballad *Johnie Scott* the mother asks her son not to leave the home. The invariable kindness and thoughtfulness of Serbian heroes towards their mothers has few parallels in the English ballads, one being, however, the ballad of *The Twa Brothers*. Nor do we find in them that great and boundless love of a mother for her children. In the ballad *Prince Robert*, a mother poisons her son because he married against her wishes. His bride comes just in time for the funeral, and the mother refuses to give her anything of her son's belongings, even the ring from his finger—all that she asked for. Such incidents are unknown in Yugoslav traditional poetry; the mothers are always anxious for their sons to marry, and to marry anyone they like.

We have mentioned how deeply sisters love their brothers, particularly the youngest, in Serbo-Croat popular ballads. It is rare that a sister does not sacrifice herself for her brother. She swears by his head, and when he is dead his sister, besides his mother, is alone allowed to mourn for him: a privilege refused even to his wife. When a brother was innocently hanged, his sister hanged herself from sorrow for him. A sister, although fastened to a pillar, tore herself away, in order to save her brother, so hard that her hair remained behind on it. When a girl expresses her love to her sweetheart, she says:

> Dearer is to me thy soul, O dearest,
> Than my brothers', all four together.

It has been mentioned, however, that there are instances

in which a Serbian girl sacrifices for her lover everything and everybody: her brother included. Such cases also occur in the English ballads.

The relations between brothers in Yugoslav traditional poetry are as a rule cordial. There are numerous examples which illustrate their friendship. Milan-beg and Dragutin-beg live on such good terms that even their horses kiss each other. Mujo and Alija are such great friends that they often exchange their horses and their weapons. Predrag, having realised that he has killed his own brother, Nenad, by mistake, stabs himself by his dead body. There are instances, however, in which even the closest friendship between brother and brother is disturbed and spoilt by the intrigues of the wife of one of them, but the intriguer suffers, in the end, the extreme penalty.

Such close friendship exists, of course, also among men who are not brothers, and is usually established by a solemn contract of brotherhood, known as *pobratimstvo*. Two men, for example, would promise each other, in church before a priest and in the name of God and St John, eternal friendship. The same contract can be established also between two women, or between a man and a woman. They bind themselves by this act to all the mutual duties of brothers and sisters. Sometimes such mutual brotherhood exists between three men: as, for instance, between the three heroes, Marko, Miloš and Relja. It also occurs that a hero concludes such a contract with a Vila.

Examples of close friendship and brotherhood are by no means a property of Serbian traditional poetry alone. In one of the English popular ballads Adam Bell, Clim of the Clough and William of Cloudesly, outlawed for breach of the game-laws, swear brotherhood.

If we think of the English and Scottish popular ballads as a whole and ask ourselves what is the predominant motif in them, we should say that it is the motif of love. It is well known how beautiful are many of these ballads in which love between a man and a woman is an outstanding feature, but many of them seem to us to have been spoiled by the indelicacy of feelings and actions expressed in them. Compared, in respect of this subject, with the Yugoslav traditional poetry, love is, as we have seen, the predominant motif in the women's songs; love is a dream of youth, of unmarried persons only. A gay, free intercourse is kept up among young people, but illegitimate love is very rare and is considered as a crime. An English reviewer of Serbian popular ballads made the following statement in the *Quarterly Review* in 1827: "We find the passion depicted, in all its stages, with a degree of delicacy for which we were by no means prepared".

A spirit of graceful roguery is prevalent among girls. A gay girl says that she is angry with her boy because he would not speak or smile at her in return for her words and smiles; she hits him with an orange and a quince, but he would not throw anything at her, not even a stone. He is hard! His mother did not bring him into this world gay, as her mother brought her.

"I was born", she says, "in the open, under the sky, on the hard ground, fairies were my godmothers, beech leaves and nettles my wrappers; a slender pine-tree my cradle. I played with the bushy tail of a squirrel, and bees fed me with honey."

Often a girl's parents or brothers want to force her to

marry an old, rich man instead of a young and poor one whom she loves. Then she implores her mother not to give her to the man she does not love. She prefers to live in the wild mountain with her sweetheart, to eat sloes and to drink water from leaves, to have a cold stone as her pillow, rather than to live in a palace with an old man she does not love, with sweets to eat and silk to sleep in.

One of the common features in both English and Serbian popular ballads, and also in many others, is that two lovers, who love each other deeply, should not be interfered with; even when forcibly separated they unite in death. In the English ballads it is usually the bridegroom's mother who interferes. She is sometimes so much opposed to her son's marriage that she herself prefers to poison him. In *Fair Margaret and Sweet William*, and also in *Lord Thomas and Fair Annet*, a lover sacrifices his inclination in order to make a marriage of interest but, having married the other girl, he dreams a bad dream about the girl he loves, Fair Margaret, and hurries to see her, but only to find her dead "for pure true love". He, too, dies of sorrow the next day. The ballads of this type end almost invariably in a typical way, to illustrate which we quote the last two stanzas of the beautiful ballad *Lord Thomas and Fair Annet*:

> Lord Thomas was buried without kirk wa,
> Fair Annet within the quiere,
> And o the tane thair grew a birk,
> The other a bonny briere.

> And ay they grew and ay they threw,
> As they wad faine be neare;
> And by this ye may ken right weil
> They were twa luvers deare.

There are several Serbo-Croat traditional songs in which a mother prevents either her son or her daughter from marrying the beloved one, with the result that both lovers die and unite in death. In one of these songs the tragic end is described as follows:

> On the eve of Saturday the maiden
> Died—and died the youth on Sunday morning:
> And they were, fond pair, together buried;
> And their hands were intertwined together;
> In those hands they placed the greenest apples:
> When, behold! ere many moons had shone there,
> From the grave sprung up a verdant pine-tree,
> And a fragrant crimson rose-tree follow'd:
> Round the pine the rose-tree fondly twined it,
> As around the straw the silk clings closely.[1]

Sometimes a rose is planted over the maiden's grave and a vine over the man's, and while growing they embrace each other as if they were the living lovers. Similar ballads exist in Russian, Rumanian, Greek, Hungarian and Albanian popular poetry. In a Moravian ballad, a bride, on learning of her bridegroom's death, jumps over four tables and alights on the fifth, rushes to her chamber and stabs herself. One would think this to be the greatest achievement in this kind of sport, but in a Croatian popular ballad a repentant husband who had planned the death of his wife, on learning that she is still living, leaps nine tables without touching the glasses on them.[2]

There is an interesting song which describes how three

[1] Translated by John Bowring.
[2] F. Kurelac, *Jačke ili narodne pěsme*, No. 479, Šuševo; mentioned also in Francis Child's collection.

young men strove for the love of a shepherdess called Mara. In order to end their quarrel, she ordered them to run up the mountain on which she grazed her sheep, and she said she would accept the one who first reached her on the summit. One remained near the foot of the mountain, the other in the middle of the slopes and the third fell in her lap, but, alas! all three were dead. Seeing this, she drew out the dagger of one of them and stabbed herself.

Turning to the *junačke pesme*, we find that love is almost excluded from them. It is seldom, if ever, the cause of a hero's action; love and heroism are kept wide apart. Heroic actions in the Serbo-Croat heroic ballads, as in those of the Russians, the Ukrainians and the Bulgars, are often animated by honour, but almost never by love.

We shall turn, in conclusion, to the Robin Hood ballads. Robin Hood has often been compared with the Yugoslav national hero, Marko Kraljević, a comparison which is misleading and erroneous. Round both these men a considerable number of ballads has been formed, so that they constitute in each case a cycle. The two heroes possess many of the usual traits of character attributed to all mediaeval champions of liberty, protectors of the poor and oppressed, and rebels against authority, whether vested in a sheriff, as is the case with the ballads of Robin Hood, or in a foreign oppressor, the Turks for instance, as is the case with the Serbo-Croat heroic songs about Marko. Nevertheless, these two heroes differ in so far that, while the latter is a "national hero", the former is distinctly a "class hero", in the sense that as such he was created for and appealed to a particular class of English people—that of the villains or serfs of the late Middle Ages.

He is not a national hero in the sense in which the Serbian Marko is, or the French Roland, or the Spanish Cid. Robin Hood is, in the words of Francis Child, "absolutely a creation of the ballad-muse". He protects the poor people merely against a sheriff; hence the strength and the means involved in this struggle cannot naturally be of the same degree as those required to fight foreign oppressors: the Arabs or the Turks. Robin Hood, therefore, is not described as a hero on the lines of Marko, Roland or Cid, true historical personages and great warriors.

All modern critics agree that there is nothing historical about Robin Hood, although several men, all named Robert or Robin Hood, are known to have lived within a period of forty years of the fourteenth century. It is probable that some of them assumed the name of the popular hero when they went "to the greenwood". His appearance was brought about, in the words of several English and American critics, when the days of chivalry, with King Arthur as their ideal knight, were gone, and under feudal conditions the English demanded an "ideal champion of liberty" (F. Sidgwick). Robin Hood thus became "a thoroughly national conception" possessing "the English love of fair play; the English readiness to shake hands when worsted in a square fight" (Henry A. Beers, Walter Morris Hart).

A closer parallel to Robin Hood and his men of the greenwood are the Serbo-Croat *hajduci* and *uskoci*. When the mediaeval Serbian Empire was overthrown by the Turks and Serbia was finally conquered by them, those indomitable men who would not bear the tyranny of the oppressor, and were eager to protect the oppressed, fled to the mountains and forests, formed bands, ambushed the Turks on the roads and robbed them of their arms and money. These men were called the *hajduci*. After the fall of Bosnia and Herzegovina, in the second part of the fifteenth century, many of these "outlaws" fled towards the north-west, into Croatia and Slavonia, where they organised themselves, under the name of *uskoci*, and often "jumped into" (= *uskočiti*) Turkish territory to inflict punishment for injustices done to their conquered brethren. They maintained the unequal fight with the oppressors for many centuries and, while the action of the *uskoci* was suppressed by Austria early in the seventeenth century and they finally disappeared, the *hajduci*, living always as outlaws in Turkish territory, kept up the spirit and the consciousness of the people and finally undertook the task of liberating Serbia at the beginning of the nine-teenth century. It is in this type of outlaw that we find an equivalent to Robin Hood and his men. There is no particular *hajduk* or *uskok* among the Serbo-Croat outlaws whom we might call a Yugoslav Robin Hood. There were, rather, many thousands among them of such Robin Hoods, and hundreds of them are mentioned by name in the Yugoslav heroic poetry.

Chapter Four

Origin and Age

I

THE question of the origin of popular ballads in general has been much discussed, and the conflicting theories can be reduced to two, distinctly opposed to each other. According to the one, which was invented by German Romanticists at the time when peoples were, so to speak, discovered behind the individuals, the "songs of the people" were a mysterious product of the people themselves, and individuals were only instruments for transmitting them. To use Sir Arthur Quiller-Couch's description of this theory, a ballad came into being much as the floating matter of a nebula condenses to form a star. With the exception of Joseph Ritson in Scotland, this theory had hardly any propagator in Great Britain. Here the opposing theory, that traditional poetry was composed by individuals, itinerant professional minstrels or bards, found many champions as soon as Bishop Percy had published his collection. He himself never doubted that they were the work of professional minstrels, and Sir Walter Scott accepted his view. It soon found followers in Germany and also in Scandinavia, with the result that the "nebular theory of the Romanticists" began to lose ground.

Remote as we are from the period when the Romanticists enthusiastically insisted upon communal authorship, spontaneity and unconsciousness of ballad production, and faced with all the modern ideas of authorship, we find it impossible to accept the German theory. But, let us remember that popular ballads, produced in one way or the other, are by no means dead yet; they naturally do not flourish now almost anywhere as they did two or more centuries ago, but they are still in being, handed down with modern additions and alterations; moreover, they are still being created by peoples remote from towns and modern influences. In studying the unwritten literary productions of these peoples, we find in their mental attitude and community feeling a reproduction, on a smaller scale, of the conditions under which the popular ballads were composed centuries ago. Thus we arrive at an understanding of the probable origin of traditional poetry in general, and see what community authorship, under conditions of improvisation and choral dance, really means.

Let us leave aside primitive tribes and turn to the Yugo-slavs among whom, in the mountain regions, the popular ballad still exists. The following incident, which occurred in Serbia proper, may serve as an example of community authorship. Some twenty odd years ago, we witnessed in a village an improvisation while a dance was in progress. Moreover, we were told two years ago that improvisations of this kind still exist in the same village. It is the village of Crna Bara in North-Western Serbia. A *kolo* was being danced at the cross-roads. The leader of the *kolo* recited, while dancing, a couple of lines with a rhyme; immedi-ately after, two more lines were added by another young man, and so on till a short, witty, but at the same time rough and "saucy ballad" was built up in stanzas of four lines, concerning one of the villagers, whose name, however, was not mentioned. The onlookers standing round the dancers would often join in the composition.

The Yugoslavs supply us also with excellent examples in support of the second theory. Some thirty odd years ago two volumes of the heroic songs of the Bosnian Moslems were published by a Yugoslav collector, L. Marjanović. His researches, and also those of Professor M. Murko, who followed him ten years later, threw new light on the origin of traditional poetry, not only among the Slavs of the Balkan Peninsula but also, perhaps, on the origin of such poetry in other parts of Europe. The study of the heroic songs of the Bosnian Moslems and Bosnian *pevači* helps us also to view more clearly the Serbian minstrels, the *guslari* and the Serbian heroic songs, which are of an earlier date than most of those of Bosnia. L. Marjanović tells us how, from 1886 to 1888, he and his assistants wrote down from twelve different Bosnians 320 songs, with a total of 255,000 decasyllabic verses. Of these, 290 were heroic and 30 women's songs. Each heroic song contained, on an average, 873 lines, though the shortest of them numbered under 100 lines, while the longest had 4000 or more lines.

One of the *pevači* recited in six weeks 102 songs, in all 80,000 lines; another, 35 songs with a total of 31,000 lines, and so on. One of these, Mehmed Kolaković, usually called Meho, related how a certain Bećir Jušić chanted once for Beg Šenčić 104 songs in six weeks, for which the Beg rewarded him with five ducats, an ox and two loads of wheat. Bećir was credited with the knowledge of

about 300 songs, which he had learned from a certain
Osmić Bušćanin, who was, in his turn, supposed to have
learned them from a book. Meho himself was called the
"chanter of Begs", because he mostly recited for them.

Sometimes he recited also for ordinary Muhammedans,
but this he did not like because their usual reward was a
few cups of coffee and cigarettes. He would also chant for
Christians on the occasion of some festival. But he was
especially pleased when Muhammedan women, the wives
of Begs, invited him to chant for them because they rewarded him in cash, better than anyone else. Like most
of the Moslem chanters, Meho accompanied himself,
while chanting, by playing a *tambura*. If he heard a song,
no matter what its length, accompanied by the sound of
the *tambura*, he remembered it after hearing it but once;
whereas it was necessary for him to hear two or three
times an unaccompanied song. When chanting he, like
most of the other chanters, would at first do it slowly,
either prolonging or merely marking the last two syllables
of each line. After the first hundred lines, he would go on
chanting, or rather reciting, so quickly that it was difficult
to follow him in writing down his recitation.

Some of the chanters did not play a *tambura* at all, but
would repeat their songs while sitting comfortably in a
chair or walking up and down a room. None of them
could repeat the same song in exactly the same way, the
difference being sometimes quite considerable. A song
chanted in 1888 was very different when repeated by the
same *pevač* in 1898; there were different names of persons,
a different order of events, different diction; moreover,
the version of ten years later was much inferior to the

original one. Some of the *pevači* greatly expanded songs which they had heard. Thus, a song of 1200 lines grew into a version of 2500 lines; another of 1500 lines extended into a variant of 4400 lines.

In the course of years, such changes could be introduced as would naturally render the original composition almost unrecognisable. Each minstrel was, therefore, a kind of creative poet, yet each one excelled in a particular way: one in describing better than all others the beauty of a woman, another the equipment of a warrior, and a third a good horse. The essential condition for a chanter was to know the material and the order of events that were to be described. Rhythm, figures of speech and simplicity of diction are the common property of the people; these presented no difficulty to him. Hence it has been credibly recorded that a Serbian peasant, who was a Parliamentary deputy, was able to recite in decasyllabic lines, about fifty years ago, the whole debate on the bill for introducing the fresh monetary system into Serbia; or that a peasant of Herzegovina could, while actually accompanying a Franciscan friar to a certain village, describe the whole journey in the metre of the traditional poetry.

For this reason, a traditional song as handed down to us in writing presents but a *Momentbild* of the epic song. As we have proofs that not only does each chanter give a different version of the same song, but that the same chanter gives different versions of the same song at different times—as well as that the song recited ten years later by the same man is hardly to be recognised—so one can imagine how different the *original* songs must have been from those that are preserved.

Yet, throughout the greater part of the nineteenth century, on the grounds of the German theory, the view was
maintained that, among the Serbs and Croats, as stated by
Vuk, jovial old men and lads recited comic songs, mostly
on marriage and weddings, while the others chanted
serious heroic songs about battles, duels and important
events, while yet no one could ascertain the original
author of any particular one, however recently it may have
been created. Among the people themselves no one was
regarded as an author, nor was it considered as something
particular or unusual, still less glorious, to compose such
poetry. The reciters and chanters never thought about
boasting of being the originators of any of the songs; and,
moreover, if one was suspected to be the author he would
calmly refuse to admit it and would say that he had heard
it from someone else.

To understand the ease with which hundreds and
thousands of lines flowed from the lips of Yugoslav *guslari*
and *pevači*, we must try to form an idea of the conditions of the period in which popular poetry was produced by itinerant singers and professional harpers among
Germanic peoples before written literary productions
existed. Bernard ten Brink tells us that at that period "the
gift of song and poetry was not the monopoly of any
guild". Heroes, kings, peasants, freedmen, and serfs cultivated songs and playing, and "at beer-feasts the harp went
from hand to hand". The essential difference between that
age and our own lies in the fact that

the result of poetical activity was not the property and not the
production of a single person, but of the community. The
work of the individual singer endured only as long as its

delivery lasted. He gained personal distinction only as a virtuoso. The permanent elements of what he presented, the material, the ideas, even the style and metre, already existed. The work of the singer was only a ripple in the stream of national poetry. Who can say how much the individual contributed to it, or where in his poetical recitation memory ceased and creative impulse began? In any case the work of the individual lived on only as the ideal possession of the aggregate body of the people, and it soon lost the stamp of originality. In view of such a development of poetry, we must assume a time when the collective consciousness of a people or race is paramount in its unity; when the intellectual life of each is nourished from the same treasury of views and association, of myths and sagas; when similar interests stir each breast; and the ethical judgment of all applies itself to the same standard. In such an age, the form of poetical expression will also be common to all, necessarily solemn, earnest and simple.

In enlarging upon Professor ten Brink's ideas, H. W. Mabie, in his excellent introduction to *A Book of Old English Ballads*, published in 1896, tells us that

in the ballad-making age there was no production, there was only reproduction. There was a stock of traditions, memories, and experiences, held in common by large populations, in constant use on the lips of numberless persons; told and retold in many forms, with countless changes, variations and modifications; without conscious artistic purpose, with no sense of personal control or possession, with no constructive aim either in plot or treatment; no composition in the modern sense of the term. Such a mass of poetic material in the possession of a large community was, in a sense, fluid, and ran into a thousand forms almost without direction or premeditation. Constant use of such rich material gave a poetic turn of thought and speech to countless persons who, under other conditions, would have given no sign of the possession of the faculty of imagination.

There was not only the stimulus to the faculty which sees events and occurrences with the eyes of the imagination, but there was also constant and familiar use of the language of poetry. To speak metrically or rhythmically is no difficult matter if one is in the atmosphere or habit of verse-making; and there is nothing surprising either in the feats of memory or of improvisation performed by the minstrels and balladists of the old time. The faculty of improvising was easily developed and was very generally used by people of all classes.

This faculty is still possessed by rural populations, among whom songs are still composed as they are being sung, each member of the company contributing a new verse or a variation, suggested by local conditions, of a well-known stanza. When to the possession of a mass of traditions and stories and the faculty of improvisation is added the habit of singing and dancing, it is not difficult to reconstruct in one's own thought the conditions under which popular poetry came into being, nor to understand in what sense a community can make its own songs.

Bearing in mind these statements, which are so aptly suited to the condition of the Yugoslav peasantry, we might safely say that only a certain primitive type of traditional poetry was originally, and among some peoples still is, produced under conditions of improvisation and dance. As to the vast number of traditional songs, the subjects of which are often based upon history, or some historical event, we believe them to have been created by individual members of unlettered communities, members particularly gifted for creating such poetry, either out of their own experience, or from a story they had heard. Thus created, they were transmitted from mouth to mouth of the community through the centuries, and in this oral transmission they underwent certain influences and suffered such changes as gave them a popular character and made them "songs of the people".

These songs, like the popular ballads in general, "are in a very real sense the songs of the people; they make no claim to individual authorship; on the contrary, the inference of what may be called community authorship is in many instances irresistible".

II

To determine the age of any traditional poetry is a most difficult question, and it seems as though no definite answer can be given to it. One conclusion seems, however, to be definite: namely, that its claim to great antiquity has been reduced. There is no evidence to prove, for instance, that the Castilian *romances* appeared before the fifteenth century. The Marqués de Santillana was the first to mention them about 1440–50, but the first printed *romances*, composed by unknown authors, date from the end of the first decade of the sixteenth century. This is the earliest edition of the *Cancioneros Generales*, published at Valencia, and is the oldest printed collection of popular ballads of any European nation. About half a century later, *romances* by known authors appeared in the early *Romanceros*, though most of the ballads contained therein were composed in the following century. At that time they began to lose their popular character and became the property of educated authors.

The oldest Danish manuscript collection dates from 1550 but, as in the case of English and Scottish ballads, there are a few which are of an earlier date. In Denmark they go back to the fourteenth, but in Great Britain to the thirteenth century, if we take into account the unique copy of *Judas*, after which no records of any popular ballads are found for about two centuries. The early sixteenth century has contributed but few ballads, so that only about ten are older than the seventeenth century. The Percy Folio, the most important of all Scottish ballad manuscripts, was written about 1650. Yet the fifteenth century has often been named as the great epoch in English and Scottish popular balladry! This, perhaps, is due to the fact that many romances, verse-tales and carols have survived from that period. Some of the Serbo-Croat heroic songs deal with true historical events which occurred in the first half of the thirteenth century, but most of them describe historical events from the battle of Kosovo onwards. None, however, of these numerous songs gives us any proofs whatsoever that any of them were contemporaneous with the events they describe. On the contrary, all the existing evidence, as will presently be seen, suggests that these songs were not composed before the end of the fifteenth or the beginning of the sixteenth century.

Frank Sidgwick wrote in his book *Old Ballads* these words:

Quite recently a ballad has been taken down, from the singing of Lincolnshire peasants, which narrates an event known to have taken place in the fifteenth century; this ballad has survived in the memories of an illiterate class, without being written down, for four hundred years.

If we accept this statement, then it would be correct to say that the English ballad *King John and the Abbot of Canterbury* originated sometime in the thirteenth century, or that the Serbian ballad *Emperor Diocletian and John the Baptist (Car Dukljan in Krstitelj Jovan)* originated in the time of the younger of these two persons, which, of course, is absurd. Traditional poetry of epic character has everywhere been founded on history or, rather, mingled and interwoven with it, but besides the events recorded fairly accurately it is well known how often historical events and historical personalities are badly confused, and gross anachronisms are to be found in popular ballads. One and the same story can be connected in one song with a well-known person of the fourteenth century and in another with an equally well-known person of the sixteenth century. The chief aim of the heroic songs being the description of a particular event, the names are of comparative unimportance. Historical personages and historical events seldom help us to determine the age of such poetry.

In trying to determine the antiquity of the Yugoslav traditional poetry, the critics, while in general agreement as regards the women's songs, have arrived at no settled opinion as to the period which saw the rise of the heroic songs. As to the priority of the former, there is no doubt; there are positive proofs that the women's songs existed as early as the middle of the thirteenth century and it is evident that their origin is of a much earlier date. The case is, however, different with the heroic songs and here, again, those of the long line, the *bugarštice*, have to be treated separately. Prominent scholars, like V. Jagić and S. Novaković, having denied their popular origin, the

question of age resolves itself into an endeavour to determine the age of the heroic songs of the short line. Their
origin is unquestionably popular, in the sense that a
variety of singers participated in both their creation and
their transmission over a long period of time. The two
groups of heroic songs are closely connected.

To prove the early existence of the Yugoslav poetry
of epic character, several sources are usually quoted, but
none of them testifies that this poetry, whether of the long
or of the short line, existed before the beginning of the
sixteenth century. If we leave aside the fantastic statement
of "Lach" K. Szyrma in his *Letters on Poland*, which we
are not able to confirm,[1] the earliest reference to the songs
of the Balkan Slavs dates from the sixth and seventh centuries. Procopius of Caesarea, the historian of Justinian,
relating the surprise of a Slav camp by the Greeks, states
that the Slavs were not aware of the danger, having lulled
themselves to sleep by singing, but if his description of
the *Sclaveni* and the *Antae* be true it is hardly believable
that they could have cultivated heroic poetry at such a low
state of civilisation. The Byzantine author and historian of
the Emperor Maurice, Theophylactos, related that in the
course of the year 590 three strangers, each of them carrying a guitar, were stopped in Thrace and explained that
they had come from the Adriatic coast. A distinguished
Slav scholar, the late Professor Louis Léger, says that

[1] His statement mentions that Attila, King of the Huns, after a battle
in which he was victorious, is alleged to have ordered two bards into his
presence, and they are said to have sung to him in a foreign, Slavonic,
language. Praises of heroes and feats of war, performed in their native
land, were the subjects of their songs and wherever these bards directed
their course they carried along with them a sort of musical harp, called
gusle.

their instruments must have been the *gusle*, and they them-selves either Serbs or Croats.

Two names of a much later date are often mentioned in connection with the age of the Serbian heroic songs in particular. A priest of Dioclea (or Zeta, later Montenegro), recording some events of his country, of no precise date but about the beginning of the twelfth century, confesses to drawing information for his "Chronicle" from oral traditions current among the people of his land. It cannot be seen from his writings whether such traditions were in the form of heroic songs or of popular stories, but the manner of his writing, especially when he is describing the victory of a local ruler, Vojislav (about 1038–50), over a combined army of his neighbours, is very similar to the way in which a traditional heroic song deals with a similar episode. To mention only the following: the Byzantine army is described as having been, alone, so numerous that there was hardly enough room in the land for it. This and some other descriptions, as for instance that of how Vojislav had organised a rising against the Greeks, lead us to think that the priest of Dioclea may have heard heroic songs chanted to him about these events and then have rendered their contents into prose. Unfortunately, not a single verse of such songs can be traced as having been recorded at the same time. The other name usually quoted is that of the Byzantine writer Nicephorus Gregoras who, in 1326, travelled in the lands of the Serbs with a Greek mission sent to the court of Stevan Uroš, the then Serbian ruler. In his *Byzantina Historia*, in describing how they were spending a night in a forest in the valley of the Strumica, he says that among their followers were people who sang tragic songs: "they sang about famous men, of whose glorious deeds we heard, but nothing saw". There is no indication that these people were Serbs and we have no proofs whatsoever that any Serbian personalities were glorified in traditional poetry before the beginning of the sixteenth century.

No mention, still less record, is to be found in any literary works of the Serbs before that date, although a considerable number of such works has come down to us. One would expect to find a reference to the heroic songs, if they really existed, in the works of the national biographers of the thirteenth and fourteenth centuries: St Sava, his brother Stevan the First-Crowned, Domentian, Theodosije and Danilo, all of whom wrote before the battle of Kosovo and before any collision took place between the Serbs and the Turks. As practically all the literary activities of those days were in the hands of the people in monastic orders and, consequently, were of a religious and ecclesiastical character, we can understand why there is no reference to the women's songs—except for two hostile ones in Domentian's and Theodosije's life of St Sava. Such ballads, besides their general worldly character, contained elements of pagan customs, and the monks, the men of letters of those days, naturally regarded them as of heathen origin. Although some such elements are to be found in the heroic songs as well, this could hardly have been the reason for which they, too, were to be treated with scorn, for national heroes and their heroic achievements constitute the main subjects of these songs.

After the battle of Kosovo and the fall of Serbia, two

more biographers were active—Grigorije Camblak and Constantine the "Philosopher". The latter has left an account of the battle of Kosovo but does not mention any kind of traditional poetry, nor is there any reference to such poetry in the writings of the former. Literary activities during the reign of Despot Stevan Lazarević (1389–1427) and under his patronage consisted mainly in translation and the copying of some earlier works; traditional poetry was not likely to attract the attention of his literary circle.

All that we may, therefore, safely say is that we have positive proofs of the existence of traditional poetry among the Serbs in the form of women's songs only, as early as the thirteenth century. They are mentioned also in the subsequent centuries. A Croatian writer, Đ. Šišgorić, mentions, in his work *De situ Illyriae et civitate Sibenici*, 1469, Serbian proverbs, the dancing of the *kolo*, lamenting, wedding and other women's songs. Busbecq, a Flemish diplomat in Austrian service, for eight years ambassador at the court of Solyman the Great, in his *Travels* describes a funeral in Serbia, witnessed by him personally, and tells how the women wailed and cried in mournful songs for the dead men. Moreover, the influence of these songs upon some of the Dalmatian poets is also marked as early as the fifteenth century. The first lyric poets, Šiško Menčetić (1457–1527) and Đore Držić (1461–1501), modelled some of their poems on the women's songs, and it appears that some actual specimens of these songs were included in their collection of lyric poems.

But of the existence of the heroic songs the first written proofs date from the sixteenth century. In July, 1530, King Ferdinand I sent to Sultan Solyman a mission led by Joseph von Lamberg and Nicolas Jurischitz, to whom a Slovene, Curipeschitz, was attached as interpreter. Curipeschitz kept a record of events on this journey and published it in 1531. In three places therein he mentions some Serbian national heroes, among them Kobilić, and tells us that heroic songs were chanted in Croatia and Bosnia, referring obviously to those about Kosovo. A Magyarised Croat, Vrančić, born at Šibenik, known as Veranzio in Italian, in describing his journey to Adrianople in 1553, incidentally mentions the Serbian heroes Lazar, Miloš and Marko. Another traveller, Stephan Gerlach, passed through Serbia in 1578, on his return journey from Constantinople to Germany. He does not say in his *Diary* that he heard any heroic songs, but he mentions the Serbian hero of Kosovo, Miloš, the alleged ruins of whose castle at Pirot in Serbia were shown to him.

The earliest written records of the heroic songs date also from the sixteenth century. A Dalmatian poet, Petar Hektorović, recorded two of these in his work, the *Ribanje* (*Fishing*), first published at Venice in 1556, and indicated also the tune to which they were chanted. He had heard them from two middle-aged fishermen, and these must have learned them from someone else. It could, therefore, be said that they had been in existence for at least fifty years before Hektorović wrote them down. One of these songs deals with Marko Kraljević and his brother, Andrijaš. Several versions of the same song exist, the oldest dating from 1614, while the latest was recorded by Vuk two hundred years later.

All these references and records of heroic songs are those of the long line. There is no doubt that they

existed throughout the sixteenth and seventeenth centuries, only in the western parts of the Yugoslav territory,
particularly Dalmatia. It is, however, not until the beginning of the eighteenth century that we find evidence
of any attempt at collecting them. It is of special importance to remember that these collections were formed
in Dalmatia, in the neighbourhood of Ragusa and Kotor,
and were written in Latin script. One of the manuscripts
(the older Perast MS.) contained also the earliest known
record of heroic songs of the decasyllabic line, gathered,
as is stated in the manuscript, from the oral tradition
of the people in the same region. It, therefore, appears
that these began to be composed about a hundred
and fifty years after the first *bugarštica* was recorded by
Hektorović. After the Ragusan manuscript was written
in 1758, no new *bugarštice* were mentioned. On the other
hand, heroic songs of the decasyllabic line seem to have
gained ground, for a large collection of them was formed
in Western Croatia in the early part of the eighteenth
century, written in Cyrillic character, known now as the
Erlangen MS. Another collection (the later Perast MS.)
was made in Latin script about fifty years later (1775),
south of Ragusa; it contained, principally, versions of
those *bugarštice* which had previously been recorded in the
older Perast MS. In 1779 the first heroic song of this
type was published in Eastern Croatia by A. Reljković in
his *Satir*. About this time, or soon afterwards, the zenith
of the production of decasyllabic heroic songs was reached,
for at the beginning of the nineteenth century they were
collected in thousands by Vuk Karadžić. Meanwhile,
the existence of the *bugarštice* remained unknown until

the manuscripts containing them were discovered and published in the second half of the nineteenth century.[1] Their total number is about one hundred.

The publication of the songs of the long line revealed that the heroic songs of the decasyllabic line were much older than was generally supposed; it also proved that the two groups of heroic songs had existed side by side for about half a century and that versions of all the historical subjects treated in the *bugarštice* appeared also in many heroic songs of the decasyllabic line. This naturally caused the question of the age of the Yugoslav traditional heroic poetry to be treated from a different point of view. New and opposing theories were put forward, but none so far has given an acceptable explanation of the age of such poetry. In our opinion, the subject of Kosovo and the connections between Dalmatia and Western Europe may help us to give a satisfactory answer.

III

The disaster of Kosovo must have made a deep impression on the minds of the people. Whatever may have been the real cause of the Serbian defeat, the people at large could not be expected to examine it critically from the historical point of view. They, therefore, looked for and found a reason in harmony with their simple pride. It appeared to them that the defeat was due to fate more than to any other reason; long before it fell upon them it was "written" that they should suffer. "If well was meant to me, Lazar would not have been killed at Kosovo", says a Serbian proverb. Adversity was only to be a trial through

[1] By Hilferding 1859, Miklosich 1870, Bogišić 1878.

which the Serbs had to pass in order to come to better days. Suffering was to be only a fresh stimulus for them to regain freedom. Hence the day of the national disaster became, strange as it may seem, the National Festival of the Serbs. To avenge Kosovo became the one aspiration of a subdued nation, until centuries later their dream was to be realised.

Following the defeat of Kosovo and the destruction of all the Yugoslav states in the fourteenth and during the fifteenth century, a large number of Serbs and Croats, including many of their nobles and priests, fled to Dalmatia, and particularly to the Republic of Ragusa, which was at that time steadily climbing towards the zenith of its prosperity. Having exchanged Byzantine domination for that of Venice at the beginning of the twelfth century, Ragusa was practically a vassal state of the Venetian Republic, but enjoyed a considerable measure of freedom throughout the period of Venetian supremacy. During the Byzantine rule, the Latin population was confined to the ancient *Ragusium*, a small part of the actual city, while the Slavs lived, almost from the time of their penetration into Dalmatia in the seventh century, outside the walls of *Ragusium*, on the other side of the bay. Their settlement was known as *Dubrovnik*, a word derived, probably, from the Serbian word *dubrava*, a wood. The Latin population having been slavicised by the end of the thirteenth century, the two settlements were encircled by a new wall into one single city. The Ragusans, being essentially a commercial people, made trade—both land and sea borne—the chief source of their wealth. By a series of commercial treaties, they were closely connected with many Italian cities, and fine Milan cloth, skins, tan and canvas for sails were brought in Ragusan ships from Italian ports and forwarded to all quarters of the Balkans and the Eastern Empire. The Arab historian, Idrisi, who wrote about the middle of the twelfth century—long before the Republic was really prosperous—praised the Ragusans as brave and enterprising people, and says that they possessed many ships sailing to distant countries. In spite of their long rule over the cities of Dalmatia, the Venetians were never able to penetrate beyond the walls of these cities; the compact masses of the Slavs and the mountain ridges at the back of them proved an insuperable barrier to Italian penetration into Yugoslav lands.

The official and, to a certain extent, the popular language was at first Italian, for the Slav vernacular, spoken outside the cities, was to come into official and literary use only when the Serbs, fleeing before the invading Turks, found refuge in Dalmatia and particularly in the Republic of Ragusa. Their arrival both increased the number of Dalmatian Slavs and strengthened the ranks of the intellectual class, who were beginning to experience the influence of Italian literature. At the time of the arrival of the Serbs, the city of Ragusa, like all other cities along the eastern shores of the Adriatic, was under Hungarian protection, in accordance with a treaty concluded between Venice and the King of Hungary in 1358. The king, while occupying the whole coast as far south as Ragusa, allowed that city to manage its own affairs with absolute liberty. Although Venetian supremacy had ceased, relations between the cities of Dalmatia, and especially Ragusa, and Italy, were by no means severed. On the contrary, the influence of Italian literature, which had been negligible during the period of Venetian rule, was fully exercised from the end of the fifteenth century onwards.

In his excellent work, mentioned in the list of "Books Consulted", Dr J. Torbarina has given an illuminating picture of the relations between Italy and Ragusa. There were numerous Italians in the service of the Republic. When the first school was opened in the fifteenth century, it was run by Italian teachers for more than a century and a half, and practically the whole book trade was in their hands and in those of professional booksellers who came from Italy to settle at Ragusa. Besides Latin and Greek works, those of Italian authors such as Petrarch, Ariosto, Aretino and Machiavelli were well represented, and by the middle of the sixteenth century their popularity had become very great. In addition, satirical poetry and Carolingian legends were especially favoured in the first half of the same century. Resident Italian archbishops exercised a great influence in both religious and literary matters. The residence of Archbishop Lodovico Beccadelli was a centre of the intellectual life of Ragusa between 1555 and 1564, and the patricians used to go to him to read Latin, Italian and Provençal poetry. A large number of young Ragusans were educated at the Italian universities, and many Italian poets were directly or indirectly connected with Ragusan poets, practically all of whose literary works in the sixteenth century were produced as imitations of Italian works, and of those of Petrarch in particular. It was through him that the troubadour influence penetrated into Ragusa, but certain Ragusan poets experienced it directly. Venice, Padua, Florence and Ancona were the chief Italian centres from which Western culture went to Ragusa.

While the Republic drew her inspiration for literary productions from Italy, her numerous ships maintained a prosperous commerce between the Turkish possessions in the Balkans, on the one hand, and the West, particularly Italy, on the other. Of all Christians outside the Turkish Empire, the Ragusans were the only ones allowed to trade freely in the Sultan's domain, in accordance with a firman granted to them by Bayezid in 1397. The Council of Basle confirmed this privilege in 1433 and the Pope followed suit in 1469. It is estimated that by the end of the fifteenth century the Ragusans possessed over three hundred ships. By that time they were known not only in Italian ports but also in those of Spain, France, England and the Netherlands. In the middle of that century, three-quarters of Ragusa's trade was sea borne and only one-quarter of it went overland, chiefly to all parts of the Balkans.

The enterprising Ragusans, having been much handicapped in their trade by the Venetians, soon established trading connections beyond the Adriatic Sea: with Spain in the first place. There is no reason to suppose that they traded only with the Catalans and the Castilians; future investigations of Moorish documents may reveal that they traded with the Caliphate of Granada as well. When the new route round Africa to the East Indies was discovered, their sea-borne trade, like that of Venice, naturally suffered a set-back, but their connections with Spain seem to have multiplied, for we know for certain that, not only were many Spanish ships manned by Ragusan officers and crews, but many of their own ships, too, were in the Spanish service. Thus, for instance, in 1531 and again in 1541 they took part in the expeditions against Tunis and Tripolis, conducted by the Emperor Charles V. That the number of Ragusan ships in these expeditions must have been large can be surmised from the fact that, owing to their loss, the Republic's Mediterranean trade was seriously depleted. Its further decline was marked after the defeat of the Great Armada, in which a large number of Ragusan ships took part. It is estimated that in the wars of Spain with England and Holland more than two hundred of them were destroyed.

To illustrate the rôle which Ragusa played in Spain,[1] suffice it to mention that a certain Michael Prazzatto, a native of Isola di Mezzo, served the Emperor Charles V with his galleys and enjoyed his favour and friendship. At his death he left his whole fortune of two hundred thousand ducats to the Republic. The sons of another Ragusan, of the Tuhel family, whose ancestors had fled from Herzegovina, entered the service of Spain in the second half of the sixteenth century. One of them, Don Pietro d'Ivelja Ohmučević-Grgurić, is alleged to have fitted out a fleet of twelve ships, manned with 3200 Ragusans and other Dalmatians, at a cost of nearly one hundred thousand pounds, to take part in an expedition to the Indies and with the Invincible Armada. On his death, Don Pietro bequeathed his fleet to the Spanish king. His sons, Don Estevan and Don Gorge d'Olisti-Tasovčić, commanded their own squadrons; the former distinguished himself in the Armada, the latter in various expeditions to Tunis

[1] See Villari, Luigi, *The Republic of Ragusa.*

and the Levant at the end of the sixteenth and the beginning of the seventeenth century. Another member of the
same family, Don Juan d'Olisti-Dinčić-Tasovčić, took part
in an attack on the shores of the Sea of Marmora in 1614,
later commanded twenty-six galleys off Catalonia and
was finally appointed Captain-General of the Neapolitan
Viceregal fleet in 1639. Don Pedro, of the same family,
led a successful expedition to Brazil and was then appointed Spanish consul at Ragusa (1623–31), while his
kinsman, Don Andrea, served Spain for fifty-seven years,
holding among others the post of Spanish admiral of the
Neapolitan fleet in the first half of the seventeenth century.
Members of the family Mazibradi were also prominent in
the Spanish service; one of them, Girolamo, held the post
of Captain-General of Spain, while his brother Nicolas
was created a Marquis and a Knight of Saint James of
Compostella. There were many more Ragusans who served
in Spain in the sixteenth century, and no doubt in the
preceding one. The Ragusans were the principal carriers
of goods in the Mediterranean for several hundred years,
before they were ousted by the Dutch in the seventeenth
century.

Some Yugoslav writers have tried to prove that the
relations between Dalmatia and Spain, and particularly
between Dalmatian Croatia and Andalusia, go back to the
period of the rule of the Caliphs of Andalusia, established
by Abd-er-Rahman III in 922, and that the *sakaliba*, or the
"Slavs" of Andalusia, were drawn principally from the
Dalmatian Slavs. Although it is probable that some of the
original *sakaliba* were Yugoslavs from the Adriatic region,
and although it appears certain that connections between

some Croat kings and Andalusian caliphs existed in the tenth century, it is impossible to accept the statement that the *Saclab*, i.e. the "Slav", Habib of Andalusia—who is alleged to have composed at the end of the tenth century a book of entertaining anecdotes interwoven with the history and adventures of the *sakaliba*—was a Yugoslav. It is still less possible to believe that his book, of which only the title has come down to us, was an anthology of "immense Yugoslav literary productions of the ninth and tenth centuries", now entirely lost. Apart from the fact that there is nothing to prove the existence of such literature among the Yugoslavs of that time, let us remember that the Moorish "Slavs" were drawn from practically every part of Europe, especially from France and the Near East, to fill the ranks of the eunuchs and the bodyguards of the Andalusian caliphs. Granted that some of them were of Yugoslav stock, there are no proofs to show that any of them preserved their original nationality, for the Islamic faith, the Arabic language and the common interests in the service of a prosperous and advanced state must have blended and fused together all the various nationalities of which the *sakaliba* were composed. A closer study of Arabic documents may throw more light on the relations between Dalmatia and Spain, but until this is done no more definite conclusions can be derived from the existing information.

Ragusa's connections with Western Europe—with Italy and Spain in the first place—on the one hand and with the Yugoslav lands held by the Turks on the other, seem to us to throw some light on the origin and development of the Serbo-Croat poetry. Through their long and close relations with Italy, where the Western popular poetry, of both the lyric and the epic character, had penetrated at an early period, the Ragusans could not help acquainting themselves not only with the troubadour poetry, but also with the popular epic as it existed in the northern as well as in the southern parts of Italy, to both of which influences Dalmatia was subject. The voluminous popular ballads of Sicily kept alive historical traditions, and all the periods of foreign rule, from the Greek down to the Spanish occupation, are recorded in them, according to Professor Salomone-Marino. All forms of popular poetry current throughout Italy, such as *strambotti* and *rispetti*, called *canzune* in Sicily, appear to have originated there. Tuscany was the first to adopt them and hand them over to Venice.

In studying the traditional poetry of West-European peoples we have arrived at conclusions similar to those of N. Banašević, but independently and in complete ignorance of his investigations. However feasible his arguments may appear it should be remembered, first, that we have no proofs whatsoever of the existence of the Yugoslav heroic poetry during the century in which the MS. of the *Chançun de Williame* was at Ragusa; secondly, that the MS. was transferred to Milan in the beginning of the fifteenth century, and lastly that, according to the proofs available so far, the earliest known heroic songs on Kosovo were composed a century later. Since we believe too that the origin of the Yugoslav heroic poetry is connected with such poetry of Western Europe, we cannot help emphasising that the Ragusans must have had a good opportunity of acquainting themselves with the French

popular poetry, either through their direct connections
with France at a later date, during the Republic's prosperity, or through their connections with Italy and
Spain. Through their connections with the latter they
must have acquainted themselves also with the Castilian
romances, and in these a prominent subject, that of the
struggle between the Christians and the Moslems, could
not have escaped their notice. Had they not repeatedly
heard of the struggle of their own ancestors with the
infidels and of the tragic story of Kosovo? Had they not
themselves witnessed and experienced the onslaughts of
the Turks on the mountains that rise above the walls of
Ragusa?

It can hardly be a mere coincidence that no trace is to
be found of the Yugoslav heroic poetry before the sixteenth century, before the time when the relations between Ragusa on the one side and Italy and Spain on the
other became so intimate. We, therefore, cannot help
concluding that the Yugoslav *junačke pesme*, in the form in
which they have been recorded, did not exist until their
creation was caused and inspired by the knowledge of the
Western heroic poems of popular origin, such as were in
vogue in France, Spain and Italy at the time when the
Dalmatians obtained knowledge of them. The vivid
memory of the oral material that had been brought to
Dalmatia by Serbian fugitives, who told of their own
ceaseless border struggles and of the great battles waged
by the Hungarians and Austrians against the Turks, in
which numerous Yugoslavs took a prominent part—all
these must have been sufficient stimulus for the Dalmatians, and for the cultured patricians of Ragusa in particular, to begin to glorify in the form of epic songs' the

momentous events of the great past of their ancestors and of their own times.

It is important to bear in mind Professor Chadwick's statement that heroic poetry "makes its appearance in various nations and in various periods of history". The conditions of the late fifteenth and the early sixteenth centuries in Dalmatia did not warrant the appearance of court poets, similar to those who appeared in the west of Europe at an earlier period, but in the sad days of tragic defeats, when stories of the great past were being told by the old to the young, the yearning for freedom, and the hope of being delivered from the enemy caused gifted men to describe in verse some of these historical events. Thus, probably, came into being the first *bugarštica* as a belated re-echo of the Western popular epics of the late Middle Ages. That the first subjects of them were fights between the Serbo-Croats and the Turks is almost certain, but we cannot say what was the particular event earliest celebrated in them. It is, however, reasonable to suppose that the battle of Kosovo was treated first, because we know that the story of Kosovo began to be recorded in Dalmatia from the sixteenth century onwards, and that the contents of various popular ballads on the subject were rendered into prose and recorded in a manuscript, the oldest known copy of which dates from the second decade of the eighteenth century.

Because of their patriotic contents, the songs of the long line seem to have become popular, their numbers increasing with the growth of national consciousness and hence the appearance of more manuscripts, and the making of collections properly so called, in the very beginning of the eighteenth century. By this time they must have been known to a large number of people, remaining, however, always the products of individual poets of a certain culture. The gifted and poetically disposed men among the common people recognised in them subjects known to them from their own traditions. While, therefore, the themes of the *bugarštice* were familiar to them, the long line must have appeared to them complicated and difficult. Since the simpler decasyllabic line had existed in popular use for the ballads of lyric type, long before the first *bugarštica* was written, it was natural that it should be adopted also for heroic songs, and that the long line should gradually disappear.

It would seem, therefore, that the material for the heroic songs of the decasyllabic line was drawn at first from the *bugarštice*, but naturally popular stories current among the people and chronicles supplied material for further composition. To these should be added fresh matter constantly supplied by contemporary events, in which the fate of the Serbo-Croat people was involved. They fought on the side of Austria-Hungary against the Turks, and contributed towards the decline of the Ottoman Empire: hence we have the glorifying of the *ćesar* (i.e. Austrian Emperor) and of Hungarian heroes in Yugoslav heroic songs; hence also the renewed hope that deliverance from the Turkish yoke was at hand. The French revolution and the Napoleonic wars also inspired the subjugated *rayah* and awakened the national conscience. Herein lies the explanation of the increase and extension of popular heroic songs all over the Serbo-Croat lands. They reached their culminating point with the First Rising of the Serbs in 1804, and it was fortunate that so many of them were collected just about that time.

Conclusion

I N the nineties of the last century Asmus Soerensen, one of the collaborators of the *Archiv für Slavische Philologie*, and a lecturer in the University of Leipzig, published an extensive treatise which may still be considered as the best on the Serbian heroic poetry. What, in his words,

gives to the really good songs of Vuk's collection—but to them alone—their value and peculiar charm is not merely the metrical correctness, the smooth diction, the harmonious rhythm, nor yet the qualities which they have in common with the poems of a later age. Their pre-eminence lies rather in the originality of invention, the consistency of the artistic composition, the characteristic turns of expression, and the variation, so happily matching the subject selected, between terseness, power and liveliness on the one hand and abundance, brilliance and majestic calm on the other. If the last-mentioned qualities give the epic Homeric tone, in the first-named we find an additional lyrical and dramatic element. Aesthetic definitions of this nature are not, however, wholly satisfactory, for all genuine arts contain an indefinable something which corresponds to the depth of soul life and is consequently more appealing. This brings us to what is most essential: there is in these songs an emotional element; they reproduce an echo of the spiritual life of man; they are not simple narratives, as Eastern tales are; they do not stand aloof from things, but are aglow with the pulsating accents of experience.

But the soul life unfolded is not that of passion; we miss in the songs the strong emotions—love and hate, joy and sorrow; in their stead we have a contemplative, artless emotion,

SYB
11

yielding rather than overpowering; a feeling of universality, a sympathy with the whole of creation, a still and quiet joy in things. There is no gloomy hatred for the foe of one's religion and people, but sincere satisfaction when the foe is hurled back, subdued and killed; no moral indignation over wrongdoing and violence, but a cheerful certainty that punishment must ensue, and full satisfaction when it is dealt; no fanatical enthusiasm for the ancestral faith, but the confident consciousness of a perfect assimilation with that faith; no fierce, passionate sentiment for nation and patriotism, but outspoken joy in deeds of strength and cunning, in deeds of violence and malice, which win for the national heroes the upper hand over the Turks.

Humour finds a fruitful soil in a mental outlook of this kind, and this is the attitude in Vuk's songs towards the world. The humour in them is not that grotesque humour which clings to the inconsistency and foibles of the world to have its joke with them, nor is it a sentimental humour which seeks to overcome these foibles and inconsistencies and holds within itself a touch of querulousness, but a naïve humour which feels at one with the world and has therefore no other object than to give expression to this comfortable frame of mind....

In the emotional world revealed to us in Vuk's songs we hark back to a quite different age: the age of to-day, an age akin and consequently near to us. We do not need to strive by study and reflection to understand any alien age and civilisation, we do not need to allow it to impress us. Is this a pure coincidence, or is perchance a satisfactory answer given to our query by the mystical ideas of nature poetry and all similar ideas?

It will be shown in the second part of this book that the interest in Serbian traditional poetry in Europe, especially in Germany, France and England, was considerable throughout the nineteenth century. The subject was sufficiently interesting to engage the attention of prominent men such as Goethe, Grimm, Pushkin, Mérimée and Mickiewicz, and the lead given by them, no doubt, contributed towards the spreading of interest in both the west and the east of Europe. Yet while this poetry exercised a very great influence on the literatures of the Yugoslavs—indeed at one time imitations of it were almost the only form of their modern literatures—and to a certain extent on those of all the other Slavs, the Czechs in particular, it cannot be said that it left any conspicuous mark on any of the West-European literatures.

Practically all those—whether poets, philologists or historians—who studied and translated Yugoslav popular ballads, drew their information from Vuk and his collection. We think we are right in saying that no other Yugoslav stood so high and was so well known in the nineteenth century as this great grammarian and collector of popular ballads.

The reader may wonder what is the present position of Yugoslav traditional poetry. To quote Lamartine, "the sombre avenues of aged oaks, and the rocks which line the torrents," still resound with the echoes of the women's songs, but the heroic songs have much declined and in most regions have practically died out. The printed collections marked the end of the spontaneous creation of heroic poetry, for they began to be read in schools and at home, so that under their influence new heroic songs came into being, composed mostly by villagers who, unlike the former chanters, were anxious to be known as the composers of such songs. Spontaneous creation survived longest in the mountain regions, especially Montenegro, Herzegovina and Bosnia.

Speaking generally, it is no longer the fashion to compose and chant the heroic songs in the manner of preceding centuries, though during the Balkan and the Great Wars it was nothing unusual to hear a peasant soldier describe in decasyllabic lines, while sitting by the camp fire in the evening, the course of the battle that had ended on that day. Such songs, however, merely related the course of the battle—often in a humorous way, at the expense of the defeated side, whichever it might be—and are no more than a poor imitation of the earlier heroic songs. Since they are of small poetical value, only a few of these modern songs have been recorded, and their existence scarcely justifies the conclusion that heroic poetry is still being created in the old fashion. Strictly speaking, the conditions that caused the creation of heroic poetry among the Yugoslavs, namely the long and gigantic struggle with the Turks, no longer exist.

The Serbo-Croat traditional heroic poetry remains, however, in the words of Professor Mathias Murko, "la plus riche, la plus parfaite au point de vue artistique, la plus réaliste et la plus humaine des poésies épiques populaires slaves".

A SERBIAN *GUSLAR*

PART II

Chapter Five

Yugoslav Traditional Poetry in German Literature

I

THE interest which the literary people of Europe took in Serbian traditional poetry was a result of the Romantic Movement, when a kind of international literary interest was awakened. The literary material of popular origin that was discovered, whether among the Germanic people or among the Balkan Slavs, whether in Spain or in Russia, was treated as common property. The Scottish popular ballads, the Castilian *romances*, the Serbian *narodne pesme*, were greeted with practically equal enthusiasm.

The origin of the Romantic Movement can be traced as far back as the first quarter of the eighteenth century, when the *Spectator* published *Chevy Chase*. It opened actually, however, with the publication of Macpherson's *Ossian* and Percy's *Reliques*. In 1760, several months before Rousseau's *Nouvelle Héloïse*, James Macpherson published his *Fragments of Ancient Poetry*, a collection of sixteen ballads. These are, as we know now, poems invented or adapted to the old Irish cycle, transmitted to Scotland in the eighth or ninth century, either in manuscript or by oral tradition. So great was the success of this book and such was the demand for it that a new edition was published before the year was out. Both of them remained anonymous until 1762, when Macpherson's name appeared as the translator of the *Fingal*, which also ran into two editions in the year of its publication. In the following year appeared *Temora*. The two latter were, in 1773, published together as the *Poems of Ossian*.

The interest that was caused in England by Macpherson's *Fragments* was very great. An unrivalled passion for unearthing archaic poetry ensued in the years between 1760 and 1765, when Thomas Percy published the *Reliques of Ancient English Poetry*. Unlike the *Fragments*, Percy's *Reliques* was at first received coldly and he was attacked as a forger. The fact was that he had drawn forty-five of the ballads, out of a total of 176, from a folio manuscript, written about 1630, which he found at the home of one of his friends, where it was being used for lighting fires. The remaining 131 were either gathered from many other manuscripts or composed entirely by Percy himself.

Rarely had a book such an immediate success in Europe as Macpherson's *Ossian*. Before the end of the century it was translated into Italian, German and French. It roused great interest everywhere, but in Germany enthusiasm for the Scottish bard went beyond all bounds. He was ranked with Homer and Shakespeare. English influence, which began to be felt soon after the publication of *Chevy Chase*, became very strong after Bürger and Herder had introduced Macpherson's and Percy's works. Herder and *Ossian* induced Goethe to study Shakespeare and the

Volkslieder. In France, a cult for the Celtic Homer was established, too, as soon as *Fingal* was translated into French. It is a fact that France's great poets of the period were full of praise for the Scottish ballads; some of their works were inspired by *Ossian.* Yet, unlike the German poets, no Frenchman attempted to dig into the past of his own people and to create a truly national literature, as the Germans did. The interest of the French poets for the Romantic past and its hidden treasures appeared later than that of the English and the Germans. When it did appear, however, it was an interest, not for France's past, but for that of other peoples.

II

What Thomas Percy did in Scotland in the sixties of the eighteenth century was done, about ten years before him, for Dalmatia by a Franciscan friar, Fra Andria Kačić-Miošić (1702–60), a Croat by birth, who died in the very year of Macpherson's publication of the *Fragments.* About the middle of the eighteenth century Kačić was performing the duties of Papal Legate for Dalmatia, Bosnia and Herzegovina, and was also in charge of all Franciscan houses in Dalmatia. He was descended from one of the oldest aristocratic families of Croatia, on which the title of *Knez* was conferred by the Emperor Maximilian I. In addition to his ecclesiastical duties, he interested himself in the history of his people, to whom he constantly refers as the "Slavs". The national heroes, whether of the Roman Catholic, the Eastern Orthodox or the Moslem confession, were the objects of his profound admiration. In order to preserve their names in the memory of his

people, he published at Venice, in 1756, a book which he
entitled *Agreeable Discourse of the Slav People* (*Razgovor
Ugodni Naroda Slovinskog*). It is a collection of poems, some
of which are preceded by short sketches in prose, all
glorifying important events and prominent personalities
among the Serbo-Croat people, from the time of Constantine the Great until the Seven Years' War. His conception of history is above all things patriotic, and in his
great enthusiasm for the heroic past of his people he
stated that Alexander the Great was descended from
Slavs! His collection consisted of nearly 140 poems, of
which but a few were really popular ballads, while most
of them were composed by himself, though modelled
upon the popular ones.

While Thomas Percy derived those forty odd genuine
ballads from the manuscript he had found, Kačić derived his few genuine ones by word of mouth from his
compatriots. As to the remaining poems, both did practically the same: they composed them themselves, but in
the spirit of the traditional ballads. Like Percy's *Reliques*,
the *Razgovor* of Kačić became very popular and many a
monk and layman busied himself with copying the book.
For a long time afterwards these poems were considered
real popular ballads. The fate of the two collections was,
however, different. Percy's book marked an epoch in
the literatures of the civilised world; the work of Kačić
naturally exercised but a local influence.

Yet, under the influence of *The Poems of Ossian* and the
Reliques, the attention of an Italian who was, in his own
days, well known, was drawn to the popular ballads of
the Dalmatian Serbo-Croats and to the collection of poems

made by Kačić. This Italian was Alberto Fortis (1741–
1803), first a monk and then scientist, naturalist, journalist,
poet and a great traveller. He often visited Dalmatia in the
'seventies of the eighteenth century, and appeared to be
chiefly interested in the Orthodox Yugoslav peasants
of the coast, known then as the *Morlachi*. In describing
their customs, he inserted now and again verses and
poems of these people, without knowing what the result
of it would be. He certainly did this with some fixed
purpose, although he spoke contemptuously of popular
poetry as matter on which no scientist should waste time.
Why, then, did he do it? One has to bear in mind that
only about ten years had passed since the time of Macpherson's *Ossian* and about five since Percy's *Reliques*
were published. Fortis was not carried away by the
general vogue that swept over Europe, but, naturally, he
must have been interested in the corresponding features
with which he came into contact among the Serbo-Croat
population in Dalmatia. He seems to have been well
acquainted with the main currents of English literature,
and it is known that he read *Ossian* in the Italian translation of the Abbé Cesarotti. Moreover, Fortis had
numerous friends in England who, as we shall presently
show, supported him financially in his work. In May,
1770, Alberto Fortis and an English friend, John Symonds (1729–1807), Professor of Modern History at
Cambridge, travelled together in Dalmatia. The result of
this journey was Fortis's book: *Observations on the Islands
of Cherso and Osero*, Venice, 1771. At the end of this work
he added a letter, addressed to John Symonds, and a
ballad, the first one in Italian translation, *Canto di Milos*

Cobilich e di Vuko Brankovic, which Fortis found in the *Razgovor*. He added this ballad to please Symonds, who was interested in popular ballads, promising to speak more about them in another work which he was preparing. The ballad of Milos Cobilich was not really popular, but was composed by Kačić on the same model. Fortis did not know Serbian and relied on the help of his Dalmatian friends, who translated it for him.

While in Dalmatia, Fortis sent to his English patrons reports on various subjects, all of which were brought together in a book which he published in Venice in 1774, three years after his *Observations*, under the title *Viaggio in Dalmazia*; a work of much greater importance, which was translated soon afterwards into German (1776), French and English (1778). Amongst other chapters there is one, perhaps the most interesting, on the *Customs of the Morlaks*, dedicated to John Symonds. Remaining true to his promise to Symonds, Fortis speaks here again of the Serbo-Croat popular poetry, describing the "Morlakian bards" and their musical instrument, the *gusle*. At the end of this chapter he added another popular ballad, *Canzone Dolente Della Nobile Sposa d'Asan Aga* (*Halosna Pjesanca Plemenite Asan-Aginize*), both in the original and in the Italian translation.

Fortis's usual source for popular ballads of the Dalmatian Serbo-Croats was the *Razgovor*, but the *Hasanaginica* is not in it and it is not known how it reached him. It is believed, however, that Fortis obtained a manuscript similar to the one that he attributed to the locality of Spalato.

III

In 1778–9 Herder, following Percy's example, published his *Volkslieder*, the first volume of which contained one, and the second three "Morlakisch" songs. Three of these, *Ein Gesang von Milos Cobilich und Vuko Brankovich, Radoslaus* and the *Die schöne Dolmetscherin*, were translated from the Italian by Herder himself, and all of them originated from the *Razgovor*. The fourth, the *Klaggesang von der edlen Frauen des Asan Aga*, was translated by Goethe, although this was not indicated. Herder's attention was drawn to the first "Morlakian" song, probably in 1773, by Professor R. E. Raspe, who was among the first of German scholars to be interested also in Macpherson's *Ossian* and Percy's *Reliques*. Goethe acquainted himself with the *Klaggesang* in 1775, when the chapter on the *Customs of the Morlaks* was translated from Italian into German, and published in Berne. This song was included in it, translated by a German poet, F. A. C. Werthes. The translation reached Goethe, and he, using it and the Serbian original—although he, like Werthes, had no knowledge of Serbian—produced an excellent translation, about 1775-6, fifteen years after *Ossian* and ten after the *Reliques*. Before it was printed, Herder "polished it up" from the metrical point of view. Eleven years later this song, slightly revised, appeared under Goethe's name as the first song in the second collection of his poems, published in 1789. It met with great approval in literary circles in Europe; Madame de Staël wrote to Goethe saying that she was enchanted with "la femme morlaque".

It was through this translation that the Serbian traditional poetry received some notice in Europe, but the
great interest aroused by it about thirty years later was
due to the publication of Vuk's large collection of the
Srpske Narodne Pesme. Having published his *Pesnarica,*
Vuk sent, at Kopitar's suggestion, a copy of it to Goethe,
along with a German translation of all the songs. Goethe
was pleased to receive it, but his interest of forty years
earlier for the Serbian ballads seemed to have vanished
for the time being.

While Vuk was busy collecting the songs, the Congress
of Vienna was sitting. A German scholar, Jacob Grimm,
was attached to the German delegacy and stayed in
Vienna from October, 1814, until June, 1815. He fre-
quented literary circles and began to interest himself in
the Slav languages. He also met Kopitar, of whom he
already knew, and Kopitar gave him Vuk's *Pesnarica* in
order to initiate him into Serbian. Grimm, having learnt
Serbian in Vienna, reviewed the book very favourably in
September, 1815. In praising the Serbian traditional
songs he compared them with Solomon's Song of Songs.
Three months before, Kopitar had reviewed Vuk's
Grammar of the Serbian Language. In November of 1815
there appeared Vuk's second volume of traditional songs.
This was reviewed at length by Kopitar himself in March,
1816. He then expressed the hope that some Goethe
would transplant into the German Parnassus these flowers
also. The new Goethe, as translator of the Serbian traditional songs, appeared in Jacob Grimm himself. While
writing the review of Vuk's first collection, he had translated a number of these songs into German. His trans-

lations were going the round of his friends until, in 1818, "Nineteen Serbian Songs, translated by the brothers Grimm", were published in Friedrich Förster's *Sänger- fahrt*. The songs were selected by Clemens Brentano, who also indicated that the translators were the "brothers" Grimm, although Wilhelm took no part in it. Even while he was rendering these songs, Jacob Grimm was conscious that they could not *really* be translated. Being a philologist and not a poet, like some of the later German translators, he aimed at giving as faithful a reproduction of the original as possible. He was a great enthusiast for Serbian traditional poetry; it reminded him often of Homer and, in fact, he asserted that "everything in them was like that in Homer". He was therefore very anxious that they should be widely known. It was under his influence that Goethe began to interest himself in them once more. It was also due to him that Talvj undertook to translate into German practically all the songs that had been published by Vuk in Serbian. Through Jacob Grimm's and Kopitar's reviews, and through Grimm's translations, Serbian folk-songs were becoming better and better known. The real enthusiasm for them, however, was aflame in the third decade of the nineteenth century, after Vuk had enlarged the first two volumes into three, published in 1823–4 at Leipzig; and after almost all the ballads contained therein had been translated into German by Talvj—but more of her presently.

Events subsequently developed as follows: In June, 1821, Vuk was ready with his third volume of the ballads and the manuscript duly reached the Censor, Kopitar, who naturally was ready to pass it. Meanwhile, unfortunately,

Vuk was denounced by his enemies at home to the Austrian Government for political reasons, and publication was consequently refused. So in April, 1823, Vuk went to Leipzig to try to publish it there, but instead of issuing the third volume he decided to publish a second revised and enlarged edition of the work, in three volumes, and this was done from the beginning of August till the end of December, 1823, the volumes appearing in reverse order. As soon as the third volume was issued in August, Jacob Grimm, without waiting for the other two to be published, wrote a review, in November, 1823, in the *Göttingische Gelehrte Anzeigen*.[1] In it he lavished praises upon both the women's and the heroic songs, giving, however, the first place to the latter and in particular to the Kosovo cycle and to the songs about Marko Kraljević. Goethe's interest in Serbian traditional songs was roused once more. Introduced by Jacob Grimm, Vuk called on Goethe at Weimar at the beginning of October, 1823. Goethe received him cordially.

Contrary to his attitude towards the Serbian traditional poetry in 1814, Goethe took a lively interest in it immediately upon Vuk's first visit to him. He published, in the next number of his *Über Kunst und Alterthum*, an heroic song that Grimm had translated and sent to him by Vuk. In November, 1823, Vuk sent to Goethe, at his personal request, from Leipzig, a number of heroic songs in German translations. One of these, describing the death of Marko Kraljević, appeared soon afterwards. Vuk presented Goethe also with his little Grammar and his *Serbian Dictionary*, published five years earlier. In his

[1] Kopitar reviewed the whole collection in 1825.

letter of thanks to Vuk, Goethe requested him to send him a few more translations of Serbian songs, the *Marriage of Hajkuna* in particular. In February, 1824, Vuk visited Goethe once more and presented him on this occasion with his new edition of Serbian traditional songs. Goethe expressed his admiration for Vuk's translations and for his Dictionary.[1] During the next few weeks, Goethe wrote an article on "Serbian Literature", which was to appear in his *Kunst und Alterthum*. It remained, however, unpublished until 1903.

IV

But the translation in bulk of Serbian traditional poetry in Germany was to be done by Talvj, a writer of long and short stories. Talvj is the literary pseudonym for Fräulein Therese Albertina Luisa von Jacob, being composed of the initial letters of her full name. She was born at Halle in 1797, ten years after Vuk, and was the daughter of Professor von Jacob. In 1806 she went with her parents to Kharkov, in Russia, where her father held a post as University professor until 1816, when they returned to Halle. Fräulein Therese acquired in this way a complete knowledge of Russian. At the age of twenty-three she began to write, and translated anonymously some of Sir Walter Scott's novels into German. In 1828 she married an American Bible scholar, Professor the Rev.

[1] In April, 1824, Vuk published his *Serbische Grammatik* with a long preface by J. Grimm in which attention was drawn to the Serbian traditional poetry. Professor Joh. Severin Vater, of whom Goethe had a high opinion, contributed to this edition some observations on the heroic songs and a survey of the most important of these. Vuk's Serbian Grammar, Grimm's preface to it and his reviews of Vuk's collection, opened the way to Serbian traditional poetry in Germany.

Edward Robinson, of Andover, Mass., and moved to the United States, where she remained until the death of her husband in 1864, having written a great deal in English and German on various subjects. During that time she wrote and published in New York a book: *Historical View of the Languages and Literatures of the Slavonic Nations, with a sketch of their popular poetry*. She then returned to Germany and died, in 1870, at Hamburg, where her son held the post of Consul-General of the U.S.A. The Austrian dramatist, Grillparzer, who met her in Goethe's house in September, 1826, when she was twenty-nine years old, calls her both young and beautiful, as well as an accomplished woman.

She was still unmarried when Vuk's collection of 1823 was published and when Grimm's review of it induced her to utilise her knowledge of Russian in studying Serbian. Some of her letters to Goethe show, however, that her primary object was not so much the study of Serbian traditional songs in themselves, but that it was the means of approaching the great master; she began translating them solely for his sake, without thinking of the public in the least, and it was due to Goethe's "gracious interest" and to his encouragement that she extended her work far more than she had at first intended. From the correspondence which passed between her and Goethe, as well as from his *Diary*, it is seen that he was not only merely encouraging her, but that he actually took a considerable interest, even a part, in her work. Having met Vuk in Halle early in 1824, she seems to have seen his collection in March of the same year for the first time, but by the next month she had already written to Goethe, sending him her first translation and requesting him—on the ground that he had been interested in Serbian traditional songs—to assist her in the undertaking. Goethe responded readily and letters and manuscripts of translations were now frequently exchanged between Halle and Weimar. In June, 1824, and then again in October of the same year, she came with her father to Weimar to visit Goethe; she seems to have made a favourable impression upon him. Soon after her first call she asked him for permission to dedicate her book to him and, a little later, asked him to write a preface to it. In answering her letter he agreed to her desire as to the dedication, but he said that he did not feel competent to write a preface; a plan as to how he thought the Serbian songs should be arranged was attached to the same letter. In drafting it, Goethe showed a remarkable understanding. The result of Goethe's renewed interest in the study of Serbian traditional poetry was his extensive article "Serbische Lieder", published in *Kunst und Alterthum* in the following spring, 1825. When Goethe wrote this article, the first and largest that he ever wrote on the subject, he was fifty years older than when he approached the Serbian poetry for the first time. The women's or love songs, as he called them, in particular met with his approval: they were admirable and of the greatest beauty, and some of them deserved, in his opinion, to be compared with the Song of Songs. On the other hand he had no liking for some of the heroic songs, especially for those of Marko Kraljević, where his cruelty towards women is expressed. He saw in Marko "a rough counterpart of the Greek Hercules, of the Persian Rustan, but of course in a Scythian and most barbaric way".

In this article Goethe also announced that the first
volume of Talvj's translations of Serbian songs was soon
to appear. The volume did appear a few weeks later at
Leipzig, entitled *Volkslieder der Serben, metrisch übersetzt
und historisch eingeleitet von Talvj*. The Dedication to Goethe
consisted of three stanzas, and he naturally was among
the first to receive a copy of it. The second volume was
published in the following year. These translations made
a considerable impression and the interest of literary
circles for them was extensive. The volumes were reviewed by well-known men of letters in a great many
newspapers and periodicals, amongst them being the poet,
Wilhelm Müller.[1] Of all the reviews, that of Jacob Grimm,
published in the *Göttingische Gelehrte Anzeigen*, in 1826,
was perhaps the most notable. Goethe himself wrote, in
December, 1826, a short note in his *Kunst und Alterthum*.
He would, no doubt, have reviewed it at length had not
Grimm done so already, and he used the draft for the
article he had intended to publish on this occasion as a
basis for his article "Serbische Gedichte" published in the
following year, when W. Gerhard's *Wila* appeared. The
actual draft appeared after his death in 1833.

Talvj, like Grimm, aimed at giving a literal translation,
though she was less successful in this because she went
wrong far oftener than Grimm. Whenever he was in
doubt as to the meaning of the text, he practically always
had at hand either Kopitar or Vuk to put him right. This
was not the case with Talvj; she preferred to be independent in labouring through the text. But even when she

---

[1] He had published in 1825 two volumes of Modern Greek popular
songs, translated from Fauriel's French translation.

called upon these Slavists for advice, she would often, sometimes obstinately, hold her own ground—she complained to Goethe about the "severe Slav press corrector of Vienna"; hence there are many more misinterpretations and mistakes in her translations than in those of Grimm. On comparing their translations, one is driven to the conclusion that Talvj never failed to consult Grimm; she borrowed from him not only words and phrases but sometimes whole lines. Goethe's translations, too, served her as a model, but she sometimes took too much liberty with the text and brought in personal feelings and expressions, thus disturbing the character of purely epic stories. These and similar drawbacks are not, however, as Dr Ćurčin rightly points out, the reasons that her translations remain far behind the original; the true reason for this was that Talvj, however hardworking and skilful, had no poetical gifts.

A recent critic, Professor G. Gesemann, is less kind to her; he calls her the "aufdringlich-geschäftige Talvj", and her translations "süsslich, klischeen-mässig, weiblich-zimperlich, klassizistisch-epigonisch", which have "die ganze deutsche Auffassung des serbischen Heldendichtes gründlichst verdorben".

The importance of her work therefore consists not in its practical value but in the success and the influence which it had upon others, within and without her country. After her marriage she continued to interest herself in the Serbian traditional poetry, but her personal influence in Europe ceased almost completely. It was, therefore, her book that remained behind to keep interest in this poetry alive and to stimulate others to study it. In 1835 she published the second edition of her translations, under the same title. When Vuk published in Vienna yet another edition of his Serbian popular ballads, in 1841, 1845 and 1846, she used it, whilst in Europe in 1850, in preparing a third, revised and enlarged, edition, published in two parts at Leipzig in 1853. The new features of this edition consisted in a fresh preface, seven additional heroic songs and about twenty women's songs. Some of the songs were slightly rearranged and revised.

Closely in Talvj's footsteps followed Peter Otto von Goetze, with a small volume of *Serbische Volkslieder*, published at St Petersburg in 1827. It contains sixty-two women's and four heroic songs, and a number of wedding and harvest songs. How closely it followed Talvj's work can be concluded from her words, "I cannot help regarding it as a most immodest plagiarism". Not only does Goetze nowhere admit that he has consulted her translations, but he says in the preface that he had translated most of these songs in 1819, from the manuscripts which Vuk himself had then brought to St Petersburg. Their publication had, however, been postponed owing to the publisher's idea of bringing out a much larger work, to contain examples of the traditional poetry of all the Slavs. There is no doubt that Goetze had been acquainted with the Serbian songs as early as 1819—in any case much earlier than Talvj herself—but on comparing their works one cannot help seeing that Goetze's translations testify unfortunately only too clearly that he had more than consulted Talvj's volumes.

V

Talvj was not the only translator, on a large scale, of the Serbian traditional songs in the 'twenties of last century. About the time when her interest in this matter somewhat relaxed, owing to her marriage, Wilhelm Christoph Leonhard Gerhard, a man of many-sided interests in poetry and the arts, developed a sympathy also for the Serbian traditional songs. He was a native of Weimar and a merchant of Leipzig. His hobbies were writing and translating poems—among others he translated those of Robert Burns in 1840—arranging musical comedies and fancy-dress processions for his friends, painting, sculpturing and, in his later days, even dancing. In 1826 he met a Serbian poet, Sima Milutinović (1791–1847), a native of Montenegro, who had come from Russia to Leipzig in that year in order to publish his epic *Srbijanka*, in which the Serbian wars for liberation were described, he himself having taken part in them. Milutinović was an adventurous and interesting man among the Serbian poets of the early nineteenth century: he was among the first to follow in Vuk's steps and collected a large number of traditional songs. On arriving at Leipzig he was in great financial trouble and Gerhard engaged him as his teacher of Serbian. With his help, he began translating songs from Vuk's collection, chiefly those that Talvj, for some reason or another, had left aside. Towards the end of 1826 Gerhard sent to Goethe, whom he had known for some ten or more years, a number of his translations and wrote to him also about Milutinović. Goethe took considerable interest in both Gerhard's

poems and his "Serbian guest" and he wrote back that
he would publish his translations in *Kunst und Alterthum*,
and that he would like to publish in it also a sketch of
Milutinović's life, as well as a short account of what his
Srbijanka contained. Having obtained these from Milutinović directly, Goethe published, in 1827, his two articles
"Serbische Gedichte" and "Das neueste Serbischer
Literatur", continuing thus to interest himself in Serbian
poetry, through Gerhard instead of through Talvj. The
article "Serbische Gedichte", after a few observations on
Grimm's and Talvj's activities in this field, says that now
Herr Gerhard appears in the same field with great skill in
rhythm and rhyme, introducing him thus to German
readers as the third translator of these songs. His second
article was an account of S. Milutinović's life and of his
Srbijanka. Goethe expressed in it, also, a desire that the
Srbijanka should be translated by Gerhard. The article is
concluded by an appeal to Grimm, Talvj and Gerhard in-
cessantly to promote Serbian traditional poetry, which is
both important and agreeable. Soon after, the *Morgen-
blatt* of Stuttgart brought out a long heroic song, *Banović
Strahinja*, in Gerhard's translation, under the title *Der
grossmütige Gatte*, and, towards the end of 1827, there
appeared at last his two large volumes of Serbian songs,
entitled *Wila: Serbische Volkslieder und Heldenmärchen*, as
the third and fourth volumes of his *Gedichte*. Goethe
published a short article about Serbian poetry, in his
Kunst und Alterthum, in the following year, as a short essay
opening a series of reviews, all included under a common
title, *Nationelle Dichtkunst*. Here Goethe announces the
appearance of Gerhard's *Wila* and, amongst other things,

says that Serbian poetry had at last spread among Western literatures to such an extent that it needed no further recommendation, and that an advertisement of the latest work was almost superfluous. Among his reviews that follow this very short essay are those of John Bowring's *Servian Popular Poetry* and of *La Guzla* of Prosper Mérimée, of which we shall speak in later chapters.

Goethe's interest in Serbian traditional poetry practically ceased after this time. His last brief essay seems to show that he began to feel a little tired of the subject. After the death of his patron and friend, the Grand Duke Karl August, and of his own son, these songs—indeed, popular ballads in general—were far from him and he would not hear of them any more, as he himself said in March, 1830, to Kanzler von Müller, "Es war doch eine schöne Zeit, als die Übersetzung der serbischen Gedichte zuerst hervortrat und wir so frisch und lebendig in jene eigentümlichen Zustände hinein versetzt wurden. Jetzt liegt mir das ferne; ich mag nichts mehr davon wissen". These are, no doubt, the utterances of an old man desirous of peace and rest.

Although Goethe bestowed lavish praises upon Gerhard's gift for translating, Gerhard in no way surpasses Talvj, who did not claim to have made a selection or an anthology out of Vuk's collection; she had "mehr herausgegriffen als gewählt", to use her own words, but a large number of songs were left aside by her on purpose, either because they were not sufficiently interesting or characteristic for German readers, or were frivolous from her point of view. With the help of his Serbian teacher, Milutinović, and during the winter evenings of 1826–7,

Gerhard laboured through most of these from Vuk's collection, and also through a number of songs which he had heard from Milutinović or taken from his *Srbijanka*. He also chose a few of the best heroic songs from the *Razgovor*, obtained for him by Milutinović. Thus, the first volume of his *Wila* contained about 140 women's songs, all under a common title, the *Kolo*. Then follow about twenty more such songs "freely formed". Lastly, there are thirty-four heroic songs entitled *Gusle*, which conclude this volume. The sources from which they had been drawn already show that not all of them are traditional songs. In the second volume there are ten more heroic songs under the same heading, while the greatest part of it is filled with an appendix and by an extensive and elaborate "Glossarium". As to the former, we shall show in the next chapter that Gerhard was one of those who were entrapped by Mérimée, because the appendix to his work consists of twenty-seven "traditional" songs translated from *La Guzla*. Gerhard, according to his own confession, actually postponed the publication of his *Wila*, awaiting the appearance of *La Guzla*. He asked Mérimée for more Serbian songs, so that he might produce a third volume. He discovered in Mérimée's prose translation the metre of Serbian traditional poetry! Had Milutinović not, by this time, left Germany, he might have opened Gerhard's eyes before he fell into Mérimée's trap.

These facts seem to show sufficiently clearly that Gerhard's translations, as such, are a different kind of work from those of his two predecessors. He may have possessed more poetical gift, but his work can in no way be regarded as superior to Grimm's and Talvj's translations.

There can be no doubt that the actual work of translating the songs, word by word, was done by Milutinović, however broken the German he spoke, and he was by no means a Vuk. Partly because he lacked a knowledge of Serbian and partly because he was evidently anxious to produce in some way a different translation from that of Talvj, Gerhard produced, on the whole, translations often poetical enough, but seldom Serbian in word or spirit. A second edition of Gerhard's *Wila* appeared in 1877, edited by Karl Brawn, as *Wilhelm Gerhard's Gesänge der Serben*, at Leipzig.

In 1857 there was published in Berlin a small book, *Stephan Duschan, Ein Guslar Poem*, translated from the Serbian by Javorin. It contains in fact three heroic songs about Tsar Dušan: in all, nearly one thousand lines.

VI

Whatever may have been Goethe's actual feelings about the Serbian traditional poetry towards the end of his life, the praises that he had bestowed upon it before remained as a stimulus to a considerable number of people, in Germany and outside it, to busy themselves with translating this poetry into German and other languages. Although Vienna was the cradle of the interest for Serbian songs— the first reviews of Vuk's collection were written in German there—yet Germany was, throughout the first half of the last century, so to speak, their home. Moreover, no Austrian, with one exception, translated or wrote anything about them before Anastasius Grün turned, in 1850, to the Slovene traditional poetry. The only Austrian who appeared in this field before him was E. Eugen

Wesely, a schoolmaster from Vinkovci, in Slavonia, but a Moravian by birth. About the time when Talvj was translating from Vuk's collection, Wesely was using the same collection in translating fifty wedding songs, published at Budapest, in 1826, under the title *Serbische Hochzeitslieder, metrisch ins deutsche übersetzt und von einer Einleitung begleitet*. Wesely's book should be regarded as a supplement to illustrate Talvj's article ".A Serbian Wedding", which she published by way of introduction to her second volume.

Like Goethe, though on a much smaller scale, Anastasius Grün interested himself for a short time in the Slovene traditional songs, before he entered the political arena against the Slovenes. He was personally acquainted with a Croat, or rather an "Illyrian" poet, Stanko Vraz, who was one of the most ardent adherents of Vuk. Under the influence of Vraz, who was himself collecting the Yugoslav songs, and in particular the Slovene, Grün translated a number of Slovene songs and published them first in a periodical and then as a separate book entitled *Volkslieder aus Krain*, 1850. Within the next two years, three other Austrians followed in his steps. These were Johann Nepomuk Vogl, August Frankl and Siegfried Kapper. Vogl dealt with a special cycle of heroic songs, those glorifying the deeds of the Serbian national hero, and called his book, therefore, *Marko Kraljević. Serbische Heldensage*. It contained twenty-nine songs, in all about 5000 lines, and was published in Vienna in 1851. They were drawn from Vuk's and Milutinović's collections. Frankl produced a small volume *Gusle. Serbische National-lieder*, published in the following year, also in Vienna, and dedicated to Vuk's daughter, "Fräulein Wilhelmine Karadschitsch, der geistvollen Serbin". It contains, besides an introduction, ten heroic songs and fifteen women's songs. Kapper, the best known and perhaps the most important of the three in this field of work, dealt also with a special cycle, that of Kosovo, and published it as *Lazar der Serbenzar*; a second, revised, edition appeared in 1852 and a third in 1853.

Here we shall pause to consider his other work, two volumes entitled *Die Gesänge der Serben*, published at Leipzig, in 1852. This is, next to Talvj's work, the largest collection of Serbian traditional songs in German. Kapper was brought up among the Czechs and had a thorough knowledge of their language. Talvj's books made an impression upon him and as a young man he published, in 1844, a collection called *Die Slavischen Melodien*, which among other songs contained two women's songs, "aus Illyrien". These were motifs taken from either Talvj or Gerhard and freely adapted. He then travelled, in the summer of 1850, through Serbia and Bosnia, thus learning the language of the Serbs thoroughly. Having done so, he proceeded to translate their traditional poetry and published *Die Gesänge der Serben*. He, too, made use of Vuk's collection, but many of the songs he had heard himself during his travels. He dwelt chiefly on the heroic songs of the more recent times, namely on the cycles of the *uskoci* and the *hajduci*, most of which had not then been translated. These filled the whole of the first volume. The second volume contains almost entirely women's songs, many of which had already appeared in preceding collections of translations. Kapper published

from time to time in various periodicals other Serbian
songs by way of supplementing his two volumes (e.g. *Die
Legenden der Serben, Die historischen Volkslieder der Mon-
tenegriner*): these, however, remained his chief work so far
as the Serbian traditional poetry is concerned. In some
ways it surpassed all other German translations. Kapper
was the only German translator who had not only learned
the Serbian language among the Serbs themselves, but
had also fully acquainted himself with the character of the
people and the spirit of their poetry. In addition to this
he was a poet. Hence one derives more pleasure from
reading his translations than those of any of the former
German translators. He has followed the Serbian metre
with greater skill than either Talvj or Gerhard.

There is only one other German translator of Serbian
traditional poetry after Kapper worthy of mention. Carl
Gröber, like Vogl, limited himself to the special cycle of
Marko Kraljević and in 1883 he published *Der Königssohn
Marko (Kraljević Marko) im Serbischen Volksgesang*. It is a
better and more complete translation of heroic songs about
Marko.[1] Two years later, in 1885, Gröber dealt with
another cycle, that of Kosovo, and produced a smaller
collection of translations.

In 1882 a very small collection of Serbian songs was
published at Eisenstadt, by the author himself, Svetozar
Manojlović, a Serb. It was entitled *Serbische Frauenlieder*,
but it contained, in addition to nineteen traditional

---

[1] Kapper's *Südslavische Wanderungen*, 1851, contains a chapter on *Marko,
der Königssohn*, which is interspersed with a number of lines in German
translation from various heroic songs about Marko. This book was
reviewed in the *Dublin University Magazine* in May, 1854, under the title
Wanderings in Servia. A short reference is made here to the "fine old Servian
poems".

women's songs, a few lyric songs, scattered amongst the former, by two or three modern Serbian poets. His little book seems to have been well received by the public. In 1888 he published in Vienna a much larger collection under the title *Serbisch-Kroatische Dichtungen*, and from the preface we see that it is the third and considerably enlarged edition of his original one—the second, which we have not been able to obtain, having been published in 1885 as *Serbische Dichtungen*. About eighty pages of this collection are allotted to a number of lyric songs by modern Serbo-Croat poets, while 180 pages are occupied by traditional songs, of which only five are heroic, concerning Miloš Obilić. Here, as in the former edition, the author endeavours to preserve the spirit and the metre of the original.

With this we might conclude the list of translators of the Serbian traditional songs in the German language, unless we mention also the translations of the traditional songs of the Bosnian Moslems. After Austria had occupied Bosnia and Herzegovina, as a result of the Treaty of Berlin (1879), interest arose in the poetry of the Bosnians, those of Muhammedan confession in particular. At the request of the Crown Prince, the Archduke Rudolf of Austria, in May, 1884, the German scholar, Dr Friedrich S. Krauss, went to the new provinces immediately in order to study the character and customs of the people. In one year he had collected about 60,000 lines of heroic songs, never previously written down. In 1889 Krauss wrote in the preface to his *Orlović* that he had collected altogether 190,000 lines of heroic songs. Among these was one song of 2160 lines. Krauss had heard it from a reciter, eighty-five years old, who in his turn had learnt it sixty years before from another peasant. In 1886 Krauss published it in Ragusa under the title *"Smailagić Meho*, a song of our Muhammedans, by order of the Anthropological Society in Vienna". In April of the same year he gave a copy of it to C. Gröber—the actual copy is now in the British Museum. Gröber translated it into German and published it in Vienna, 1890, entitled *Mehmed's Brautfahrt (Smailagić Meho). Ein Volksepos der südslavischen Mohammedaner*. Gröber has almost invariably rendered line for line, but divided it into twelve parts, while in the original no division is made.

Three years after *Smailagić Meho* was published in the Serbo-Croat language, Krauss himself translated another Muhammedan heroic song. It appeared in 1889, in Freiburg im Breisgau, under the name *Orlović der Burggraf von Raab. Ein Mohammedanisch-Slavisches Guslarlied aus der Herzegovina*. The book contains also the text in the original language on the opposite pages to the translation. There are 672 lines in the original and to each corresponds a line in German.

In 1908 Krauss published sixteen more heroic songs of the Bosnian Muhammedans, as the second part of his work *Slavische Volksforschungen*.

Chapter Six
Yugoslav Traditional Poetry in French Literature

I

IF the temporary enthusiasm for *Ossian* be excepted, there was no interest in France for traditional poetry in general before the opening of the nineteenth century. Even Percy's *Reliques* seem to have remained unnoticed until that time. The interest for such poetry began to develop about 1820, at the time when the *Romancero* of the Cid was translated into French. Widespread interest was aroused among literary people only when Claude Fauriel published his two volumes of the *Chants populaires de la Grèce moderne* in 1824–5. Greece, with her ancient traditions, her heroic struggle for freedom from the Turks, and Byron's part in it, was an attractive subject enough for the Romantic poets. Hence the interest of the French Romanticists for the songs of Greece's past. A series of articles greeted Fauriel's work enthusiastically. An English and two German translations of it appeared in the following year. Then followed a number of other translations and imitations of foreign traditional poetry. Of these, the *Ballades, légendes et chants populaires de l'Angleterre et de l'Écosse*, by Sir Walter Scott, Thomas Moore and Campbell—translated into prose by A. Loéve-Veimars, 1825—had the greatest success. *Le Globe*—the best known of the three main organs of the

French Romanticists—threw open its pages to articles on the subject of traditional poetry in particular. It was at this time that the Serbo-Croat traditional songs, too, penetrated into French literature.

In France, as in Germany, the first interest in Serbo-Croat traditional poetry was caused by A. Fortis's book on Dalmatia. A French translation of it was published in Berne in 1778, in two volumes entitled "*Voyage en Dalmatie*, par M. L'Abbé Fortis". Ten years later, a certain Justine Wynne, of Anglo-Italian birth, who became "Comtesse des Ursins et Rosenberg", published, in 1788, at her own expense, a novel called *Les Morlaques*. For the "local colour" she drew information mainly from Fortis's book. She was also personally acquainted with him. Her husband was Graf Rosenberg und Orsini, the Austrian ambassador at Venice. Of her many writings in English and French, only a few were published. She is no longer known as an authoress, but in her own days she had a considerable reputation. Goethe was one of her many readers who bestowed praises upon her books, and her novel *Les Morlaques* in particular. Mme de Staël used it as a model when writing *Corinne*. On the whole, this novel illustrates Rousseau's ideas and is one of the first novels in French to describe the life and customs of a foreign primitive people. At the same time, it reflects also the ideas of the time, in which *Ossian* was glorified. This latter fact is due perhaps mainly to her close friendship with the Abbé Melchior Cesarotti, the Italian translator of *Ossian*. Through him and through the Abbé Alberto Fortis,[1] Justine Wynne was led to the *Morlakian*

---

[1] Also through Giovanni Lovrich's *Osservazioni*, etc., 1774. Venice.

Ballads, ten of which she quoted in her book. Like Mérimée, she never saw the land of the Morlacks. Some modern critics thought it a sufficient reason to declare these ballads as unoriginal and mere hoaxes, yet it is probable that a few of them were drawn from A. Kačić's collection of songs and that, therefore, they are not hoaxes.

When writing his article, the "Serbische Lieder", Goethe said that he had translated, fifty years before, the song of *Hasanaginica* from Justine Wynne's *Les Morlaques.* It has since been proved that this was a *lapsus memoriae* on Goethe's part, for neither did *Les Morlaques* contain this song, nor were they published at the time when Goethe occupied himself with it.

With the establishment of the "Illyrian Provinces" by Napoleon in 1809 these lands and their peoples, formerly practically unknown in France, became the subject of large numbers of books, chiefly books on travel, and articles written during and after his regime. Thus they became widely known.[1] Laibach, the capital of Slovenia —by the Slavs then, as now, called Ljubljana—was made the seat of the French Governor. A Napoleonic court was set up with all due splendour; French manners and customs made their way rapidly. An official paper, *Le Télégraphe officiel des provinces illyriennes,* was conducted in four languages. A library was instituted, and, towards the end

[1] A book, "*Voyage pittoresque et historique de l'Istrie et de la Dalmatie, rédigé d'après l'itinéraire de L. F. Cassas,* par Joseph Lavallée", had already been published in 1802. Cassas, an artist and architect, the author of this exquisitely illustrated work, travelled through Istria and Dalmatia in 1782. He gave, among other things, a brief account of the Morlacks, but without recording any of their traditional songs. A small edition of this book was published in English in 1805.

of 1812, the Provincial Governor called Charles Nodier from Paris to fill the place of librarian and to take charge of the *Télégraphe officiel*. He remained at Laibach in this capacity for eight months. Having spent another month in Trieste, he returned to France, Laibach having been abandoned to the Austrians in August, 1813. Nodier never learnt the Slovene language, still less that of the Serbo-Croats. Nevertheless he became, after his sojourn in Illyria, and remained all his life, an authority upon all Illyrian matters. He acquired this reputation by publishing a number of articles on Illyrian traditional poetry, first in the *Télégraphe officiel* and then in the *Journal des Débats*. He conducted in the latter also a critical study of various works relating to Illyria and poured out his severe criticism upon their authors for having improvised hurried writings about the people, i.e. the "Illyriens", of whose language even they knew nothing! No wonder that he was considered such an authority on Illyria!

His reputation became still greater after he had published a few novels, all of which were connected with this province. In 1818 he published *Jean Sbogar*. He said that the hero of this novel, Jean Sbogar, was a true Illyrian brigand, and described him as a dreamer and philosopher who protested against Napoleon's and every other government; who lived in a castle in Istria and who spoke French, Italian, German, modern Greek and practically all the Slav languages. The hero, however, does not possess any such traits as would show him to be a true Illyrian and, in fact, is modelled, with all the due romantic touches, on the hero of Schiller's *Räuber*; the book shows also a remarkable likeness to Byron's *Corsair*, which led

Nodier's critics to accuse him of plagiarism. The only "local colour" in *Jean Sbogar*—which is a Czech and not a Jugoslav name—consists of very beautiful descriptions of the land and the costumes of the people, for which, naturally, no knowledge of the language was necessary. But on the ground of these alone Nodier could not claim for himself the privilege of being the first to introduce "local colour" into French literature.

In 1821 Nodier published a strange work, the second of his Illyrian stories: *Smarra, ou les démons de la nuit, songes romantiques*. He tells us that it was but a translation from a modern and even recent work—yet one still unpublished while he sojourned in Illyria—attributed to a noble Ragusan, disguised under the name of Maxime Odin. Nodier informs us, further, that he obtained it thanks to his own friend M. le Chevalier Fédorovich-Albinoni. As V. M. Yovanovitch says, the very name Fédorovitch, which is not Serbo-Croat, but Russian, makes one suspect the genuineness of Nodier's statement. No such person then existed in the Illyrian provinces, but a certain Count Kreglianovich-Albinoni did exist, whose memoirs Nodier mentioned in the *Télégraphe officiel* in 1813. Having explained that the word "smarra" was a "Morlakian" name for an evil night spirit that went round and tormented people—the actual Serbo-Croat word for it is *mora*—Nodier spins his strange story. With this, however, we need not deal here. It corresponds in no way to the character of the people to whom he attributes it. But we are concerned with "un poème de tradition" which is incorporated in the book under the title of *Spalatinbey*, and with *La Femme d'Asan*, in which we recognise the

Hasanaginica. Nodier says of the former that it was an unpublished and a very beautiful story, chanted to an accompaniment by the *gusla*, while in fact this "traditional poem of the Morlacks" is only a free composition of the author's own imagination, but with more "local colour" than in *Jean Sbogar*. Like Justine Wynne before, and Prosper Mérimée after, he borrowed geographical names from Fortis's *Voyage en Dalmatie* and copied out from it many Serbo-Croat words. The hero received the name of the "Comte Spalatin", the president of the law-court in Laibach during Nodier's stay in that town. Mérimée, believing in the authenticity of the name, borrowed it for one of his ballads.

As to *La Femme d'Asan*, it is a free, drawn-out, prose version done not from the original but from Fortis's Italian and from the French translation of the unknown translator of Berne.

In 1823 Nodier obtained a copy of Justine Wynne's *Les Morlaques*. He pronounced it "the best book on the subject", expressing at the same time his regret at having misjudged it ten years earlier, without having read it.

In September of the following year *Le Globe* remarked that Germany's great poet, Goethe, interested himself in the traditional poetry of the Serbs and, in November of that year, it undertook to publish a series of articles on the "Poésies nationales des Serviens", of which only two appeared. In 1825 Mme Panckoucke included in her translation of *Poésies de Goethe* also *La Complainte de la noble femme d'Asan Aga*. In the same year G. B. Depping published an article, "Chants populaires serbes", in the *Bulletin des sciences historiques*. He explained in it that the

Serbs possessed a rich popular poetry, almost unknown before Vuk published his collection. He then gives a brief, dry account of this collection. The following year the *Volkslieder der Serben* by Talvj were mentioned in the same periodical.

French interest in Serbian traditional poetry began to grow steadily from the time it became known that Goethe himself was its champion. Thus Baron Ferdinand von Eckstein, the editor of *Le Catholique*, published two long articles of an informative character, covering about sixty-five pages, in February and June, 1826, on the "Chants populaires du peuple Serbe". A number of extracts were quoted from Talvj's translations; and an excellent analysis of the heroic song *Noces de Maxime Tsernoyévitch* was given. About the same time (June, 1826) *La Bibliothèque Allemande*, at Strasburg, published a brief note about Talvj's book. *Le Globe* objected, three months later, to the *Bibliothèque* for having treated the subject too summarily. Also, at the same time, the *Revue Encyclopédique* mentions *Serbische Hochzeitslieder* by E. Wesely, and the *Nekolike pjesnice* by S. Milutinović. A few months later, in the same *Revue*, Talvj's book was described, giving mainly a résumé of her introduction.

In 1827 the *Journal général de la littérature étrangère* published four notes relating to Serbian poetry.

II

But Serbian traditional poetry in France in the nineteenth century is especially connected with several names: Prosper Mérimée, Mme Élise Voiart, Auguste Dozon, Baron Adolphe d'Avril, Achille Millien and Mme la Comtesse

M. Colonna. Each of them, except Mérimée, contributed
to the French literature either a collection or a number of
traditional songs translated, with few exceptions, from
the original Serbo-Croat. Some of these, as well as other
people, wrote articles and treatises on this subject. Among
the others Xavier Marmier, V. de Mars, Ida von Dürings-
feld, H. Valmore, Mme la Comtesse Dora d'Istria, Émile
Pricot de Sainte-Marie and René Millet should be mentioned. With the establishment in Paris of the chair of
Slavonic literatures, in 1840, courses of lectures on Serbo-
Croat traditional literature were delivered. Claude Fauriel
was the first to speak on the subject, but his successor, the
great Polish poet, A. Mickiewicz, was the first to give a
systematic course of lectures on Serbian poetry. This
tradition was continued during the past century by
Cyprien Robert, Alexandre Chodźko and Louis Léger.
Of the periodicals, in which most of the above-mentioned
people wrote, the following, besides the *Globe* and those
already mentioned, published one or more articles on the
Serbo-Croatian traditional songs, or literature in general:
Le Correspondant, *Revue Contemporaine*, *Revue des Deux
Mondes*, *Revue Européenne*, *Bibliothèque Universelle*, *Revue de
Géographie*, *La Nouvelle Revue*, *Revue Britannique*, *Revue de
l'Orient*, *de l'Algérie et des colonies*, *Revue International* and
Journal des Savants.

The story of Mérimée's literary fraud in the matter of
the Serbian traditional songs is treated at full length by
V. M. Yovanovitch in "*La Guzla*" *de Prosper Mérimée*.
Towards the end of July, 1827, there appeared in Paris a
book of some 255 pages, entitled *La Guzla, ou choix de poésies
illyriques, recueillies dans la Dalmatie, la Bosnie, la Croatie et*

l'Herzégowine. The anonymous author informs his readers, in the preface, that he was by origin an Italian, by education a Frenchman and by birth a Dalmatian, while in fact he was none other than Prosper Mérimée, then a promising young man of letters, aged twenty-three. A frontispiece was also added. It represents a man seated, with crossed legs, and playing the *gusle*. His name is given below as Hyacinthe Maglanovich. The "Notice" that follows the preface gives his biography and explains who he is. He is said to be the Illyrian minstrel from whom the author was supposed to have heard most of the twenty-eight ancient songs rendered in prose. The author had met him at Zara for the first time in 1816. In the following year, he said, he had spent two days at his home. It was on those occasions that Mérimée heard him recite the songs which he gives in French prose translation, and learned all about his past. The book concludes with a literal translation, in prose, of the *Triste ballade de la noble épouse d'Asan Aga*, the only authentic song in *La Guzla*.

When this collection appeared, it was received, on the whole, coldly in France, although everyone believed it to be a genuine translation. Many people outside France were deceived, too; amongst others the Polish poet, Mickiewicz, and the Russian, Puskhin. The latter, with his great gift of versification, made very good translations of thirteen of Mérimée's Illyrian songs. Two months after the publication of *La Guzla*, John Bowring, of whom we shall learn more presently, wrote to Mérimée, whose identity as the author had by then become known to some, and asked him for the original verses from which the translation had been made. We are told this by Mérimée himself, in his preface to the new edition of his book in 1842, though Bowring's actual letter has never been found. An unknown author who reviewed *La Guzla* in the *Monthly Review* in November, 1827, did not hesitate to give a decided preference to this collection over that of Bowring, especially as Bowring was "indebted for his specimens altogether to the industry of a celebrated Serbian, Vuk". On the other hand, he says of the little volume of Mérimée—whose name, of course, was not yet generally known as that of its author—that it was "the work of an industrious and persevering stranger who saw the minstrel and listened to his strains; and who was guided in his selection of the traditional songs of Illyria by the impressions which they immediately made upon his own heart and imagination". About nineteen months later, in June, 1828, Mérimée's collection was the subject of another article in the *Foreign Quarterly Review*. It was written by M. Thomas Keightley. He, too, was taken in and believed the translator to be "an Italian, but born of a Morlachian mother"—although by that time it was known that Mérimée was the author of *La Guzla*. He also said that "the Illyrian poetry, as might be expected, presents a great resemblance to the Servian", as if the two names did not denote one and the same poetry!

It has been shown in the previous chapter how badly W. Gerhard, in Germany, was misled by *La Guzla*. Goethe was the only one not to be entrapped. Although he devoted a note to Mérimée's collection, he called it, at the very beginning of the note, "a publication which at the first is interesting, but, when closely examined, of problematical genuineness". The mystery was solved by

Mérimée himself, several years later. Pushkin began at last to doubt the authenticity of *La Guzla* and asked his friend, S. A. Sobolevsky, to write to Mérimée and find out where he had obtained the original. In January, 1835, Mérimée answered that *La Guzla* was composed by himself, for two reasons. First, "de me moquer de la couleur locale dans laquelle nous nous jetions à plein collier vers l'an de grâce 1827". As to his second reason, he gave the following story. In the same year, he and his friend, Ampère, planned to travel to Italy. They spread out a map and, with a pencil, traced an itinerary as far as Venice. Having been annoyed at the thought of the English and the Germans they met there, they made with their pencil for Trieste and then for Ragusa. The plan was accepted, but—they had no money for the journey! To surmount the difficulty it was decided to write beforehand the description of this journey, produce a book, sell it and use the profit for seeing personally whether they had gone far wrong in their description. Mérimée's rôle was to collect traditional songs and translate them. The following day he showed five or six of them already to his friend, and while spending the autumn in the country Mérimée went on with this work. He consulted a pamphlet by a French consul in Bosnia and carefully copied the Illyrian words quoted in it. Then he read the chapter on "The Customs of the Morlacks" in Fortis's *Voyage en Dalmatie*. With the help of a friend who knew Russian, he obtained a literal translation of the ballad *Hasanaginica* and, comparing it with the Italian text, gave a prose translation of his own. In order to make it look like an original work, Mérimée interspersed his translation with explanatory notes and essays on the Evil Eye and Vampirism. For the same reason he attached the picture of H. Maglanovich.

In making his investigation as to the sources of *La Guzla*, V. M. Yovanovitch begins by suspecting Mérimée's statement. "Il ne faut pas accorder à son récit une entière confiance. Mérimée, c'est trop évident, se donne une attitude; ce n'est qu'un jeu d'écrire *la Guzla*; il le fait pour relever un défi." On comparing Mérimée's letter to Sobolevsky with the preface to the second edition of *La Guzla*,[1] in which Mérimée makes practically the same confession, Yovanovitch found that the tone of the passage referring to this matter was quite different from that in his letter of 1835. "Non seulement on ne le mit nullement au défi, mais c'est en rechignant—autre affectation—qu'il se vit infliger par son ami Ampère cet étrange métier de collectionner des ballades." Yovanovitch concludes that the truth was neither in the first nor in the second statement—sincerity being no eminent quality with Mérimée —and he proves that the plan for a trip to Dalmatia could not have been formed in conjunction with Ampère in 1827, for the simple reason that the latter was far away from France in that year and that he returned three months after *La Guzla* had been published. Mérimée could not have written *La Guzla* in the autumn of 1827, because it was published in July of that year. There seems to be no doubt, however, that it was written, if not actually in collaboration with Ampère, as suggested by F. Chambon,

[1] *La Guzla* was published for the second time in 1842, in the same volume with *Chronique du règne de Charles IX*. The "Avertissement" to *La Guzla* is dated 1840. In 1853 the *Chronique* was translated into English but *La Guzla* remained untranslated.

at least in his presence. Therefore it must have been composed before Ampère left France in August, 1826.

Briefly stated, one arrives at the conclusion that *La
Guzla* was written either in 1825 or 1826, but after the
idea of writing it had been in Mérimée's mind for some
three or four years. Having read Nodier's *Jean Sbogar* in
1820 and *Smarra* in 1821, Fauriel's *Chants populaires de la
Grèce moderne*, and also *Ossian*, having studied Fortis's
Voyage en Dalmatie and consulted L. F. Cassas's *Voyage
pittoresque*, Mérimée sat down and composed a number of
songs in prose, probably within a fortnight, with or
without Ampère's help.

According to Mérimée's own confession, the sale of
La Guzla was very poor: hardly a dozen copies of the
first edition were sold. "Le cœur me saigne encore en
pensant au pauvre éditeur qui fit les frais de cette mystifi-
cation." The book, however, was well received abroad
and favourably reviewed in many periodicals at home, in
August and September, 1827. Louise Swanton Belloc,
translator of Thomas Moore, wrote a notice, in August,
1827, in both the *Revue Encyclopédique* and the *Journal
général de la littérature de France*, in which she praised *La
Guzla*. "Ces chants ont un caractère très original, et dont
on ne peut guère donner l'idée. Moins nobles, moins
austères que les chants grecs, ils sont peut-être plus
spirituels et plus vifs." One has to bear in mind that Mme
Belloc was supposed to be one of the few persons who at
that time had the reputation of being well acquainted with
the Serbian traditional poetry. She had announced the
publication of a volume of Serbian songs only a few
weeks before Mérimée published *La Guzla*. Instead of

this volume, *Le Globe* brought out in August, 1827, several Serbian heroic songs, which were supposed to be translated from Vuk's collection, whereas in fact they were translated from J. Bowring's *Servian Popular Poetry*. In June, 1827, she reviewed Bowring's book in the *Revue Encyclopédique*.

In September, 1827, *Le Globe* and *Le Journal des Savants* fell into Mérimée's trap, too. The former said that "it appeared as if the *Guzla* of the Slavs was soon to be as celebrated as the harp of Ossian", while the latter assured its readers that the "ballads" were of popular origin. The same journal returned to the subject of *La Guzla* in February, 1829, and pointed out that it had obtained "un assez joli succès auprès des critiques", but that the publisher had practically no success at all.[1]

In this month the *Bibliothèque Universelle* of Geneva published the second part of a lengthy review of Talvj's two volumes of *Volkslieder der Serben*. The first part appeared in the volume for January of the same year, over the signature "A. P.". The author discourses first upon popular poetry in general, gives next a short survey of the history of the Serbs and of their traditional poetry, and concludes by showing its characteristic features and analysing it according to Talvj's translations. Less than two years later, an exhaustive review, occupying nearly fifty pages, also signed "A. P.", of Talvj's *Volkslieder* appeared in the *Bibliothèque Universelle des sciences, belles-*

---

[1] When *La Guzla* was reprinted in 1842, in one volume with the *Chronique du règne de Charles IX*, it naturally had a much greater success, and in such company it was frequently reprinted. It was, of course, known then who was its actual author, yet a number of notable French poets remained in ignorance of it even in the 'fifties.

lettres et arts, vol. XL of the series on literature. It contains
a number of the *ženske pesme*, several fragments of the
junačke pesme, and the whole heroic song on the *Death of
Marko Kraljević*, all in prose translation. The author
thinks that the German language, which, he says, "by
numerous analogies" stands close to the Slavonic languages, can render the naïve simplicity of the Serbian
traditional poetry far better than the French. In illustrating the Serbian traditional songs, the author often refers
to analogies in the Greek popular songs.

In 1834 Élise Voiart published her two volumes of the
Chants populaires des Serviens. Her aim was to give a selection of songs, taken from Talvj's much larger collection,
in faithful translation, line for line. In doing this, she did
not follow Talvj's plan absolutely. Thus, for instance, her
petits poèmes are a selection from those that Talvj called
either *Grössere Gedichte* or *Heldenlieder*. While in Talvj's
collection the heroic songs of Marko are to be found both
in the first and the second volumes, under two slightly
different headings, Voiart collected them all together and
with them opened her second volume. Of 147 women's
songs, which in Talvj's volume are called either *Kleinere
Gedichte* or *Scherz- und Liebesgedichte*, Voiart selected
seventy-three, calling them *poésies légères*. While she thus
left out a large number of women's songs from Talvj's
book—hoping to publish some of them "si cet essai est
couronné de quelque succès"—she translated all the
heroic songs about Marko, about the battle of Kosovo,
and about the First Rebellion. In fact, she left out few
heroic songs on the whole. Her book contains also a
survey of Serbian history. Most of this consists of a trans-

lation of two articles published in *La Revue Germanique*, 1829. Numerous "notes" and "renseignements géographiques" are attached to each of the two volumes.

Voiart's translations are good, she did the work with both considerable skill and talent. It was well received by the critics, but it had no general success. With few exceptions, hardly anyone took any notice of it. Lamartine read it and inserted a few of her translations in a later edition of his *Voyage en Orient*, 1861, by way of a "commentaire". His *Souvenirs, impressions, pensées et paysages pendant un voyage en Orient* 1832–1833 were published in four volumes in 1835. Although the fourth volume opened with "Notes sur la Servie", in which reference is made to the traditional songs, none of them was quoted at that time by Lamartine.

III

Twenty-five years were to pass before another collection of Serbian traditional poetry was to appear in French translation, by Auguste Dozon, but during this period the Serbs and their poetry were not forgotten. A number of articles, though mainly translated from English and American periodicals, were published on the subject. The *Revue Britannique*—whose object was, as its larger title says, to publish a selection of articles from the best written periodicals of Great Britain and America—brought out in 1837 an article on the "Poésie populaire des nations Slaves". It contains a brief account of the Serbs, their language, "le plus sonore, le plus mélodieux, le plus énergique", and their traditional poetry, of which one specimen is given in prose translation. The author, curiously, calls the heroic songs the "natcké pjesné". This article was translated from the *North American Review*. In vol. XLIII of this *Review*, for 1836, Vuk's fourth volume of *Serbian Popular Songs* was reviewed, probably by Talvj, who lived in the United States at that time.

In 1843 the poet Sebastien Rhéal published in his book, *Les Divines Féeries de l'Orient et du Nord*, three women's songs in very free verse. In the *Notice sur les ballades Serviennes*, which precedes them, he explains that the first one was composed according to the translation of É. Voiart; the second was entirely original, while the subject for the third was drawn from the ballad *The Maiden of Kosovo*.

Three years later the great French traveller and prolific writer Xavier Marmier dedicated a chapter of his book, *Du Rhin au Nil, souvenirs de Voyages*, to Belgrade and while speaking of Serbian popular poetry says that Marko is for the Serbs what Arthur is for the Bretons, Parsifal for the Germans and Sigurd for the Scandinavians.

More important than these articles were six lectures on the history of the Serbs and their poetry delivered, in 1840–1, at the Collège de France by the great Polish poet, Adam Mickiewicz, already mentioned. He was the first official holder of the chair of Slavonic literatures in Paris. Two years later, A. Lebré published in the *Revue des Deux Mondes* an excerpt from them, under the title "Mouvement des peuples Slaves". Little reference is made to the Serbs in particular. It is rather an article of informative charac-ter on the Slavs in general. They were coming into promi-nence more and more. "Les peuples slaves présentent un des plus grands spectacles de notre époque.... La question

slave touche à toutes les grandes questions de l'époque."
They were, however, little known. Consequently a chair
of Slavonic literatures was founded in the Collège de
France, following the example of several universities in
Germany. In 1849 Mickiewicz's lectures were published
in four volumes from shorthand notes. All the lectures on
the Serbian traditional poetry were fully recorded here,
containing the lavish praises which he had bestowed
upon them.

Between 1845 and 1857 the chair of Slavonic literatures was occupied by Cyprien Robert, one of the most
active correspondents of the *Revue des Deux Mondes*.
Before filling the chair he had published, in 1844, his two
volumes on the *Slaves de Turquie*,[1] dealing with their re-
sources, their tendencies and their political progress. In
the introduction Robert speaks of the picturesque appearance of the Slavs and of their customs, including, of
course, those of the Serbs. In the chapter on the Mon-
tenegrins, he speaks about their traditional poetry. Their
history forms one long epic, which is the subject-matter
of all their popular songs. The author says, amongst other
things, that the Montenegrin songs will, perhaps, some
day become an *Iliad* as well as an *Æneid*, because they
celebrated both the triumphs of a race of heroes equal in
their exploits to the primitive races, and the efforts of their
warriors to reconstruct a destroyed city, an empire wiped
out. Robert quotes, in prose translation, a number of

----

[1] A second edition of it was published in 1852. *Les Slaves de Turquie,
Serbes, Monténégrins, Bosniaques, Albanais et Bulgares, leurs ressources, leurs
tendances et leurs progrès politiques: édition de 1844 précédée d'une introduction
nouvelle sur la situation de ces peuples pendant et depuis leurs insurrections de
1849 à 1851.*

heroic songs illustrating the Montenegrin wars with the Turks. The second part of the first volume deals with the Serbs—in particular with their history under Prince Miloš. Robert does not refer to the traditional poetry in this chapter, but deals with it again in the one following, that on *Les Bosniaques, Serbes de langue et de mœurs*. He gives here prose translations of several songs: *La Moba, Une orgie d'hiver, Ce que coûte le plaisir* and *La Justice des haidouks*, the hero of all these being Tomitj Miiat, one of the most celebrated of the modern *hajduci*. A few more songs, mainly in fragments, are quoted, by way of illustrating recent history in Bosnia.

Of Cyprien Robert's other works, *Le Monde Slave, son passé, son état présent et son avenir*, published in two volumes in Paris, in 1852, which is in fact a continuation of his preceding work, is perhaps one of the most important of all. It was intended to fill one of the serious gaps in the political and scientific literature of France. The author was interested chiefly in the origin of the Slavs, their history and their institutions. Only a small part of the work is dedicated to their literatures. Their traditional poetry is touched upon now and then, but no translations of it are given.

In December of the same year, the *Revue des Deux Mondes* published C. Robert's article "Les quatres Littératures Slaves", the second part of which dealt with Ragusan literature; but no mention is made of the traditional poetry. In June of the following year Robert printed, in the same periodical, an extensive article, covering forty pages, "Le Gouslo et la poésie populaire des Slaves". The greater portion of it dealt with Serbo-Croat popular ballads, quoting part or the whole of many of them in prose translation, from Vuk's collection, which he calls "la source vive au minerai le plus pur de la poésie nationale en Slavie".

In the same year, Xavier Marmier published in the *Revue Contemporaine* a very good account of Serbian songs. After giving a short survey of the history of the Serbs from the earliest days, he deals with their traditional songs and quotes a number of both lyric and epic songs in prose translation. He had studied such songs among other peoples, the Nordic ones especially, and he was perhaps the only student of Serbian traditional poetry to remark rightly at this time that this poetry, and its love songs in particular, bore more likeness to the Swedish and Danish ballads than to the corresponding poetry of any other peoples. But at the same time he also points out that both the women's and the heroic songs of the Serbs were fundamentally different from the traditional poetry of all other European nations. His article is interspersed with a number of prose translations of Serbian songs. A few months later appeared his two volumes, *Lettres sur l'Adriatique et le Monténégro*. The last chapter of the second volume contained his article "Les Chants Serbes". Marmier seems to have studied the Serbian songs fairly closely, mainly through É. Voiart's translations, Cyprien Robert's books and Mickiewicz's lectures. He knew of Vuk, of course, and of German, Italian and French translations of Serbian poetry, but he does not appear to have read many of them. He does not give the impression of having seen Talvj's book, or else he would not repeatedly have called her "Mme Talwig", nor that of A. Frankl, whom he calls "Frank". On the other hand, he knows more of Kapper's *Lazar der Serben-zar* and J. N. Vogl's *Marko Kraljević*, both of which were published in 1851. In dealing with the heroic songs, Marmier dwells chiefly on the songs of the battle of Kosovo and on those of Marko Kraljević. He supported his statements with prose translations, based on those in verse by Kapper and Vogl.

IV

In the 'fifties the semi-independent Principality of Serbia was gradually being stabilised under the rule of Prince Alexander Karađorđević. Europe began to pay more attention to its attitude in international matters, especially during the Crimean War. The allies had sufficient cause to believe that Serbia might join Russia: hence they were pleased when she decided to remain neutral. In February, 1854, the *Revue des Deux Mondes* points to the "very wise" attitude of this remarkable principality. The author, V. de Mars, of a short article, "Les poètes serbes et les chrétiens d'Orient", finds that their literature "reflète très fidèlement la pensée du pays", because the Serbs had not yet emerged "de cette ère de spontanéité durant laquelle l'homme pense et agit en quelque sorte tout d'une pièce. Dans la Serbie, le poète ou le publiciste, l'écrivain et le citoyen ne sont qu'une seule et même personne". The author deals here also with a small book, *Slaves du Sud ou le Peuple Serbe avec les Croates et les Bulgares*, published in Paris several months before the outbreak of the Crimean War. Its authors were two young Serbians, M. Janković and J. Grujić, who were studying in Paris at that time. It is a book of an informative character, but its authors, although maintained by the Serbian Government, did not fail to criticise some of its actions severely, with the result that, soon after their book had been published, they had to forfeit their government scholarships. We are interested in their book in so far as it mentions, though briefly, the Serbian traditional poetry. V. de Mars does not, however, refer to them in his article.

Two months later, Cyprien Robert returned to the subject of Serbian popular ballads once more in his article "La Poésie Slave au dix-neuvième siècle", which appeared in the *Revue des Deux Mondes*. Besides a whole lyric song of Bosnia, which he gives in prose, he quotes parts of several other women's songs. About the same time the *Revue de l'Orient, de l'Algerie et des Colonies*, tome xv, published in prose a heroic poem *Miliza la zarina*, called *Carica Milica i Vladeta Vojvoda* in the original, and a lyric song *La jeune fille et le poisson*, without indicating who was the translator. It is probable, however, that it was Auguste Dozon who translated them, since the same volume contains his review of the third edition of Vuk's collection, and his line translation of the heroic song *Le Tsar Lazare et la Tsarine Militsa*.

About two years afterwards, in 1856, M. Chopin published his book *Provinces Danubiennes et Roumaines*, in the work called *L'Univers*.

v

Of all Frenchmen who interested themselves in the subject of Slav poetry, Louis Auguste Henri Dozon (1822–90) is the most closely associated with the Serbian traditional poetry. In addition to a constant study of the

Classical, Sanskrit and Arabic languages, he took a great interest in modern foreign languages from his early youth. Between 1850 and 1853 he had an opportunity of being initiated into the Serbian language and the Serbian poetry by J. Ristić and J. Grujić, during their stay in Paris. Dozon's serious study of Serbian popular ballads began in 1853 when he was sent to Serbia as "chancelier" of the French consulate in Belgrade. The result of his study was a collection of songs entitled *Poésies populaires Serbes traduites sur les originaux avec une introduction et des notes*. The book was published in Paris towards the end of 1859. In the introduction—which in parts consists of quotations from Vuk—he points to the likeness between the Serbian *pesmas* on the one hand and their Spanish sisters, the *romances*, the Greek *chants klephtiques* and the English ballads of Robin Hood on the other. In this introduction, Dozon showed a sound knowledge of the subject with which he dealt. His translations, both in verse and in prose, revealed his thorough mastery of the Serbian language. The five heroic songs on the battle of Kosovo, and the *chants domestiques*, which conclude the collection, are in verse, without rhyme, of course. The other heroic songs on *Marko Kraljevitch*, *Les Haïdouks* and *Poésies héroïques diverses* are in an excellent prose translation.[1]

Dozon's larger and, perhaps, better and more important work, *L'Épopée Serbe, chants populaires héroïques*, was published nearly thirty years later, in 1888. It is usually regarded as a new, enlarged edition of his first collection. In fact it is, as he himself says, a new work in its contents,

---

[1] H. Valmore, in writing an article "Poésies Serbes" in the same year in the *Revue Européenne*, refers to Dozon's book.

its scope and its character. The heroic songs alone constitute the new collection; the women's songs are left out,
to form a separate volume which, however, never appeared. All the heroic songs of the first collection, except
those about Kosovo, were here reprinted, but many new
ones were added, especially those about Marko Kraljević.
The introduction to the new book is a scholarly piece of
work. Dozon's knowledge of the subject was more extensive than that of any of his predecessors. He had spent
about thirty years of his life among the Jugoslavs. Perhaps no foreigner was so well acquainted not only with
their language, but also with their history and literature.
Hence, *L'Épopée Serbe* can be regarded as truly the best
translation of Serbian traditional songs in a foreign language. It might be mentioned that between 1859 and 1888
Dozon translated (in 1874) and edited (in 1877) for the
first time some Bulgarian traditional songs, translated
some Albanian folk-tales in 1881, wrote a Grammar of
the "Chkipe", or Albanian, language, and translated songs
from the Hungarian, under the pseudonym d'A. Argonne.

VI

Between the two collections of Dozon's translations of
Serbian traditional songs, there appeared in 1868 Baron
d'Avril's excellent translation, *La Bataille de Kossovo.
Rhapsodie Serbe. Tirée des chants populaires et traduites en
français*, already mentioned.[1]

In 1876 d'Avril published his *Voyage Sentimental dans
les Pays Slaves*, under the pseudonym "Cyrille". It con-

---

[1] Reviewed in the *Revue des Deux Mondes*, for 15 July, 1868, by J. de
Cazaux.

tains chapters on the modern history and social conditions of various Slav countries, the Jugoslavs in particular. The chapter on Serbia is especially interesting to us, for it includes a number of heroic songs, mainly on Kosovo, rendered into French line for line. These songs are the same as those of his preceding work and are here simply reprinted. The only difference consists in the number of songs, the *Voyage Sentimental* containing eleven as compared with twelve of *La Bataille de Kossovo*. None of the original twelve songs is, however, left out, d'Avril having blended two of *La Bataille* into one, namely those concerning the Kosovo heroes Miloš, Ivan and Milan, and the Maiden of Kosovo.

There is another of d'Avril's works that contains a number of Serbian heroic songs, chiefly about Marko Kraljević. It is his *Slávy Dcéra* ("Daughter of Sláva"),[1] his *fille Slave*, with the sub-title *Choix de poésies Slaves*, published in 1896. The title was borrowed from the Slovak poet, J. Kollár, who so called one of his best known works. In his *Voyage Sentimental*, d'Avril had already mentioned that the Marko and "heidoques" cycles were the two to be ranked with the classical cycle on Kosovo. Having, however, been too much absorbed in the latter, he did not give any translations of the songs about Marko, but seems to have left these to be dealt with in the *Slávy Dcéra*. He did not, however, attempt to give here another rhapsody similar to that of *La Bataille de Kossovo*, but he chose one "cantilène de Marko" which seemed to him to be the most epic of the whole cycle. In the original it is called *Uroš and the Mrljavčević* and it runs

[1] Sláva = glory.

into about 250 lines. D'Avril's translation is a faithful rendering, line for line, but he divided the whole song into nine short parts, with a special title for each one. He was, naturally, well acquainted with Dozon's *Épopée Serbe* and leaves it to readers who wish to know more about the legendary history of this hero to consult this capital work. D'Avril calls Marko one of the "representative men" in the sense of Emerson's recognised phrase, i.e. Marko is a representative of Serbia, as "Guillaume Bras-de-Fer, le marquis au court nez" was of France of the Middle Ages, and as the Cid is for Spain.

In this work d'Avril once more returns to the subject of Kosovo. The songs on Kosovo and Marko are, in his words, the two principal cycles in the heroic epics of the Serbs. He boldly compares the former with the *Iliad* and the latter with the *Odyssey*. He did not repeat the whole cycle on Kosovo but reprinted the two songs on the Monastery of Ravanitza, with which his *La Bataille de Kossovo* respectively opens and closes. As he expressed it, the whole epic of Kosovo is, as it were, concentrated in the history of this monastery. The two songs are here entitled *Comment Lazare fonde un monastère* and *Comment Lazare reçut la sépulture*.

In 1881 C. Courrière returned to the traditional poetry of the Serbs, when he published, in the *Revue Britannique*, "Les Chants Tsernogoriens", i.e. the Montenegrin Songs. The translation is in prose but each line of the original is separated by a hyphen from that following. He does not say where he found the originals. In 1887 and the following year Courrière busied himself with the Slavs once more. It was again the *Revue Britannique* that published his articles, most of which are but an annual account of the political conditions of all the Slav peoples. In his opinion, they were no longer "une quantité négligeable" but peoples who were becoming more and more important in political combinations in Europe. He finds in them the natural allies of France against Germany, their common enemy. "Nous devons étudier leur développement, assister à leurs luttes et nous réjouir de leurs succès."

In the 'sixties La Comtesse Dora d'Istria, a Russian princess, Kolzoff-Massalsky, contributed towards the spreading of knowledge of Serbian traditional songs, by bestowing praises upon them in an extensive article, "Nationalité Serbe d'après les chants populaires", which appeared in the *Revue des Deux Mondes* for January, 1865.

VII

Among recent French writers, the greatest champion of the Slav peoples was the late Professor Louis Léger (1843– 1923). He met, in 1867, the famous Croatian bishop, Strossmayer, who invited him to Zagreb, to be present at the inauguration of the Academy. Léger utilised this visit for a trip through the lands of the Yugoslavs in the hope of acquainting himself with the peoples. He was in Belgrade the day after the fortress had been evacuated by the Turks. From 1868, when his doctor's thesis was presented, his name constantly figured in the press in connection with his studies of the Slavs. In the same year Léger was appointed to teach Russian at the Sorbonne. He also lectured on Czech, Polish and Serbian literature between 1868 and 1870. From 1874 he was in charge of the Russian Department in the School of Oriental

Languages in Paris. In 1885 he was nominated professor of Slavonic languages and literatures in the Collège de France. Professor Léger contributed to French literature a number of valuable works on the Slavs, but he did not busy himself with translations of their traditional poetry; *Chants héroïques et chansons populaires des Slaves de Boheme* was his only contribution of this kind, in 1866.

One of the most active collaborators of the *Revue des Deux Mondes*, Saint-René Taillandier, published in 1872, while a professor of the University of Paris, a book entitled *La Serbie, Kara-George et Milosch*, which he dedicated to Milan Obrenović, the ruling Prince of Serbia. As the title of the work indicates, the author's aim was to give an historical account of modern Serbia, but he also speaks of some customs of the Serbs and their traditional poetry. In connection with the last-named subject, he quotes in prose translation an heroic song of the cycle on the *hajduci*, and another from the Kosovo group, in the translation of Auguste Dozon.

Gaston Thomson acted similarly in his book *L'Herzégovine*, published in 1875. Speaking of the traditional songs recited by blind rhapsodes, he bestows due praise upon the heroic songs on Kosovo and gives in prose translation the whole of the *Car Lazar i carica Milica*, a ballad which was mentioned by most French translators. He lays due emphasis on the heroic songs of the *hajduci* and quotes a few in prose translation. When speaking of the women's songs he too, like several of his predecessors, quotes in full a few typical lyric songs, among which are the very beautiful ones *La belle Militza a des sourcils trop longs*, which is called by Vuk *A Serbian Maiden*, and *La*

Trahison, called in the original *Ništa se sakriti ne može* (*Nothing can remain hidden*).

Joseph Reinach, who was the chief editor of *La Republique Française* in the 'eighties, had made a name for himself in 1876, with the book *La Serbie et la Monténégro,* in which a whole chapter deals with Serbian poetry. A number of women's and heroic songs in prose translation illustrated his text. In his opinion "le Serbe est naturellement poète, il chante comme un autre parle; c'est un besoin pour lui", and he quotes Mickiewicz's statement about the Serbs that they are the people "destiné à être le barde et le musicien de toute la race Slave".

Among the many periodicals interested in Serbian political and literary conditions was also *La Nouvelle Revue.* In October, 1884, it published an article "Mœurs et chants de Bosnie et d'Herzégovine", by É. de Sainte-Marie. It contains a few translations of the most recent women's songs of the Muhammedan Serbo-Croats of these provinces. The writer claims to have been the first to publish them. To these the author adds three heroic songs, the first of which, *La Perte des neuf Yougovitch,* is from the Kosovo cycle. The second, *La Veuve Jania,* is a story of the "tribute in blood" that the Christians were forced to pay to their conquerors and oppressors, the Turks. The third describes a similar subject: how a son of an Herzegovinian duke, Stephen, was taken as a prisoner to Constantinople in 1454, and how he was converted to Islam under the name of Ahmed Pasha. The first two were translated from a collection of Bosnian and Herzegovinian traditional songs published by I. F. Jukić in 1858. Sainte-Marie's translations are fairly good. He is anxious to preserve the literal sense of the originals. In the heroic songs he renders, practically always, line for line, but often, when he is not sure of what the original means, he leaves out the line. Hence his translations are slightly shorter than the originals. Sometimes, too, he misunderstands the texts.

In September,1886, the *Nouveaux Mélanges Orientaux* published A. Dozon's extensive study and a translation of the longest Yugoslav heroic song recorded by Vuk Karadžić, the *Marriage of Maksim Crnojević*, which runs into 1226 lines and which the French translator called "un des plus precieux monuments". His translation is preceded by an elaborate "Notice historique et littéraire".

Towards the end of the century, Achille Millien, "le delicat poète nivernais", published, in Paris, in 1891, *Chants populaires de la Grèce, de la Serbie et du Monténégro*, consisting of twenty-eight poems, mainly women's songs. Knowing no Serbo-Croat, Millien used the translations of Mme Voiart, Cyprien Robert and Auguste Dozon. While preserving the gist of the originals he, like Owen Meredith, gave them an entirely different form, namely, that of modern verse and rhyme. He has, therefore, given them a grace which they do not possess in the original. They are very good, pleasant verses, but hardly to be called Serbian.

In conclusion, M. Colonna's *Contes de la Bosnie*, published in Paris in 1898, might be mentioned. V. M. Yovanovitch has referred to this book in "*La Guzla*" *de Prosper Mérimée* under a separate heading, "Un Plagiat". Suffice it to say that the collection contains a dozen Bosnian ballads, in prose translation. Yovanovitch says that some of these songs are of true popular origin, but the translator has mutilated them so much, in order to preserve their simplicity and *naïveté*, that they are hardly recognisable. Others are simply manufactured by the author. Four of them are but paraphrases of Mérimée's Illyrian ballads. Almost all these "Bosnian ballads" were reprinted in the *Revue d'Europe, économique, financière et littéraire*, in 1899–1900.

Chapter Seven

Yugoslav Traditional Poetry
in English Literature

I

SIR WALTER SCOTT has often been mentioned as
the first British author to be interested in Serbian
traditional songs, because of his translation of
The Lamentation of the Faithful Wife of Asan-Aga, i.e. the
Hasanaginica, but we feel bound to recognise that he
translated this song not because he was in the least interested in the Serbs and their poetry, but solely because
of his interest in the work of Goethe, whose German
translation of this song came into his hands. In 1796
Scott translated Burger's *Lenore*. His interest in the
German ballads grew steadily afterwards, so that in the
next few years he was busily engaged in translating them.
These translations, however, remained unpublished for a
time. In 1799 he translated Goethe's *Goetz*, and it was
about this time that he rendered into English also the song
of Asan-Aga's wife.

There was a kind of mystery about this translation and
the mystery was at last revealed in December, 1924, when
the *Slavonic Review* published D. H. Low's article on "The
First Link between English and Serbo-Croatian Literature". The story, briefly stated, goes as follows: It must
be familiar to most people how young Scott, at the age of
twenty-eight, negotiated with James Ballantyne, towards

the end of 1799, "to print off a dozen copies or so" of as many of his "little ballads" as would make a pamphlet, sufficient to let his Edinburgh acquaintances judge of Ballantyne's skill for themselves. This is what Lockhart said in his *Life of Sir Walter Scott* and he, Lockhart, was of opinion that exactly twelve copies were struck off accordingly, with the title, alluding to the long delay of Lewis's collection, of *The Apology for Tales of Terror* (1799). Relying on what Lockhart had mentioned, namely that among the "recent pieces designed to appear in Lewis's collection", which Scott took to Ballantyne's office, there was also "the Morlachian Fragment after Goethe", i.e. the *Hasanaginica*, Professor A. Brandl of Berlin concluded in 1882 that this ballad was one of those published in the *Apology*. Professor Miklosich, like several other prominent critics, accepted this and stated that the twelve copies of the *Apology* had all been lost. V. M. Yovanovitch, however, has proved that both Brandl and Miklosich were wrong: he traced one of the twelve copies of the *Apology* in the library at Abbotsford and found that Sir Walter Scott's translation of the above-mentioned ballad was not printed in it. Yet that the translation existed in manuscript was not to be doubted, because the manuscript seems to have been exhibited at Edinburgh in 1871, at the centenary of Scott's birth. Yovanovitch expressed the hope that some day it might be found and it *was* found by D. H. Low. "It is hard to see", he says, "why the whereabouts of the MS. should have remained so long concealed from those interested. It is safely preserved in the library of Edinburgh University (Laing collection)." In Sir Walter Scott's translation it is printed, for the first

time, in the *Slavonic Review* under the original heading:
The Lamentation of the Faithful Wife of Asan-Aga (*from the Morlachian Language*).

To turn to the ballad itself, its content, stated as briefly as possible, is as follows. Asan-Aga is lying dangerously wounded. His mother and sister visit him but his wife cannot do so because she is too bashful. Upon his recovery, Asan-Aga orders his wife to leave his home and the children. Her proud brother comes with the letter of divorce and takes her away after her pitiful farewell to the children; soon afterwards he marries her to a Cadi, against her will. Before the marriage, she implores the Cadi to bring a veil for her that she may not see her children on passing Asan-Aga's home. This he does, but as she rides past her old home her two boys ask her to call, while her two daughters are looking out of the window. She cannot forbear to visit them and give them presents. Asan-Aga, who seems to have repented of his injustice to his wife, and to have expected her to return to him even at this late moment, which she could not do, calls the children back, which breaks her heart and she falls dead.

In the original, the ballad consists of ninety-three lines without rhyme. Sir Walter Scott produced twenty-six stanzas, rhyming *a b*, *a b*, in all 104 lines. In the words of Mr Low: "Scott's version is only a translation of a translation of a translation, and it would be a sorry task to compare this wishy-washy verbosity with the spare, lean virility of the Serbian—or even of the German".

Since Scott's day the *Hasanaginica* has been translated into English by twelve known and one unknown persons, and printed no less than nineteen times. Of all the translators of the nineteenth century, only two—John Bowring and Owen Meredith—were directly interested in the Serbian popular ballads. The remaining translators of the same century—James Clarence Mangan, 1836, 1845; W. Edmondstone Ayton, 1844, 1859; Edgar Alfred Bowring, 1853, 1874; Mary Anne Burt, 1853, 1856; George Bancroft, 1855; Edward Chawner, 1866, 1879; and William Gibson, 1883—were interested mainly in Goethe's work and, in translating his poems and ballads into English, also translated the ballad of Asan-Aga's wife under slightly varying titles. The translation of the unknown author appeared in a small collection entitled *Selim and Zaida*, published in 1801 and also in 1802.[1]

II

In the nineteenth century, two names were chiefly associated with the Serbian traditional poetry in English literature: those of John Bowring in the first, and of Owen Meredith in the second half of the century. It is known to but few people that John Gibson Lockhart showed an equal interest in this subject and that he, too, prepared a volume of Serbian songs in English, which, however, has never been found.

But neither Bowring nor Lockhart were the first to publish in English the Serbian traditional songs. Since Scott's translation of the *Hasanaginica* was not published until quite recently, the translation of the same song by an anonymous author in *Selim and Zaida* is the first Yugoslav popular ballad to be published in the English language.

[1] The most recent translations of the *Hasanaginica* are by G. R. Noyes and M. A. Mügge.

It was translated from the German of Goethe, but the translator also possessed the original, of which he quotes the opening and concluding lines. It is a good translation and is much better than that of Scott. A reprint of it was published in the *Slavonic Review* in December, 1927.

The naturalised Pole, K. Szyrma, was the first known author in England to write about half a page in English on the "South Sclavonian" popular poetry and on the *Wife of Asan-Aga*, a ballad he called "undoubtedly the finest specimen of elegiac traditional poetry", written in the "Morlaco-Sclavonic dialect". This short reference was included in his article published in the form of a letter on the "Sclavonic Traditional Poetry" in *Blackwood's Edinburgh Magazine* for September, 1821. In January, 1823, he published his *Letters on Poland*, in which, amongst other things, he dwells, in the first two chapters, on the same subject, including the popular songs of the Serbs, and on the "Sclavonic" music. Moreover, he quotes one, *The Nightingale*, which he probably translated from the original, published by Vuk in 1814 under the title *Natural Freedom*, in six rhymed stanzas. Szyrma adhered to the original but gave seven stanzas. Having misunderstood a word in the original text, he went slightly wrong in two places. It is possible that Szyrma also came across J. Grimm's German translation of this song, published in 1818 by F. Förster.

The publication of Talvj's volumes of Serbian traditional songs had been noticed in England almost immediately by Lockhart and Bowring, both of whom set themselves to translate a considerable number of them. John Bowring, afterwards Sir John, was a business man by profession, whose hobby was the study of foreign languages and literatures and the publishing of anthologies of popular poetries. He learned French, Italian, Spanish, Portuguese, German and Dutch; he acquired a sufficient knowledge of Swedish, Danish, Russian, Serbian, Polish and Czech; he also studied Magyar and Arabic, and while residing in the East as British Consul he made good progress in Chinese. Enjoying the advantage of personal acquaintance with most of the eminent authors and poets of his time, he secured their assistance in his purpose of writing a history of the literatures of the Continent and giving translated specimens of the popular poetry, not only of the Western but also of the Oriental world. He was a Fellow of the Royal Society and the recipient of many foreign insignia.

Knowing of the success of Talvj's *Volkslieder der Serben*, Bowring wrote in July, 1826, a review of Vuk's three volumes of Serbian folk-songs, in the *Westminster Review*, a monthly founded in 1824, of which Bowring was one of the first editors. In fact it was more than a review; it was an article illustrated by about a dozen Serbian ballads in Bowring's translation, in which he quoted also a few passages of Goethe's translation of the *Hasanaginica*. His intention was "merely to give a few specimens of the poetry of the Serbians", in the hope that the subject would be treated more elaborately thereafter.

Eight months later the *Monthly Literary Adviser* announced, on the 10th March, 1827, that Bowring had in the Press a volume of "the poetical and popular Literature of the Servians, intended to fill up one of the Chasms" which had hitherto "prevented the English reader from taking a comprehensive view of modern as contra-

15-2

distinguished from Classical Minstrelsy". A month later
the same paper advertised, on the 10th April, John Bowring's "just published" book, *Servian Popular Poetry*, a
collection of seventeen "historical, traditional and religious ballads", and sixty-four "lyrics, songs and occasional poems", in all, 235 pages, preceded by a longish
introduction by way of giving an account of the "Servians", their history and their literature, the popular
ballads and their customs. The introduction shows a fair
amount of knowledge, yet it is written in anything but a
scholarly way, not to mention many inaccurate statements.
For instance, in giving an account of the "various idioms
of the Slavonian language", he says that the "southern
stream" that "flowed forth" from the old, or Church
Slavonic, is "composed of the Hungarian (!), Bulgarian
and Servian tongues". One would naturally expect "a
competent Slav scholar" to know that the Hungarian
language has no linguistic connection whatsoever with
the Slavonic languages, or indeed with any of the Indo-
European tongues. This much he could have derived
from a book which he quotes on page xxxiii, as a footnote,
namely: *A comparison between the Servian and other Slavonic
idioms*, by Vuk Karadžić, Vienna, 1822. As to the "Servian
idiom", he finds it "the most cultivated, the most interesting and the most widely spread of all the Southern
Slavonic dialects", but says that the vicinity of Greece
and Italy had modified and mellowed it to such an extent
that it was, in fact, "the Russian hellenized, deprived of
its harshness and its consonant terminations and softened
down into a perfect instrument for poetry and music".
Bowring does not, of course, omit to mention that the

"Servian language has been considerably influenced by the Turkish", yet all his utterances on the language, as well as those that he states so briefly on the history and literature of the Serbs, are not such as a scholar would use. Not only are they sometimes inaccurate and unreliable, but on the whole they are superficial and, at best, were no more than useful information for people who at that time knew nothing about the subject. He says, for instance, that "the Servians must be reckoned among those races who vibrated between the north and the east; possessing to-day, dispossessed to-morrow; now fixed, and now wandering; having their headquarters in Sarmatia for many generations, in Macedonia in the following ones, and settling in Servia at last". He concludes, therefore, that "to trace their history, as to trace their course, is impossible"!

Bowring evidently had an inadequate and inaccurate knowledge of the Serbs, but we must make allowance for the fact that in those days no proper history of this people existed and that those few works which he calls "the best sources of Servian history" have ceased long ago to be considered as such. That the Serbs and their literary activities were practically unknown at the time Bowring's collection appeared is seen also from a review of this book, published in *The London Magazine* in April, 1827. "The Servians—the Servians—who are the Servians?" asks the reviewer, and says that their language and their literature were things "wholly unheard of here" until the appearance of the two articles in the *Westminster Review* and the *Quarterly Review* respectively. The popular poetry of the Serbs at length revealed its character in the most agreeable manner. The delicacy, elegance and fancy of much of it was not to be excelled by the lyrical poetry of any other country. It was, moreover, remarkable for its affectionate and amiable turn of thought. The songs celebrated in general "the feminine charms, or the manly beauties of the beloved; the pure delights of intimacy and the blessings of affection". The love was not only the love of lovers, but also the love of brothers and sisters and mothers; "in short, nothing can be more remarkable than the purity of these compositions, their amiable simplicity, and their agreeable fancies".

There is no doubt that Bowring was prompted to translate the Serbian traditional songs by the success of Talvj. It seems also beyond doubt—he himself admits it in his letters—that he had translated them more from her German version than from the original Serbian, yet he wisely kept silent in his book about it. In February, 1828, Talvj said she had at last in her hands Bowring's book, and, on comparing her own translations with his and seeing no mention of her name, she was indignant and hurt. She said that she could not but agree with one of her friends, who called Bowring a "literary dandy". She pointed out that this mania to be "universal" not only in the Slavonic sphere but in everything that was foreign was ridiculous, judging from his superficial knowledge of languages.

In the introduction to his collection Bowring says that most of the popular songs which constituted it were taken from that of Vuk, to whose writings he often refers throughout the book. As to Talvj's translations, he calls

it "the work of an amiable woman", and he adds that he
had employed *the Notes* attached to her translations without any special reference to them. Yet, when comparing
Bowring's translation with that of Talvj, it is very obvious
that he must have been indebted to her for more than the
notes alone. He duly admits that he endeavoured to avail
himself of all the authors who had written on the subject,
"particularly of the valuable criticisms of Dr Kopitar...
of the works of Goethe, J. Grimm and Joh. Severin
Vater", the last of whom was also interested in Serbian
traditional poetry.

To prove that Bowring translated some and probably
all of the songs in his collection from Talvj's German
translations and not from the original, suffice it to dwell
upon a few lines of the following song. It is called in the
original, *Of the Wedding of Hajkuna, the sister of Beg Ljubo-
vić*. Talvj calls it simply *Hajkuna's Wedding* and Bowring
Ajkuna's Marriage. We.shall see presently that this song
was translated by Lockhart, too, but we cannot tell under
what name. In a footnote to this song Bowring says he
pays "cheerful homage to the poetical beauties of the
translation of this ballad", but that the "tasteful author
(i.e. Lockhart) has no doubt greatly embellished the
original". He then quotes about fifteen lines of Lockhart's translation, putting into italics the words that are
not to be found in the original.

> Never, never, since the world's beginning,
> Never, never bloomed a fairer blossom
> Than was reared of late beneath the shadow
> Of the noble Lubovitzi's fastness.

White and high o'er Nevesinya looking
Stands the tower wherein they reared Hainuka,
But it holds no more the flower of beauty,—
Far away lies Lubovitzi's sister.

Fair she was, there could be nothing fairer;
Stately was she as the *mountain* pine-tree;
White and rosy-coloured *intermingled*
Were her cheeks, as *she had kissed* the dawning;
Dark and flashing, like two noble jewels,
Were her eyes; *and over them were* eyebrows,
Thin and black, like leeches *from the fountain*;
Dark the lashes too; *although the* ringlets
Hung above in clusters *rich and golden*;
Softer were her eyelids *than* the pinions
Of the swallow *on the breeze reposing.*
Sweeter were the maiden's lips *than* honey;
White her teeth, as pearls *in ocean ripen'd*;
White her breasts, two little *panting* wild doves;
Soft her speaking, as the wild dove's murmur;
Bright her smiling, as the *burst* of sunshine.
Wild through Bosnia and Herzegovina
Went the story of her wondrous beauty.

If by the "original" Bowring really meant Vuk's Serbian version and not the German of Talvj—the only one
that Lockhart used—then we must say that some of the
words of his own, i.e. Bowring's, translation are not to
be found in the Serbian text either. In the original it runs
into 126 lines, for which Talvj and Bowring have given
127 each, but which Lockhart has extended into 132 lines.

Let us pause and compare these lines with the original
and Talvj's translation. Bowring says that the word

"mountain" in the line "Stately was she as the mountain pine-tree" does not exist in the original, and he is right. He himself has rendered the same line as "She was tall and slender as the pine-tree". Yet in the original there is no mention of "pine-tree" either, but simply that she was "In her figure slender and tall". Again Bowring is right in finding the line "White her teeth, as pearls in ocean ripen'd" not to correspond to the original. He has translated it: "And her teeth were pearls *array'd* in order", which is not what the Serbian texts say, namely that her "White teeth (are) two rows of pearls". The explanation is to be found as soon as Bowring's translation is compared with that of Talvj. We shall find that she has inserted the words "like a pine-tree" (= wie die Tanne) in the first line quoted above and that the word "array'd" is the nearest translation of the German "aufgereihte", and not of the Serbian *dwa niza* (two rows). There is another proof of Bowring's literal translation of Talvj's version; lines 20 and 21 of her translation are not to be found in the Serbian original at all. Had Bowring really consulted the Serbian text he would have seen this and, as he was so particular about rendering the original in as literal a fashion as possible, he would naturally have omitted the two lines instead of giving a literal translation of the German text. We could give numerous examples which would show that Bowring really translated his collection of Serbian songs from Talvj's German version. Suffice it, however, to give the following. In the song *Ništa se sakriti ne može*, which Talvj translated literally as *Es kann nichts verborgen bleiben*, and which Bowring calls *Secrets Divulged*, there is a line as follows: *putnik kaza na vodi vozaru*, which means, in literal translation, "the wanderer said on the water to the ferryman". Bowring renders it as: "he to a sailor on the restless ocean tells it", which is obviously a translation from the German: "auf dem Meer dem Schiffer sagt's der Wanderer". That Bowring, however, had a Serbian text before him can be seen from the following. In a song entitled, in Serbian, *A Shepherd and a Girl*, the first line in Serbian runs: *Žetvu žela lepota devojka*, which means, "a beautiful girl reaped the corn". Talvj calls the same song *Schlaue Ausrede*, while in Bowring's book it is entitled *Lepota*. He explains correctly, in a footnote, that "*Lepota* is the Servian word for *Beauty*". This word, viz. *lepota*, is not once mentioned by Talvj. She translated the phrase *lepota devojka* with "Schönheits-mädchen". It is, therefore, obvious that Bowring found the word *lepota* in the Serbian text. As to the translation of the whole song, it is by no means a literal one.

A careful examination will show, moreover, that there is not a single song in Bowring's collection that does not exist in that of Talvj.

Numerically, Bowring's collection of Serbian popular poetry is much smaller than that of Talvj and still more so than that of Vuk. While Vuk gives 406 women's songs and 73 heroic ones, Talvj presents us with 204 and Bowring with but 107 "various songs and ballads". In all the narrative poetry, to quote his own words, he had preserved the original measure. In the rendering of shorter lyrical pieces he had allowed himself "some latitude of expression". D. H. Low thinks that "he had a certain fluent and agreeable knack which, although it urged him sometimes to the verge of the namby-pamby,

is employed, upon the whole, effectively enough".
Bowring insisted that, above all things, the wish to preserve most faithfully the character of the original had
prevented his introducing many very obvious decorations
and his veiling many equally obvious defects. He says:
"To fidelity, at least, this volume may lay an honest
claim". As to the choice of the songs, it is now clear that
he had looked rather for characteristic than for beautiful
ones. From the aesthetical point of view, his "lyrics,
songs and occasional poems" are a better choice than the
heroic ballads. From Bowring's introduction as well as
from the numerous footnotes in his book of Serbian
translations, in which he often refers to the original, nay,
even quotes some verses in Serbian, one must, however,
conclude not only that he possessed a fair knowledge of
the subject with which he dealt, but also that he must have
had some Serbian texts before him. It is another question
as to how much he knew of the Serbian language and still
another how accurate he was in referring to it. One thing
is certain, however—that he translated *Ajkuna's Marriage*
from Talvj's German translation and that, in criticising
Lockhart's translation of the same ballad, he had compared it with the German *only*, although mentioning the
original.

As to Bowring's further linguisitic competence, it is
interesting to view V. M. Yovanovitch's criticism. He
recalls Professor G. Saintsbury's statement in the *Encyclo-
paedia Britannica* that Sir John Bowring was "a competent
Slav scholar", and emphatically denies it. Not only was
he, in Yovanovitch's opinion, NOT a competent Slav
scholar, but he was never recognised as such by those who

were competent Slav scholars. In reality, while the "juge compétent" in Germany, i.e. W. Gerhard, was but a silk merchant, the "juge compétent" in England, i.e. Bowring, was only a drapery merchant. He was a well-known polyglot: "un polyglotte quelque peu pressé".

Not only does Yovanovitch deny him the knowledge of Serbian, but also that of Russian, for the following reason. In December, 1826, Bowring wrote to Vuk in French and Vuk answered in Russian in January, 1827. Yovanovitch obtained, in 1908, a copy of Vuk's letter from Bowring's son—the late Lewin Bowring, then an old man of 84, living in Torquay—and published it in July of that year in Belgrade.

He pointed out then that to Vuk's Russian letter an English translation was attached, written by someone else and not by Bowring himself, and that this translation had a "servile tone". Hence Yovanovitch concluded that Bowring probably did not understand Vuk's letter properly and that he had it translated into English first. On the back of this translation, as well as on the back of Vuk's letter, Bowring himself wrote: "an(swer)d May 10th".

Yovanovitch's argument on this point does seem to be strong. Bowring may or may not have known Russian any better than he knew Serbian. This is not for us to examine here. But Yovanovitch cannot state categorically that Bowring did not know Russian because he did not himself translate a letter from the Russian. For all we know, the letter may have been illegibly written, or Bowring may not have been good enough to read Russian in handwriting. Most Serbs find it easier to read a letter written in French, German or English than one written by a Croat in Latin characters, yet who could deny a Serbian a complete knowledge of the Croatian language?

When publishing Vuk's Russian letter to Bowring, Yovanovitch published at the same time a letter which Talvj wrote to Bowring from Halle, on the 4th April, 1827, and while commenting on these letters, in 1908, he found that Talvj "otherwise spoke unjustly about John Bowring". Yet when writing, a few years later, his work "*La Guzla*" *de Prosper Mérimée*, he changed his opinion of Bowring and concluded his judgment of him as follows: "Mr Bowring was an *amateur d'autographes* and, like most English people, maintained an enormous correspondence. He exhausted (*accablait*) with his letters all the *grands hommes du jour*".

Yovanovitch obviously wishes to be humorous at the expense of Bowring and his countrymen. He had admitted in 1908 that Bowring was greatly interested in the Serbs, that he took much trouble in producing his anthology of Serbian folk-songs, and that he also had some success and exercised a certain influence in England. His anthology was warmly reviewed in many periodicals, and a part of it translated into French and published in *Le Globe* in 1827. Goethe too reviewed it in his *Kunst und Alterthum*. As to his enormous correspondence, suffice it to point to the vast correspondence of Vuk Karadžić— of which so far seven volumes, or more than 5500 quarto pages, have been published, and at least three more volumes, containing over 2000 pages, have yet to appear —and of numerous other scholars and public men and women of those days, when writing long letters was by no means regarded as a drawback.

Since Yovanovitch's pronouncement on Bowring, a dozen letters exchanged between him and Vuk have been published in the State edition of Vuk's correspondence, and these throw a fresh light on the work of this English *amateur d'autographes*. It appears that Bowring came into touch with Vuk through the famous Czech philologist and archaeologist, Professor P. J. Šafařík (1795–1861). On the 10th December, 1826, he wrote to Vuk that John Bowring, the man who had published in the previous year a Russian, and in that year a Polish, anthology, had just translated several ballads and songs from Vuk's collection and that these had been received in England with "roaring applause" (mit rauschendem Beifall). Bowring had also intended to translate and publish them all, "being over head and eyes in love with Serbian folk-songs". Šafařík adds that Bowring wrote to him on the 20th November (1826) and amongst other things asked him several questions which he could answer, but said that he would also refer him to Vuk and Kopitar. "Wait, therefore," he goes on, "for his letter and be careful that his wish is fulfilled."

It will be remembered that the reference above to Bowring's translations of several ballads and songs from Vuk's collection relates to his review of Vuk's three volumes of songs, published in the *Westminster Review* in July, 1826, as already mentioned.

A few days later (19th December) John Bowring duly wrote to Vuk in French. Having apologised for doing so, he informed him of his intention of publishing a volume of Serbian ballads: he would add to it also such information as he could find in the works of Talvj and Grimm, and especially in those of Vuk. He asked him, therefore, for information, advice and help. He explains at the end of his letter that he was a merchant and that it was through some business friends of his in Vienna that he had tried to approach him. His friends had applied to Kopitar, who was good enough to say "it would not displease you to come in touch with me. If you encourage me our correspondence might become more interesting. In what way could I be useful to you in this country? Please consider my services as fully at your disposal". Vuk was in possession of this letter at the beginning of January, 1827, and was very delighted, as is to be seen from his letter in Russian, addressed from Vienna on the 12th of the same month, to "Dear Sir, Ivan Karlovitch",[1] i.e. John Bowring. Vuk said that he considered it an honour for the Serbian people and a reward for all his work that Bowring was about to publish an English translation of Serbian ballads. He also used this opportunity to ask Bowring to recommend him to the London Bible Society and see that it invited him to London to publish his Serbian translation of the Bible, a matter on which Vuk and Bowring corresponded for many years after.

In his second letter, that of the 30th March, 1827, Bowring told Vuk that he had fulfilled his promise, namely that a volume of Serbian traditional songs had already been published, of which two copies had been sent to Vuk through Kopitar, and one to Prince Miloš Obrenović, the then ruler of Serbia. Fearing that the two volumes might be late in reaching Vuk, he sent him in his letter a copy of the dedication, in verse, to Vuk, printed at the beginning

[1] Because Charles was the name of Bowring's father.

of his *Servian Popular Poetry*. He also expressed the hope that, as all indications pointed, his book would be well received by the English public and that either another edition of it would be seen, or he would be encouraged to publish another volume. He therefore asked Vuk to send him new material and also to supply him with a few small pictures of Serbian costumes, as well as some patterns of the language and its writing at various epochs ("quelques échantillons de la langue et de son écriture à différentes époques").

It is interesting to notice that Bowring in this letter said that he owed to Kopitar, without knowing him, his first knowledge of Serbian literature.

From Bowring's next letter, of the 18th June, 1827, we see that Vuk had written to him in the previous May, telling him that the copy of Bowring's translations had been forwarded to Prince Miloš. On hearing that the prince wás about to establish a Press at Belgrade, Bowring was extremely pleased. He also asked Vuk to inform Kopitar of the great progress he had made in Bohemian translations, and that he was also busying himself with Bulgarian translations.

Six months later (15th February, 1829) Bowring acknowledged Vuk's letter of the previous 29th September and told him that he had received nothing—on account of which he was extremely angry—"because an interesting moment was passing and yet he found himself unable to do that which he especially wanted to do". It looks as if Bowring had expected an acknowledgment from Prince Miloš for the copy of his translations sent to him a year before, for Vuk says in his letter of the 5th March, 1829, that the reason for his not having received an answer to his letter was that "they did *not* understand it"; there was not a single man in Serbia who knew English.

From another letter of Vuk, sent to Bowring several weeks later (15th April), it is clear that Vuk had asked Bowring to translate into English *Die serbische Revolution*, by Leopold von Ranke. Bowring agreed to do this and to try to have it published in English, but the copy Vuk promised to send him never reached Bowring, as he says in his letter of a year later (15th March, 1830). The correspondence was broken off temporarily and Bowring seems to have lost touch with Vuk for nearly two years, when Vuk sent him a letter on the 15th December, 1831, explaining that his silence was due to his stay and work for the Government in Serbia. Bowring, meanwhile, had been busily publishing his translations of Hungarian folk-songs and preparing his Scandinavian songs. As there was no answer from Bowring, Vuk wrote once more in April (28th) of the next year (1832), but the next and last letter of John Bowring that is published in Vuk's correspondence is dated sixteen years later, the 3rd August, 1848. The subject of this letter is still the same with which Vuk opened his correspondence with Bowring twenty-one years before, namely, the publication of Vuk's translation into Serbian of the Bible, through the London Bible Society.

The existing correspondence between Bowring and Vuk shows that Bowring started it first, having been impressed by Talvj's German translation of Serbian poetry and the warm reception it had found among the literary people of Europe. As long as he was interested in them, and as long as he had hoped that his own translations would be received in England with the same enthusiasm, he was anxious to secure Vuk's assistance in supplying him with new material. He intended even to visit Serbia in 1828. Kopitar and Vuk expected him in Vienna and Vuk hoped to be his interpreter in Serbia. Governmental business, however, called Bowring to Holland and his journey to Serbia never took place.

His expectation of producing either another edition or an additional volume of Serbian ballads in English was not fulfilled. Soon afterwards he became interested in the traditional poetry of other peoples and the subject of Serbian ballads disappeared from his correspondence altogether, a year or two after he had published *Servian Popular Poetry*. Vuk was for him first "Monsieur le Docteur", then his "digne maître", his "cher ami", his "cher M. Vuk" and, lastly, his "cher M. Karadzich", while for Vuk he remained throughout their correspondence "Dear Sir, Ivan Karlovitch".

As to Vuk, the correspondence shows that, while he was always ready to place his services at Bowring's disposal, he never relapsed from trying to secure through him an invitation to London from the London Bible Society to publish his Serbian translation of the Bible, in which Bowring failed.

Another matter in which Vuk untiringly tried to secure Bowring's assistance was that concerning Ranke's book on the Serbian revolution which, as is well known, Ranke wrote with Vuk's help; Vuk supplied the material and Ranke did the rest. They met in Vienna, probably through Kopitar, towards the end of 1827. Ranke, like all those who knew Vuk, was very fond of him and regarded him as the most learned Serb of those days. In the story of the Serbs, which Vuk related to him, in the patriarchal life, their poetry, their fight for freedom, Ranke found a very great attraction. When his little book, *Die serbische Revolution*, was published in 1829, Niebuhr himself wrote that Ranke's little book was, as a history, the most excellent book that German literature possessed and shortly before he died he proclaimed its author "a Thucydides of the present time". It was no wonder that Vuk was so anxious to have it translated and published in English, a thing that did not take place until 1847.

III

We can give only a brief account of Lockhart's translations of Serbian traditional poetry.

In January, 1827, the *Quarterly Review* gave an account of the *Translations from the Servian Minstrelsy: to which are added some specimens of Anglo-Norman Romances*, supposed to have been printed in London in 1826—i.e. about a year before Bowring's collection. The reviewer mentions that "of this volume a very small edition only has been printed for private circulation", and that a copy had been laid upon the editor's table with leave to do with it as he might think fit. He further expressed the hope that the use they had made of that *Minstrelsy* might lead to its publication. He also pointed out that "some of the minor songs of the Serbians" had already been very prettily translated in a late number of a contemporary journal—meaning by this Bowring's review in the *Westminster Review* of July, 1826, and that from that quarter also they might look "for further exertions on a field which is wide enough to employ, and rich enough to reward, many labourers".

In *Chambers's Edinburgh Journal* of the 17th May, 1845, it is said in a footnote to an article, "The Servians and their Songs", that the translator of the *Servian Minstrelsy* was the editor of the *Quarterly Review* himself, John Gibson Lockhart. Whether a few copies of his translations were really published is doubtful, for none has been found so far. It appears as if Lockhart himself had written the above article in order to sound the feelings of the reading public, and to encourage subscription towards publishing his book of *Servian Minstrelsy*. What his translations are like, we can judge only from the few songs, in all 456 lines, quoted in the review. We see further, from the pagination quoted at the foot of each ballad, that Lockhart's little book possessed at least eighty-three pages of Serbian songs: of these about sixty are covered by "metrical romances and historical ballads" while those remaining are occupied by "poetical compositions more strictly within the class which we moderns describe by the term *lyrical*", the greater part of which were, of course, amatory. The reviewer finds in the specimens before him few traces "of that Turkish kind of love" which predominates in the historical ballads of the collection. Lockhart has not adhered to the original metre either in the women's or the heroic songs, with the exception of the one of *Hajkuna's Wedding*. The author of the article in the *Chambers's Edinburgh Journal* just mentioned seems to have been unaware of this fact. The whole song is quoted in the review for the following reasons, given by the reviewer: first, on account of the state of manners which

it describes in its narrative and which is equally indicated
in the Oriental imagery of its diction; secondly, because it
is the only Serbian ballad in the collection that professes
to be rendered in the metre of the original; and thirdly,
for the extraordinary resemblance which the story of Suko,
the hero of the ballad, bears—down even to the taunt of
the closing verses—to that of *Young Lochinvar*. The same
fact is pointed to in *Chambers's Edinburgh Journal* when it is
said also that the description, in the opening lines, of a
high-born Serbian lady bears a likeness to that of a
Scottish maiden in Burns's song: *On Cessnock banks there
lives a lass*. The beginning of the song has been quoted
above (pp. 231–2). The rest runs as follows:

> Lovers many came about the maiden;
> Two above the rest came late and early;
> One, the hoary-bearded Mustaph-Aga,
> Lord of Kraina, lord of Castle-Novi.
> Mustaph-Aga, at her brother's portal,
> Met another that was come a-wooing,
> Young and noble Suko of Ubeina.
> Mustaph-Aga and the fearless Suko
> Once they met at Lubovitzi's portal,
> As the sun went down on Nevesinya.
>
> Mustaph-Aga brought a thousand pieces
> Virgin gold upon a golden basin;
> Round the basin twined a golden serpent—
> Eyes of diamond glittered in its forehead;
> Eyes of diamond, glittering so splendid
> Men might feast at midnight by their shining.
> Suko offered but a dozen ducats,
> All he had he offered for the maiden;

Lord was he of little but his sabre
And the targe that hung upon his shoulder.
Noble Suko made the border feed him,
As the air is fain to feed the falcon.

Lubovitzi spake unto his sister,
"See, my sister, see, my dear Hainuka,
In the hour in which thy mother bore thee
It was written somebody should wed thee;
Many lovers came to me a-wooing,
But this night the two that are the noblest
Both are here, within the court together.
Here is hoary-bearded Mustaph-Aga,
Come from Kraina, from his Castle-Novi;
Wealth on wealth hath lordly Mustaph-Aga,
All in silk and satin would he clothe thee,
Every day with honey would he feed thee.
Close beside is Suko of Ubeina;
Lord is he of little but his sabre,
And the targe that hangs upon his shoulder.
Choose, Hainuka, choose to-night, my sister,
Choose and tell me which of them shall wed thee".

Thus the sister spake to Lubovitzi,
"Thine the choice is, thine alone, my brother;
He to whom thou givest me is my husband;
But for me, I'd rather have a bridegroom
Young and bold, with nothing in his girdle,
Than the richest that is hoary-bearded;
Wealth is not to have gold and silver,
Wealth is there where lover meets with lover".

Lubovitzi heard his sister's answer,
Yet he gave the maid to Mustaph-Aga;

Sore against her will he gave Hainuka.
Mustaph-Aga swiftly rode to Novi;
Mustaph bade his kinsmen to the wedding;
Suko too was bid by Mustaph-Aga,
Noble Suko was to ride the foremost
With the banner, bringing home the maiden;
Richly clad came Mustaph-Aga's kindred,
Noble Suko rode among them proudly.

White days three they feasted in the fastness;
But they mounted early in the morning,
When they led her from her brother's dwelling.
When her home lay far behind the maiden,
Far within the plain of Nevesinya,
Fair Hainuka whispered to the bridesman:
"Tell me, kinsman, tell me true, my jewel,
Which is he that Lubovitzi chose me?"

Softly whispered back again the bridesman,
"Lovely maiden, beautiful Hainuka,
Right and left I pray thee look around thee!
Seest the old man riding far before us?
Him that stately sits, like an Effendi;
Him that sits upon the crimson cushion,
With the white beard hanging to the girdle;
Mustaph-Aga, with the beard of silver—
Whom besides could Lubovitzi choose thee?"

Right and left the maiden looked around her,
Heavy heart had beautiful Hainuka,
And again she whispered to the bridesman—
"Who is he that rears aloft the banner,
Riding yonder on the snowy charger,
Curly-bearded, blacker than the raven?"

Softly whispered back again the bridesman—
"Lovely maiden, Suko of Ubeina,
He that sorely struggled with thy brother
In the hour when Mustaph-Aga won thee".

Swift she dropt as if a dart had pierced her,
Black the ground, and like a corse her falling;
All came round to lift the lovely maiden,
Mustaph-Aga came himself to raise her;
But she lay as if her blood was frozen,
Until Suko struck the banner-halbert
Deep in earth, and bent him from his saddle;
Swiftly then, O, swiftly sprung Hainuka,
Swiftly leapt she on his horse behind him;
Swiftly Suko gallops for the woodland,
Swiftly, swiftly, never star more swiftly
Sunk in gloom, across the clear sky darting.

Mustaph-Aga screamed unto his kindred,
"Noble guests I've bid unto my wedding—
Ha! the robber seizes on my maiden!
Ne'er a hand is lifted to avenge me!"

"Aga, Aga," answered all the kindred,
"Welcome be the wild hawk to his pigeon,
It was written she should be his booty;
White and stately in the Castle-Novi,—
There repose thee, with thy beard of silver—
Old man, dream not of the flower of beauty."

In Lockhart's translation, "Hainuka" and "Ubeina"
are misspelled throughout for "Haikuna" and "Ud-
bina".

The following fragment illustrates the metre in which Lockhart translated one of the Kosovo songs:

That night came two black ravens   from Kossova field,
And round about the tower   in the red dawn they wheeled;
Round it, and round it,   with many a croak, they flew,
When they perched them on the turret   more loud their
     croaking grew.
Ho! is this the castle   of that famous king?
It is a silent castle—   it holds no living thing.

The solitary lady   heard them where she lay,—
Up went she to the turret,   in the dawning gray;
"Ye two black ravens,   God greet ye well this hour,
Why come ye here so early,   to croak about the tower?
Over Kossova field   was it your luck to fly?—
Saw ye two mighty hosts   that thereupon did lie?—
Saw ye the meeting, ravens?   —Did ye hear the din?—
Tell me the truth, black ravens,   which of them did win?"

"Fair thanks for such a greeting",   said the ravens black,
"We have been to Kossova,   we are just come back;
Two mighty hosts, fair lady,   it was our luck to see,
Yesterday they fought,   and near enough were we;
The princes of the armies   are slaughtered, both the two,
And all the Turks are dead   except a very few;
Some of the Servian warriors   still remain in life,
But every breast among them   is gashed with lance or
     knife".

That Lockhart no doubt had a very high opinion of Serbian popular ballads can be seen from the following tribute which he paid to them:

"No English ear", he says, "will ever be persuaded that there is any ballad in the world to be compared with 'Chevy

Chase'; no Spaniard will ever believe that any other chivalries have been sung as nobly as those of Castile and Grenada: nor can it be expected that we should meet with a Scandinavian critic less strongly prepossessed with the superiority of his own Svend Vonveds and Reddar Olles. We suspect, however, that when these various fountains of romance are all equally familiarized, as it appears likely they soon will be, to the general 'reading public' of Europe, the ballads of the long-trampled *Servians* may be found entitled to a place not very far below those of haughtier nations, whose ancestors have been enabled to hand them down inheritances more valuable than ditties 'old and plain', for the benefit of

'The spinsters and the knitters in the sun,
And the free maids that weave their thread with bones'."

Nearly twenty years were to pass before Serbian popular poetry was mentioned again in English. In May, 1845, *Chambers's Edinburgh Journal* printed an article entitled "The Servians and their Songs".

Its author may have seen the second edition of Ranke's book on Serbia that had been published in Germany in the previous year, and in which a chapter dealt with the poetry of the Serbs. He may have known also of Vuk's second volume (the first appeared in 1841) of the third edition of his collection of Serbian folk-songs, published in Vienna at the beginning of 1845. These books probably prompted the author of the article to turn to the Serbian popular songs.

The article is short and is, as we now see, more amusing than interesting, because it reveals how little the English people then knew of the Slavs, and shows also its author's very vague knowledge of the subject of which he treated.

For instance, he says in the beginning of the article about "Russia and its inhabitants", for whom "just and natural curiosity" had been aroused during the last few years in the English mind, that this mind would never be "finally satisfied with anything less than a thorough comprehension, not of the Russians only, but of the other interesting nations and tribes who, along with them, compose the great Slavonian family". Reading this one cannot help feeling that he considers Russia a newly discovered country. "It was but the other day", says the author, "we heard a friend predict that in thirty years a knowledge of Russian would be as common an accomplishment among us as a knowledge of German is at present. And strange as it may appear to many of our readers, we believe the prediction to be a correct one." Still, the author knew something of their growing political and commercial importance and something of their intellectual achievements, for he says, "in one important department, the poetry of the people, the Slavonians have already immeasurably outstripped us; and by competent judges it is decided that the collective minstrelsy of all other countries must yield, both in wealth and in beauty, to that of the nations of Slavonian origins".

The author is evidently cautiously feeling his way through this unknown domain of the "Slavonian tribes", but coming to the subject of the "Servian" poetry, he seems to let his imagination work more freely. He rightly points out that among the Slav languages that of the Serbs stands pre-eminently for power, flexibility and music; "nay," he says, "we have even seen somewhere quoted an opinion of the historian Niebuhr, to the effect that

theirs is altogether the noblest of European languages".
He also has an idea of their popular poetry and of Talvj's,
Lockhart's and Bowring's works, and quotes some of the
latter's translations, but he goes wrong when, in conclusion, he says that "cheerfulness—a serene and cheerful
transparency—is the principal characteristic of the Servian
poetry". It is true that Talvj also wrote: "Cheerfulness
is the fundamental element of Servian poetry—a serenity
clear and transparent, like the bright blue of a southern
sky", but she said this when speaking of the women's
songs; and this cannot hold good of the heroic ballads
as well, though cheerful incidents are not rare among
these, too.

However, the author may be forgiven for this slip.
Where he really goes wrong is with regard to the geo-
graphy of Serbia. He rightly says that its population consisted of about a million people, but he squeezed this
unfortunate million into a space of only 400 square miles,
instead of letting them breathe freely on a territory of
about 10,000 square miles, which they actually covered at
that time. Again, we can accept as reasonable the statement that the country was "traversed and intersected by
innumerable streams and mountains" which were "covered with forests of oaks on all sides towards the interior,
of almost impenetrable thickness", but we fail to find on
any map of Serbia of those days any justification for his
remark that "the brawling torrents collect themselves
into peaceful lakes", for there were no lakes in the Serbia
of that time. As he, however, mentioned Lamartine, who
passed through Serbia in 1833, the explanation of this
error is to be found in the following description in

Lamartine's *Travels in the East*: "The numerous rivers and streams, which descend from the mountains, meander in the valleys and form at intervals lakes in the midst of the woods".

Serbia, though still a vassal country under Turkish suzerainty, was at this time coming more and more into European politics, and, before Ranke's book on Serbia was translated into English by Mrs Alexander Kerr in 1847, there was published, in July, 1845, a book called *Servia, the Youngest Member of the European Family*, by Andrew Archibald Paton, and in 1861 this was included in his larger work *Researches on the Danube and the Adriatic*, published at Leipzig. Paton, as Mrs Kerr rightly pointed out in the preface to Ranke's *History*, had been the only writer who had made English readers acquainted with Serbia, almost a *terra incognita* at that time. The English public, she said, was indebted to the ability and intelligence of this gentleman "for a lively and faithful account of the present state of the Servians and their country". Indeed, Paton's book on Serbia is a good and interesting account of Serbia and the Serbs of those days, under the rule of Prince Alexander Karadordević. Paton saw a close resemblance in character between the Serb and the Scottish Highlander. The Serb was brave in battle, highly hospitable, delights in simple and plaintive music and poetry, his favourite instruments being the bagpipe and fiddle: but, unlike the Greek, he shows little aptitude for trade and, unlike the Bulgarian, he is very lazy in agricultural operations. All this corresponds with the Scottish Celtic character; and without absolute dishonesty, a certain low cunning in the prosecution of his material interests completes the parallel.

Mrs Kerr's translation of Ranke's *History* and especially
Paton's book on Serbia contributed very much to spreading a knowledge of Serbia. But, in practically the whole
of the first half of the nineteenth century, the interest
shown in Great Britain for the Serbs was, on the whole,
sporadic and inconsiderable. The Western world knew
very little of the Balkan peoples. Once they were all
styled, in the British Parliament, as "Greeks". In the
'forties and 'sixties—after the publication, in 1862, of a
third work on Serbia, *Servia and the Servians*, by the Rev.
W. Denton, quite a few articles appeared in *Blackwood's
Magazine*, the *Quarterly Review*, *Fraser's Magazine*, *Macmillan's Magazine*, *Leisure Hours*, the *Nation* and other
journals, based mainly on these three works. In February,
1846, the *Dublin University Magazine* published an article
drawing information from Ranke's and Paton's works.
Amongst other things, the author mentions the popular
ballads of the Serbs. In *Chambers's Journal* for May, August
and September, 1855, three articles appeared, in which
reference is to be found to the Serbs and their traditional
songs. In one of them, entitled "Servian Ballads", the
anonymous author gives a short account of the blind
Serbian ballad-singers. He mentioned, moreover, the
blind bard Philip, in an incident during the first rebellion
of the Serbs, and paid a tribute to the women of Serbia,
"faithful, industrious, domestic, brave, even to sharing in
the battles of their country". This author is not ignorant
of Bowring's translations and in order to illustrate "the
Homeric force, directness and *objectivity*" of the Serbian
original he gives, in addition to Bowring's work, two
"literal versions" which he rendered "in the unrhymed

trochaic metre of the original". The two ballads are *The Fatal Shot* and *The Bounden Brothers*, both translated from Mérimée's prose collection and inspired probably by W. Gerhard's German translations of Serbian popular songs. He knew that the second ballad was referred to by Leopold Ranke but, even at this late date, he was not aware that, among others, Ranke, too, was taken in by Mérimée. This ballad, however, was translated by this unknown author chiefly, as it appears, because of "its allusion to the custom of entering into bonds of brother-hood, one of the most singular institutions of the Servian people". Persons unite with one another in the name of God and St John, he quotes from Ranke, for mutual fidelity and aid during their whole lives. A man, it is con-sidered, will make the safest selection for his brother, in choosing one of whom he may at some time have dreamed that he had solicited assistance in some case of need. The allied designate themselves "brothers in God", "brothers by choice", *pobratimi*.

IV

The other champion of Serbian traditional poetry in English literature was Edward Robert Bulwer, first Earl of Lytton (1831–91), better known in literature under his pseudonym of Owen Meredith. He was a son of the well-known novelist, educated at Harrow and then privately at Bonn, and was a statesman and a poet. At the age of eighteen he accepted his uncle's offer to join him at Washington as an unpaid *attaché* and in October, 1850, he sailed for America. It was not until he reached the age of fifty that he settled again in his own country, except for a few holiday months. His uncle, Sir Henry Bulwer (1801–72), afterwards Lord Dalling, had some connection with Serbia in the course of his diplomatic career, while secretary to the Embassy and then Ambassador to the Porte (1858–65). From Washington, Robert Lytton went to Florence, the Hague and then to Vienna, whence he was sent to Belgrade in January, 1860, to take temporary charge of the Consulate. Serbia was being ruled for the second time by Prince Miloš Obrenović, whose character was full of interest to the young poet-diplomatist.

At this time his uncle was at Constantinople and was highly pleased with his nephew's despatches during his mission. In October of the same year he was again sent to Belgrade unexpectedly by the Foreign Office. It was immediately after the bombardment of Belgrade, and his mission to "keep the peace between the Turks and the Servians till the close of the Conference at Constantinople" was "highly commended" by the Embassy at Vienna and the Government at home.

The poetical outcome of his mission to Belgrade was his *Serbski Pesme, or National Songs of Servia*, published in 1861, under his pseudonym Owen Meredith, which he had assumed in 1855, and for the ballads he says, in the introduction to this collection, he was largely indebted to Monsieur Dozon's "able and interesting little work upon the poetry of the Serbs". It is, therefore, not correct to say that he "had forgotten to indicate his source", as V. M. Yovanovitch informs us, and that he passed it over in silence. It is, however, true that the introduction to these poems conveyed a misleading impression, because he spoke of the character of the Serbs and their poetry in such a way as to imply that he possessed both personal knowledge of the country and of the Serbian language, the latter of which he did not possess. He apologised soon afterwards, amply and chivalrously, first in a letter and then in the note to his *Servian imitations and phrases* attached at the end of his work *Orval*.

When his little volume appeared early in 1861, he was soon attacked "with vehemence, bordering on virulence", in the *Saturday Review* in March of the same year, by Lord Strangford, an able and competent linguist, though practically unknown during his life (d. 1869). He was a frequent contributor to some periodicals, but he published no books during his lifetime. Prince Lucien Bonaparte called him "a very distinguished linguist" and it is said, elsewhere, that he credited him with an acquaintance with Slav tongues. But whoever reads his review of Owen Meredith's *Serbski Pesme* would undoubtedly be impressed by how very well, and perhaps thoroughly, Lord Strangford must have known Serbian. Moreover, his *Occasional Notes upon Turkey* reveal his great knowledge of the political and social conditions in the Balkans and the much-discussed Eastern Question. His death was lamented by the *Saturday Review* (16th January, 1869), wherein he often wrote, and it is said in that number that he "knew the state of things in South-Eastern Europe better than any other man living".

In his introduction to the *National Songs of Servia*, Meredith said that in the poems no attempt had been made at accurate verbal translation from the original language and that they could not, indeed, be called translations in the strict sense of the word. He left it to the reader to

decide what they are. What they were intended to be was
nothing more than a rude medium through which to convey to other minds something of the impression made
upon his own mind by the poetry of a people amongst
whom literature was as yet unborn. He found this poetry
inferior to that of the Persians, inasmuch as it was less
intellectual, had less fancy, less wisdom and less art, but
that it was the "primitive *universality*" which gave to the
poetry of the Serbs its freshness and its force. And then,
amongst other things, he also mentions Monsieur Dozon,
"to whose able and interesting little work upon the
poetry of the Serbs" he was largely indebted and from
whose "excellent cricitism on the poetry of the Serbs" he
had "adopted many statements entirely confirmed" by
his own experience in the country. Lastly, he concluded
his introduction with the following passage, which left
him open to severe criticism: "I will only add of the contents of this little volume that, whether they be weeds or
wild flowers, I have at least gathered them on their native
soil, amidst the solitudes of the Carpathians, and along
the shores of the Danube".

Lord Strangford, considering it his bounden duty fully
to establish Meredith's ignorance of Serbian, opens his
criticism of Meredith's book with an ironical remark on
the wrongful wording of the title.

"It would appear", he says, "that when Mr Owen Meredith was in Serbia he lost no time in inquiring what was the
native name for Servian. He was told 'Serbski'. On asking
further what might be the Servian for 'poems' he was told
with equal correctness 'Pesme'. He then combined his information and the result of his research gleams before us all

over his gorgeous little volume....Its correctness, however, is equal to that of the words 'Latinus poemata' in Latin. 'Serbski' is a masculine singular and 'Pesme' is a feminine plural."

The correct title should be "Srpske Pesme".

This was not, however, the weakest spot that Lord Strangford had discovered in Meredith's collection. He concentrated his attack on the statement that the poems, whether they be weeds or wild flowers, had at least been gathered on their native soil. This pretty metaphor, Lord Strangford went on to say, did not indeed state directly that the poems were taken down by him from the mouths of Carpathian and Danubian bards. The point was guarded with sufficient dexterity and would meet the contingency of his having culled the flowers from the *hortus siccus* of M. Dozon, which was delightfully portable and may, or rather must, have formed part of his Carpathian travelling kit. Considering that the true seat of Serbian popular poetry was elsewhere, not in the range of the Carpathian mountains or along the shores of the Danube, he ironically remarks that Meredith had not the least occasion to go farther than his bookseller's shop, as all the songs, without one exception, were to be found in M. Dozon's excellent little work. Mr Meredith had transferred these to his own pages in a different order from that of M. Dozon, having first shuffled them elaborately like a pack of cards, and then dealt them out to the printer.

In comparing the two collections, one comes to the same conclusion as Lord Strangford. To begin with the introduction, in which Meredith gives a brief sketch of the Serbian people and their poetry, he undoubtedly borrowed freely from Dozon and Bowring, who again in their turn had borrowed, directly or indirectly, from Vuk's introduction to his own collection, to which, after all, everyone went, and still goes, for information. As to the manner in which Meredith executed his poetical versions, contrary to the French original, which is an excellently literal prose translation from the Serbian original, Meredith adopted a metrical version but, instead of adhering, like Bowring, to the long-drawn, uniform harmony of the familiar trochaic rhythm, he replaced it, in the words of Lord Strangford, "by a variety of tripping metres". Meredith rightly described Serbian popular ballads as especially "objective", meaning by this a poetry dealing with, not thoughts and feelings, but outward things. Yet by rejecting the trochaic rhythm Meredith, in the opinion of Lord Strangford, threw away the best garment that suits such a poetry. He even went still further and introduced abstract expressions of subjective and self-conscious modern poetry, things not only out of place but jarring when used to represent a vigorous popular poetry. So there is much truth in Lord Strangford's words that "they may be very pretty but they are not Servian"; it is equally true, however, to say that they do not lack Serb spirit entirely, but that what they do lack is simplicity, both of exposition and of verse. The very skilful and elaborate versification of Owen Meredith is antagonistic to the Serbian popular ballads.

Lord Strangford's criticism followed rapidly upon the heels of an accusation of plagiarism in the *Literary Gazette* of March, 1861. Here it was stated that his *Lucila*, in so far as regards Part I of that poem, was beyond a doubt nothing more than *Lavinia* by George Sand, published in 1844. The critic ironically asked whether Mr Owen Meredith's "Songs of Servia", which he had been preparing for publication, would prove to be a translation from Bérenger. Hardly two months had elapsed since Lord Strangford's criticism, when *Chambers's Journal* published (25th May) an article, the "Songs of Servia", in which Owen Meredith's *Serbski Pesme* were referred to once more. "This prince of plagiarists" rightly called himself *Owen*, since he *borrowed* so largely, but in his rage for plagiarism he adopted the title of another writer, George Meredith, who must have felt rather uncomfortable "at this continual calling out of 'stop thief'". The critic says, however, that O. Meredith, notwithstanding his obligations to Dozon and to Bowring, had plenty of natural talent and excessive adaptability of mind. But he adds ironically that this last gift had been the main cause of his divergence from the legitimate road,

just as litheness of limb and nimble fingers too often tempt the Whitechapel (*sic*) into pocket-picking. He is keen to catch not only the meaning, however hidden and subtle, of a writer, but his very spirit. This faculty especially qualifies Mr Meredith for the work of translation; and his *Songs of Servia* are a pleasing proof of what he can do, even with somewhat barren materials.

In conclusion a few heroic songs on the battle of Kosovo are quoted, as well as one of the women's songs, in Meredith's translations.

As Lord Lytton himself admitted in a letter, Lord Strangford's attack alone would not have done much harm, but, taken with the preceding onslaught, it had

proved most injurious. At the same time he considered
this criticism quite justifiable, for he admitted that his
preface to the Servian poems, very hurriedly written, had
been ill considered, reckless and so far charlatanic in that,
although it recorded his acknowledgment of Dozon's
book and openly referred the reader thereto, an idea was
suggested which he had not really intended to convey,
namely that the poems were the result of personal dis-
covery on the spot and that he appeared to assert a knowledge of the language which he did not possess. He concluded that "any amount of hard hitting, therefore, on
that blot was fair play".

Owen Meredith apologised fully in 1869, when his
collection of the *National Songs of Servia* was reprinted as
the last part of *Orval*, preceded by the motto *Omne meum :
nihil meum*. In his Note, which Lord Strangford did not
live long enough to see, Lord Lytton paid first a high
tribute to Strangford's knowledge of the languages, the
literature and the social life of the East and then went on
to say that the Serbian ballads he had published in 1861
were neither translations nor paraphrases—strictly speaking not even imitations, "for they attempt neither the
imitation of Servian metres, nor the treatment of subject
in purely Servian forms, nor even the faithful expression
of purely Servian sentiment". In fact, they represented
nothing more than the result of a passing wish to embody
in forms of his own the personal impressions made upon
himself by the popular poetry of a people amongst whom
he had lived when they had been written. He sincerely
deplored that he had conveyed, "in that unlucky preface",
to the mind of his accomplished critic an impression that

he intended to pass off his own verses as derived from original sources and as translated by himself from the recitation of the native singers. He had intended nothing of the kind. All he meant to imply was that his verses "had been prompted, and were characterised, by the local influences of a period passed in contemplation of much of the scenery to which they often refer and in personal contact with the people from whose history, habits and sentiments" the subjects of them were derived.

In short, the publication of these ballads was occasioned only by a belief that "the freshness of impressions, thus directly received, might possibly have imparted to them some of the qualities which ought to be found in original verse". He pointed further to a merit which belonged to accurate translation and to a merit which belonged to spiritual paraphrase, and he said there was yet another kind of merit, belonging neither to the one nor to the other "in the vividness in which a writer may succeed in imparting to the minds of his readers sensations added to the stock of his own individuality by contact with a literature embodying the thoughts and fancies of an experience unfamiliar to himself and to his countrymen". It was the attainment of this kind of merit which was aimed at in the *Serbski Pesme*. He also repeated on this occasion that he was greatly indebted both to Dozon's book and to his personal assistance in giving him information about a country in which he had long resided, although as to the composition of those versions of Serbian songs he also had received assistance from others of his acquaintance in that country. However, he admitted that had he never been to Serbia those verses would never have been written.

V

Between the publication of O. Meredith's *Serbski Pesme*
and the 'seventies, Serbian poetry appears to have been
entirely forgotten. It is true that owing to Serbia's
political and economic development a number of political
articles on Serbia was published, but none except the one
in the *Quarterly Review* for January, 1865, touches the
subject of the songs. In the 'seventies, especially during
the few years prior to the Congress of Berlin—during the
war between Serbia and Russia on the one side and
Turkey on the other—the "National Poetry of Servia"
again became the subject of articles published in *All the
Year Round* for November, 1875, *Temple Bar* for November,
1876, *Macmillan's Magazine* for January, 1877, *Westminster
and Foreign Quarterly Review* for April, 1878 and in the
Dublin University Magazine for September, 1879. On account
of Great Britain's Turkophil, or rather her Russophobe
policy, the editors of *Temple Bar* thought it necessary to
add a footnote to the article on "The Poetry of Servia",
in which they say that this interesting paper was inserted
without endorsing its political tendency. It is of interest
to point to the few traditional songs quoted in this article
from Bowring's and Meredith's translations respectively.
Its author, who had travelled in Dalmatia six months before,
also gives an interesting description of a Montenegrin
wandering professional minstrel whom he had heard
chant some heroic songs. He, like the author of the
article "The Literatures of the Servians and the Croats",
published in the *Westminster and Foreign Quarterly Review*,
is full of praise for the traditional songs. In publishing his

article the author's aim was also to show to his own people, some of whom had said that this branch of the Slavonic family was absolutely without culture, that the Serbs are not an uncivilised "nation of pork-butchers", for their traditional songs "are exquisite and show great refinement of feeling". In speaking of foreign translations of Serbian songs, he criticised those of both Bowring and Meredith. Those of the former were "diffuse and inaccurate", the latter's were "carelessly executed and utterly false to the spirit of the original".

The Serbian songs are not less praised in an article published in the *Dublin University Magazine* by Kate Freiligrath Kroeker. She deals chiefly with "short lyrics", which she finds of "unexpected beauty, pathos and tender grace". She gives fourteen songs in an English translation. On comparing them with the corresponding songs in Talvj's collection and with the original, one is easily convinced that she had translated them from the German.

In an article about "Marco Kraljevitch: the mythical hero of Servia", published in *Macmillan's Magazine*, 1877, about 270 lines are quoted in English from various heroic songs about Marko.

Before the close of the nineteenth century, only one more reference to Serbian traditional poetry is to be found, in spite of the publication of a considerable number of books and articles on the Serbs and their lands. They are mentioned by J. D. Bourchier in his article "The Great Servian Festival", published in the *Fortnightly Review* for August, 1889.

Perhaps we should mention yet another collection of Serbian heroic songs, published in London in 1881. This is entitled *Kossovo*, by Elodie Lawton Mijatovich. Mme Mijatovich was an Englishwoman and wife of M. Cedo Mijatovich, Minister Plenipotentiary of Serbia to the Court of St James's for many years. As the title itself shows, her collection deals with one particular event of Serbian history. She herself calls it "an attempt to bring Serbian national songs into one poem", and in this way resembles similar attempts which have already been mentioned. Mme Mijatovich relied on A. Pavić's book, *National Poems about the Battle of Kossovo*, already mentioned, and adhered as strictly as possible to the originals, desiring to give simply a literal translation of the Kosovo cycle. She devotes about fifty pages to an introduction in which she tries to show how the battle of Kosovo is recorded both in history and in the heroic songs. Among the fourteen songs there is also the remarkable one about *Banović Strahinja*, omitted from most other collections of Kosovo songs.

Books Consulted

I. BIBLIOGRAPHICAL WORKS

List of Works in the New York Public Library, relating to folk-songs, folk-music, ballads, etc.

Polybiblion, Revue bibliographique universelle. Paris, 1868 et seq.

Catalogue Général de la Librairie française, rédigé par Otto Lorenz.

Essai de Bibliographie française sur les Serbes et les Croates, 1544–1900, par N. S. Petrović. Édition de l'Académie Royale de Serbie, Belgrade, 1900.

Essay on French, English and German bibliography concerning Serbia and the Serbs, by Ivan Ivanitch. London, 1907.

Essai de Bibliographie française de la Littérature Yougoslave, par Pavle Popović et Miodrag Ibrovac. Le Monde Slave, tome II, mai, 1931, Paris.

Essai de Bibliographie française sur les Serbes, Croates et Slovènes depuis le commencement de la guerre actuelle. Paris, 1918.

An English Bibliography on the Near Eastern Question, 1481–1906, by Voyslav M. Yovanovitch. Belgrade, 1909.

Bibliographie der deutschen Zeitschriften-Literatur. Bd. I, Bd. II. Leipzig, 1896, 1899.

Srpska Bibliografija za noviju književnost, 1741–1867, compiled by Stojan Novaković. Belgrade, 1869 (in Cyrillic).

Bibliografija hrvatske i srpske narodne pjesme, by J. Milaković. Sarajevo, 1919.

II. GENERAL

ANONYMOUS. The Fairy Mythology. 2 vols. 1828.

ANONYMOUS. Südslavische Wanderungen im Sommer 1850. 2 vols. Leipzig, 1853.

ARBUTHNOT, G. Herzegovina or Omer Pacha and the Christian Rebels, with a brief account of Servia, its social, political and financial conditions. London, 1862.

ARSENÉV, S. V. "Khozhdenie Ignatiya Smoliyanina, 1389–1405". Pravoslavni Palestinsky Sbornik, tome IV. S. Petersburg, 1887.

ASBÓTH, JÁNOS. An official tour through Bosnia and Herzegovina, with an account of the history, antiquities, agrarian conditions, religion, ethnology, folk-lore and social life. London, 1890.

AVRIL, ADOLPHE D'. La Bataille de Kossovo: Rhapsodie Serbe, tirée des chants populaires et traduite en français. Paris, 1868.

BALFOUR, LADY BETTY. Personal and Literary Letters of Robert, First Earl of Lytton. 2 vols. London, 1906.

BAYNES, NORMAN. The Byzantine Empire. London, 1925.

BEHRNAUER, W. F. A. Quellen für Serbische Geschichte. Aus Türkischen Urkunden im Originaltext redigirt und in's Deutsche übertragen. In das Serbische übersetzt und herausgegeben von A. T. Berlić. Wien, 1857.

BÖCKEL, OTTO. Psychologie der Volksdichtung. Leipzig, 1913.

BOGIŠIĆ, VALTAZAR. Narodne pjesme iz starih, najviše primorskih zapisa. Biograd, 1878 (in Cyrillic).

BOWRING, JOHN. Narodne Srpske Pjseme. Servian Popular Poetry. Translated. London, 1827.

BRINK, BERNHARD TEN. Early English Literature, translated from the German by H. M. Kennedy. 3 vols. London, 1883–96.

BROCKELMANN, C. VON. Geschichte der arabischen Literatur. Leipzig, 1901.

BRUTUS, STEPHANUS JUNIUS. A Defence of Liberty against Tyrants. A translation (by W. Walker) of the Vindiciae contra Tyrannos. London, 1924.

BRYANT, FRANK EGBERT. A History of English Balladry and other studies. Boston, 1913.

BURY, J. B. Romances of Chivalry on Greek Soil. Oxford, 1911.

BUSBEQUIUS, AUGERIUS GISLENIUS (Seigneur de Busbecq). Travels into Turkey, translated from the Original Latin. Glasgow, 1761.

CARRÉ, JEAN-MARIE. Goethe en Angleterre. Étude de littérature comparée. Paris, 1920.

CHADWICK, MUNRO H. The Heroic Age. Cambridge, 1912.

CHALCOCONDYLAS, LAONICUS. L'Histoire de la decadence de l'Empire grec, et establissement de celuy des Turcs; comprise par Nicolas Chalcondyle Athenien. Paris, 1584.

CHILD, FRANCIS JAMES. The English and Scottish Popular Ballads. 5 vols. Boston and New York, 1882–98.

—— English and Scottish Popular Ballads. Cambridge Edition, edited by Helen Child Sargent and George Lyman Kittredge. London, 1904.

CHODŽKO, ALEXANDER. Specimens of the Popular Poetry of Persia. Orally collected and translated. London, 1842.

CHOPIN, M. Histoire et description de tous les peuples. Provinces Danubiennes et Roumaines. Bosnie, Servie, Herzégovine, Bulgarie, Slavonie, Illyrie, Croatie, Dalmatie, Monténégro, Albanie. Paris, 1856.

CLARKE, A. BUTLER. Spanish Literature. An elementary handbook. London, 1893.

COLONNA, M. Contes de la Bosnie. Paris, 1898.

ĆURČIN, MILAN. Das serbische Volkslied in der deutschen Literatur. Leipzig, 1905.

CURIPESCHITZ, BENEDICT. Itinerarium der Botschaftsreise des Josef von Lamberg und Niclas Jurischitz durch Bosnien, Serbien, Bulgarien nach Konstantinopel, 1530. Aus einer gleichzeitigen Handschrift neuherausgegeben von Eleonore Gräfin Lamberg-Schwarzenberg. Innsbruck, 1910.

CYRILLE. Voyage sentimental dans les pays Slaves. Dalmatie — Monténégro — Herzégovine — Croatie — Serbie — Bulgarie — Galicie — Bohême — Slovénie. Paris, 1876. ("Cyrille" was a pseudonym of Baron Adolphe d'Avril.)

DENTON, THE REV. W. Servia and the Servians. London, 1862.

DIETERICH, KARL. Geschichte der byzantinischen und neugriechischen Litteratur. Leipzig, 1902.

DIXON, W. MACNEILE. English Epic and Heroic Poetry. London, 1912.

DOZON, AUGUSTE. Poésies populaires serbes traduites sur les originaux avec une introduction et des notes. Paris, 1859.

—— L'Épopée Serbe, chants populaires héroïques. Paris, 1888.

DUCAS, MICHAEL. Histoire des Empereurs Jean, Manuel, Jean, et Constantine Palaeologues. Paris, 1672.

—— Michaelis Ducae Nepotis, Historia Byzantina. Recognovit et interprete italo addito supplevit Immanuel Bekkerus. Bonnae, 1834.

EDWARDS, GEORGE WHARTON. A book of Old English Ballads. Introduction by Hamilton W. Mabie. New York, 1896.

ENGEL, JOHANN CHRISTIAN VON. Fortsetzung der Algemeinen Welthistorie der neuern Zeiten durch eine Gesellschaft von Gelehrten in Teutschland und England ausgefertigt. Ein und dreyzigster Theil, 2. Band: Geschichte von Dalmatien. Halle, 1797.

—— Geschichte des Freystaates Ragusa. Wien, 1807.

FARRER, J. A. Literary Forgeries. London, 1907.

FORSTER, CHARLES THORNTON. The Life and Letters of Ogier Ghiselin de Busbecq, Seigneur of Bousbecque, Knight, Imperial Ambassador. 2 vols. London, 1881.

FORSYTH, WILLIAM. The Slavonic provinces south of the Danube. London, 1876.

FORTIS, ALBERTO. Viaggio in Dalmazia. 2 vols. Venezia, 1774.

—— Travels into Dalmatia. London, 1778.

—— Saggio d'osservazioni sopra l'isola di Cherso ed Osero. Venezia, 1771.

FRANKL, LUDWIG AUGUST. Gusle. Serbische Nationallieder. Wien, 1852.

GARDNER, EDMUND G. The Arthurian Legend in Italian Literature. London, 1930.

GAYANGOS, PASCUAL DE. Translation of the History of the Mohammedan Dynasties in Spain by Ahmed ibn Mohammed Al-wakkari. 2 vols. London, 1840.

GERLACH, STEPHAN. Stephan Gerlachs dess Aeltern Tage-Buch, etc. Franckfurth am Mayn, 1674.

GESEMANN, GERHARD. Erlangenski Rukopis starih srpskohrvatskih narodnih pesama. (Zbornik Srpske Kraljevske Akademije knjiga, XII.) Sr. Karlovci, 1925 (in Cyrillic).

—— Studien zur südslavischen Volksepik. Reichenberg, 1926.

GIBB, E. G. A History of Ottoman Poetry. 6 vols. London, 1900–9.

GOETZE, P. VON. Serbische Volkslieder in's Deutsche übertragen. St Petersburg-Leipzig, 1827.

GONZALEZ DE CLAVIJO, RUY. Narrative of the Embassy of Ruy Gonzalez de Clavijo to the court of Timur at Samarcand, A.D.1403–6. Translated by Clements R. Markham. London, 1859. (The original was published in 1582 in Seville.)

—— Historia del gran Tamorlan. Madrid, 1782.

ÐORÐEVIĆ, TIH. Naš Narodni Život. Vols. I–V. Beograd.

GRIMM, W. C. Altdänische Heldenlieder, Balladen und Märchen übersetzt. Heidelberg, 1811.

GRÖBER, CARL. Der Königssohn Marko (Kraljević Marko) im Serbischen Volksgesang. Wien, 1883.

—— Die Schlacht am Amselfelde (Kosovo, 1389). Epische Dichtung mit Benützung von Bruchstücken Serbischer Volkspoesie. Wien, 1885.

GRUNDTVIG, SVEND. Dänische Volkslieder der Vorzeit. Aus der Sammlung von Svend Grundtvig. Translated by Rosa Warrens. Hamburg, 1858.

GUMMERE, F. B. Old English Ballads. Boston, 1894.

—— The Beginnings of Poetry. New York, 1901.

—— The Popular Ballad. Boston and New York, 1907.

HART, WALTER MORRIS. Ballad and Epic. A Study in the Development of the Narrative Art. (Studies and Notes in Philology and Literature, vol. XI.) Boston, 1907.

HAUFFEN, WOLFGANG. Das serbische Volkslied in der tschechischen Literatur. Reichenberg, 1928.

HENDERSON, T. F. The Ballad in Literature. Cambridge, 1912.

HERDER, Johann Gottfried von. Volkslieder. 2 vols. Leipzig, 1778–9.

HÖRMAN, KOSTA. Narodne pjesme Muhamedovaca u Bosni i Herzegovini. Sarajevo, 1888–9.

JAVORIN, VON. Stephan Duschan. Ein Guslar Poem aus dem Serbischen übersetzt. Berlin, 1857.

JIREČEK, CONSTANTIN. Geschichte der Serben. 2 vols. Gotha, 1911, 1918. (Allgemeine Staatengeschichte, herausgegeben von Karl Lamprecht.)

JUKIĆ, IVAN FRANJO, i HERCEGOVAC, LJUBOMIR. Narodne Pjesme bosanske i hercegovačke. Osjek, 1858.

KAČIĆ MIOŠIĆ, A. Razgovor ugodni Naroda slovinskog. Zagreb, 1846.

KAPPER, SIEGFRIED. Die Slavische Melodien. Leipzig, 1852.

KARADŽIĆ, VUK STEFANOVIĆ. Srpske narodne pjesme. Beograd, 1891–1902. State edition in 9 vols. (in Cyrillic).

KELLY, JAMES FITZMAURICE. A New History of Spanish Literature. London, 1926.

KER, W. P. Epic and Romance. Essays on Mediaeval Literature. London, 1908.

—— "On the History of the Ballads 1100–1500." Proceedings of the British Academy, vol. IV. London, 1909.

KNOLLES, RICHARD. The General History of the Turks. London, 1603.

KOVAČEVIĆ, LJ. Vuk Branković. Beograd, 1888 (in Cyrillic).

KOWALSKY, H. Ukrainian Folk Songs. Boston, 1925.

KRAUSS, FRIEDRICH S. Slavische Volksforschungen. Leipzig, 1908.

KRUMBACHER, KARL. Geschichte der byzantinischen Literatur von Justinian bis zum Ende des oströmischen Reiches, 527–1453 München, 1897.

KURELAC, FRAN. Jačke ili narodne pěsme. Zagreb, 1871.

LAMARTINE, M. ALPHONSE DE. Souvenirs, impressions, pensées et paysages pendant un voyage en Orient 1832–1833, ou Notes d'un Voyageur. 4 vols. Paris, 1835.

LAVALLÉE, JOSEPH. Voyage pittoresque et historique de l'Istrie et de la Dalmatie. (Rédigé d'après l'itinéraire de L. F. Cassas.) Paris, 1801. (An English edition of this book appeared in 1805 in the collection of Modern and Contemporary Voyages and Travels, vol. I.)

LÉGER, LOUIS. Les Anciennes Civilisations Slaves. Collection Payot. Paris, 1921.

—— Serbes, Croates et Bulgares. Paris, 1913.

LEVY, PAUL. Geschichte des Begriffes Volkslied. Berlin, 1911. (Acta Germanica, Bd. VII.)

LEWIS, M. G. Tales of Wonder. 2 vols. London, 1801.

—— The Monk. A Romance in 3 vols. London, 1796.

LOW, D. H. The Ballads of Marko Kraljević. Cambridge, 1922.

LUCCARI, GIACOMO. Copioso Ristretto degli Annali di Rausa, libri quattro. Venetia, 1605.

LUCIO, GIOVANI. Joannis Lucii de regno Dalmatiae et Croatiae, libri sex (Presbyteri Diocleatis Regnum Slavorum). Amstelaedami, 1666.

MACPHERSON, JAMES. Fragments of Ancient Poetry, a reprint of the first edition of 1760. Edinburgh, 1917.

MANOJLOVIĆ, SVETOZAR. Serbische Frauenlieder. Eisenstadt, 1882.

—— Serbisch-Kroatische Dichtungen. Wien, 1888.

MARETIĆ, TOMISLAV. Naša Narodna Epika. Zagreb, 1909.

MARJANOVIĆ, LUKA. Hrvatske Narodne Pjesme. Sakupila i izdala Matica Hrvatska. Junačke Pjesme (Muhamedovske). Knj. 3 i 4. Zagreb, 1898.

MARMIER, XAVIER. Lettres sur l'Adriatique et le Monténégro. 2 vols. Paris, 1853.

MARTINEGO-CESARESCO, E. Essays in the study of Folk-Songs. London, 1914.

MENÉNDEZ Y PELAYO, D. MARCELINO. Romances viejos castellanos. (Primavera y flor de romances.) Publicada con una introducción y notas por D. Fernando José Wolf y D. Conrado Hofman. 3 vols. Madrid, 1899.

—— Tratado de los romances viejos. 2 vols. Madrid, 1903.

MENÉNDEZ PIDAL, RAMÓN. El romancero español. (The Hispanic Society of America.) New York, 1910.

MEREDITH, OWEN. Serbski Pesme, or National Songs of Servia. London, 1861.

—— Orval, or the Fool of Time. London, 1869.

—— The National Songs of Servia. Boston, 1877.

MÉRIMÉE, ERNEST. A History of Spanish Literature. London, 1931.

MÉRIMÉE, PROSPER. La Guzla, ou choix de poésies illyriques recueillies dans la Dalmatie, la Bosnie, la Croatie et l'Herzégowine. Paris, 1827.

—— Chronique du règne de Charles IX suivie de la Double Méprise et de la Guzla. Paris, 1847.

MICKIEWICZ, ADAM. Les Slaves. Cours professé au Collège de France, 1840–1841, et publié d'après les notes sténographiées. 4 vols. Paris, 1849.

MIJATOVICH, ELODIE LAWTON. Kossovo. An attempt to bring Serbian National songs about the fall of the Serbian Empire at the battle of Kossovo into one poem. London, 1881.

MIKLOSICH, FRANZ. Über Goethe's "Klaggesang von der Edlen Frauen des Asan Aga". Wien, 1883.

MILADINOFF, DIMITAR i KONSTANTIN. Blgarski Narodni Pjesni. Zagreb, 1861.

MÜGGE, MAXIMILIAN A. Serbian Folk Songs, Fairy Tales and Proverbs. London, 1916.

MURKO, MATTHIAS. Geschichte der älteren südslawischen Litteraturen. Leipzig, 1908.

—— "Bericht über eine Bereisung von Nordwestbosnien und der angrenzenden Gebiete von Kroatien und Dalmatien behufs Erforschung der Volksepik der bosnischen

Muhamedaner." Sitzungsberichte der Kais. Akademie der Wissenschaften in Wien, Philosophisch-historische Klasse, Bd. 173, Abhandlung 3, 1913.

MURKO, MATTHIAS. "Bericht über eine Reise zum Studium der Volksepik in Bosnien und Herzegovina im Jahre 1913." Sitzungsberichte der Kais. Akademie der Wissenschaften in Wien, Philosophisch-historische Klasse, Bd. 176, Abhandlung 2, 1915.

—— La poésie populaire épique en Yougoslavie au début du XXe siècle (Travaux publiés par l'Institut d'études slaves.—x). Paris, 1929.

NEIGEBAUER, J. F. Die Süd-Slaven und deren Länder in Beziehung auf Geschichte, Kultur und Verfassung. Leipzig, 1851.

NICHOLSON, R. A. A Literary History of the Arabs. Cambridge, 1930.

—— Studies in Islamic Poetry. Cambridge, 1921.

NIEDERLE, LUBOR. La Race Slave. Paris, 1911.

—— Manuel de l'Antiquité Slave. Paris, 1923.

NOVAKOVIĆ, S. Kosovo. Srpske narodne pesme o boju na Kosovu. Epski raspored Stojana Novakovića i drugih. Beograd, 1906 (in Cyrillic).

NOYES, GEORGE RAPALL and LEONARD BACON. Heroic Ballads of Servia. Translated into English verse. Boston, 1913.

ORBINI. Il Regno de gli Slavi, etc. Pesaro, 1601.

PATON, ANDREW ARCHIBALD. Servia, the Youngest Member of the European Family. London, 1845.

—— Researches on the Danube and the Adriatic. 2 vols. Leipzig, 1861. (This work includes the above mentioned.)

PATTERSON, ROBERT STEWART. Romanian Songs and Ballads. London, 1919.

PAVIĆ, ARMIN. Narodne pjesme o boju na Kosovu, godine 1389. Zagreb, 1877.

PETRANOVIĆ, BOGOLJUB. Srpske narodne pjesme iz Bosne i Hercegovine. Epske pjesme starijeg vremena. Beograd, 1867 (in Cyrillic).

POPOVIĆ, PAVLE. Pregled srpske književnosti. Beograd, 1913 (in Cyrillic).

—— Iz Književnosti. Vol. III. Beograd, 1926 (in Cyrillic).

POUND, LOUISE. Poetic Origins and the Ballad. New York, 1921.

PRODANOVIČ, J. M. Ženske narodne pesme. Antologija. Beograd, 1925 (in Cyrillic).

PUSHKIN, ALEXANDER. Pesni zapadnykh slavyan. Sochineinya. Vol. II. Petersburg, 1859.

PYPIN, A. N. and SPASOVIČ, V. D. Geschichte der Slavischen Literaturen. Leipzig, 1880–4.

RAMBAUD, ALFRED. La Russie Épique, étude sur les chansons héroïques de la Russie. Paris, 1876.

REDHOUSE, J. W. On the History, System and Varieties of Turkish Poetry. London, 1879.

REINACH, J. La Serbie et le Monténégro. Paris, 1876.

ROBERT, CYPRIEN M. Les Slaves de Turquie, Serbes, Monténégrins, Bosniaques, Albanais et Bulgares. Paris, 1844.

—— Le Monde Slave. 2 vols. Paris, 1852.

ROLLINS, HYDER E. Old English Ballads, 1553–1625. Cambridge, 1920.

—— Cavalier and Puritan Ballads and Broadsides illustrating the period of the Great Rebellion 1640–1660. New York, 1923.

ROOTHAM, HELEN. Kossovo. Heroic Songs of the Serbs, translated from the original. Oxford, 1920.

SCHURÉ, ÉDOUARD. Histoire du Lied ou la Chanson populaire en Allemagne. Paris, 1903.

SETON-WATSON, R. W. Serbian Ballads. Published by the Kossovo Day Committee. London, 1916.

SIDGWICK, FRANK. The Ballad. London, 1915.

SIMMONS, LUCRETIA VAN TUYL. Goethe's lyric poems in English translation prior to 1860. Madison, 1919.

SLAWIJKOFF, P. Bulgarische Volkslieder, übertragen von Georg Adam. Leipzig, 1919.

—— The Shade of the Balkans: being a collection of Bulgarian folk-songs and proverbs, here for the first time rendered into English, together with an essay on Bulgarian popular poetry. London, 1904.

SMITH-DAMPIER, E. M. Danish Ballads. Cambridge, 1920.

STANOJEVIĆ, STANOJE. Vizantija i Srbi. 2 vols. Novi Sad, Matica Srbska, 1903 (in Cyrillic).

STEFANOVIĆ, S. Legenda o zidanju Skadra. Beograd, 1928 (in Cyrillic).

STOJANOVIČ, LJ. Život i Rad Vuka Stef. Karadžića. Beograd, 1924 (in Cyrillic).

STOJKOVIČ, S. J. Kosovska Epopeja. Pregled pokušaja za sastav narodnog epa o boju na Kosovu. Beograd, 1901 (in Cyrillic).

STRANGFORD, THE VISCOUNTESS. The Eastern Shores of the Adriatic in 1863, with a visit to Montenegro. London, 1864.

—— A Selection from the writings of Viscount Strangford on political, geographical and social subjects. 2 vols. London, 1869.

—— Original letters and papers of the late Viscount Strangford upon philological and kindred subjects. London, 1878.

SZYRMA, K. Letters, Literary and Political, on Poland; comprising observations on Russia and other Sclavonian nations and tribes. Edinburgh, 1823.

ŠREPEL, M. Akcent i metar junačkih narodnih pjesama. Agram, 1886.

ŠTREKELJ, K. Slovenske Narodne Pesmi. 3 vols. Ljubljana, 1895–8, 1900–6.

TAILLANDIER, SAINT-RENÉ. La Serbie, Kara-George et Milosch. Paris, 1872.

TALVJ. Volkslieder der Serben, metrisch übersetzt und historisch eingeleitet. 2 vols. Halle u. Leipzig, 1835. Second enlarged edition, Leipzig, 1853.

—— Versuch einer geschichtlichen Charakteristik der Volkslieder germanischer Nationen mit einer Uebersicht der Lieder aussereuropäischer Völkerschaften. Leipzig, 1840.

—— Historical view of the languages and literatures of the Slavic nations with a sketch of their popular poetry. New York, 1850.

THOMAS, HENRY. Spanish and Portuguese Romances of Chivalry. Cambridge, 1920.

THOMSON, GASTON. L'Herzégovine. Paris, 1875.

TICKNOR, GEORGE. History of Spanish literature. Boston, 1872.

TOMIĆ, J. Boj na Kosovu. Novi Sad, 1908 (in Cyrillic).

TONNELAT, ERNEST. Les Frères Grimm. Leur œuvre de jeunesse. Paris, 1912.

TORBARINA, JOSIP. Italian Influence on the poets of the Ragusan Republic. London, 1931.

VASILJEVIČ, JOV. HADZI. Muslimani naše krvi u Južnoj Srbiji. Beograd, 1924.

VERKOVIČ, STEFAN I. Narodne pesme Makedonski Bugara. Beograd, 1860 (in Cyrillic).

VILLARI, LUIGI. The Republic of Ragusa. London, 1904.

VODNIK, BRANKO. Narodne Pjesme hrvatsko-srpske. Zagreb, 1918.

VOGL, JOHANN NEP. Marko Kraljević. Serbische Heldensage. Wien, 1851.

VOIART, ÉLISE. Chants populaires des Serviens, recueillis par Wuk Stéphanovitsch et traduits, d'après Talvj. 2 vols. Paris, 1834.

VRČEVIĆ, V. S. Hercegovačke narodne pesme (koje samo Srbi Muhamedove vjere pjevaju). Dubrovnik, 1890.

WATT, L. M. The Scottish Ballads and Ballad Writing. London, 1923.

WHITTE, JAMES. A visit to Belgrade. (Translations from
S. Kapper's Südslavische Wanderungen.) London, 1854.

WÜSCHER, GOTTLIEB. Der Einfluss der englischen Balladen-
poesie auf die französische Litteratur, von Percy's
Reliques of Ancient English Poetry bis zu De la Ville-
marque's Barzaz-Breiz, 1765–1840. Trogan, 1891.

WYNNE, JUSTINE, COMTESSE DES URSINS ET ROSENBERG. Les
Morlaques. 2 vols. 1788. Printed privately.

YOVANOVITCH, VOYSLAV, M. "La Guzla" de Prosper Mérimée.
Paris, 1911.

III. PERIODICALS

Archiv für Slavische Philologie, Berlin:

Bd. III, 1879, Novaković, St., "Die serbischen Volkslieder über die Kosovo-Schlacht"; also "Ein Beitrag
zur Literatur der serbischen Volkspoesie".

Bd. IV, 1880, Jagić, V., "Die südslavische Volksepik
vor Jahrhunderten".

Bd. V, 1881, Jagić, V., "Kraljević Marko kurz skizzirt
nach der serbischen Volksdichtung"; also Wesselofsky,
A., "Die Rolandsage in Ragusa".

Bd. IX, 1886, Wollner, W., "Untersuchungen über den
Versbau der südslavischen Volkslieder"; also Novaković,
St., "Über die Entstehung mancher Volkslieder".

Bd. XIII, 1891, Jagić, V., "Aus dem Leben der serbischen Volksepik".

Bd. XIV, 1892; Bd. XV, 1893; Bd. XVI, 1894; Bd. XVII,
1895; Bd. XX, 1898, Soerensen, Asmus, "Beitrag zur
Geschichte der Entwickelung der serbischen Heldendichtung".

Bd. XXVIII, 1906, Maretić, T., "Prosper Mérimées
Mystifikation Kroatischer Volkslieder".

Bd. XXXVI, 1915, Simonović, Mirko, "Beitrag zu einer
Untersuchung über einige der deutschen und serbischen
Heldendichtung gemeinsame Motive".

Bd. XXXVIII, 1923, Gesemann, G., "Die Asanaginica
im Kreise ihrer Varianten".

The Biblical Repository, conducted by E. Robinson, Nos. xiv, xv, 1834, New York, "Historical view of the Slavic language in its various dialects".

Bibliothèque universelle des sciences, belles-lettres et arts, faisant suite à la Bibliothèque Britannique, XIVme année, tome xl, Genève, Paris, 1829, A. P., "Volkslieder der Serben par Talvj".

Brastvo, iii, 1889, Beograd, Đorđević, P. P., "Kratak pregled srpskih narodnih pesama".

The British and Foreign Review or European Quarterly Review, vol. xii, No. xxiv, 1841, 1. "Die serbische Revolution; aus serbischen Papieren und Mitteilungen von Leopold Ranke (The Servian Revolution, from papers and oral communications)"; 2. "Serbiens Neuzeit von Emanuel Thal (The Regeneration of Servia)".

Le Catholique, tome i, No. 2; tome ii, No. 6, 1826, "Chants du peuple serbe".

Chambers's Edinburgh Journal, vol. iii, May, 1845, "The Servians and their songs"; Chambers's Journal, vol. iii, May, 1855, "The Slavonic races"; vol. iv, August, 1855, "The Servians"; September, 1855, "Servian Ballads"; vol. xv, May, 1861, "The Songs of Servia'.

Le Correspondant, tome iii, 1843, Paris, "Les chrétiens en Bulgarie et en Bosnie".

Dublin University Magazine, May, 1854, "Wanderings in Servia"; October, November, December, 1876, January, 1877, "Servia and the Slavs"; September, 1879, "The National Poetry of Servia", by Kate Freiligrath Kroeker.

The Foreign Quarterly Review, vol. ii, No. iv, Paris, 1827, "La Guzla ou Choix de Poésie Illyrique...".

Glasnik Srpskog Učenog Društva, knj. 75, 1892, Belgrade, "August Dozon od Stojana Boškovića".

Jahresberichte für neuere deutsche Litteraturgeschichte, 1890, Schischmanov, J. D., "Lenorenstoff in der bulgarischen Volkspoesie".

Journal des Savants, 1886, "Le chant populaire du frère mort", par N. G. Politis, Athènes, 1885.

The London Magazine, vol. VII, April, 1824, "Servian Popular Poetry". (A review of John Bowring's book.)

Mitteilungen der schlesischen Gesellschaft für Volkskunde, Bd. VI, 1907, Heft XII, Nehring, W., "Die slovenischen Volkslieder"; Bd. IX, Heft XVII, Nehring, W., "Serbische Volkslieder insbesondere serbische Volksepik".

The Modern Language Review, vol. XIII, No. 1, January 1923, "Goethe's lyric poems in English translation", by H. D. Fiedler.

Modern Philology, vol. XXI, August, 1923, "The Making of Ballads", by Gordon Hall Gerould.

The Monthly Review, November, 1827, "The Guzla, a selection of Illyrian Poetry".

The North American Review, vol. XLIII, 1836, Boston, "Narodne Serpske pjesme, izdao Wuk Stef. Karadjich" (Servian Popular Songs, published by Vuk Stef. Karadjich), vol. IV, Vienna, 1833.

La Nouvelle Revue, tome trentième, 1884, "Mœurs et chants de Bosnie et d'Herzégovine", par E. de Sainte-Marie.

Nova Evropa, Br. 3, March, 1930, Zagreb, Subotić, D., "Jugosloveni u službi španskih Arapa".

The Quarterly Review, vol. XXXV, January, 1827, London, "Translations from the Servian Minstrelsy: to which are added some specimens of Anglo-Norman Romances, London, 1826".

Rad Jugoslovenske Akademije Znanosti i Umjetnosti, Zagreb: 7 (1869), 15 (1871), Matković, Petar, "Prilozi k trgovačko-političkoj istoriji republike dubrovačke".

77 (1885), 79, 81, 85, 89, 91, 94, 99, 101 (1890), Nodilo, N., "Religija Srba i Hrvata, na glavnoj osnovi pjesama, priča i govora narodnog".

97 (1889), Rački, Fr., "Boj na Kosovu"; Maretić, T., "Kosovski junaci i događaji u narodnoj epici".

166 (1906), Tropsch, Stjepan, "Njemački prijevodi narodnih naših pjesama".

168 (1907), Maretić, T., "Metrika narodnih naših pjesama".

182 (1910), Scherzer, Ivan, "Bugarštice".

229 (1924), Maixner, R., "Charles Nodier i Ilizia".

Revue Britannique, ou choix d'articles traduits des meilleurs écrits périodiques de la Grande Bretagne, tome VII, quatrième série, 1837, Paris, "Poésie populaire des races slaves" (translated from the North American Review); cinquième série, 1841, "Le Passé et l'Avenir des Slaves" (translated from the British and Foreign Review).

Revue des Deux Mondes:

Tome 4, Dec. 1843, "Mouvement des peuples slaves, leur passé, leur tendences nouvelles, cours de M. Mickiewicz", par A. Lebré.

Tome 6, Avril, 1854, "La poésie slave au dix-neuvième siècle", par Cyprien Robert.

Tome 55, Janvier, 1865, "La nationalité serbe d'après les chants populaires", par Dora d'Istria.

Tome 76, Juillet, 1868, "La poésie légendaire chez les Serbes", par J. de Cazaux.

Revue des Études Slaves, tome VI, 1926, Paris, Banašević, N., "Le cycle de Kosovo et les chansons de geste".

Spomenik, XXXVI, drugi razred 32, 1900, Beograd, Srećković, P. S., "Pregled istorijskih izvora o knezu Lazaru i Kraljeviću Marku".

Srpski Književni Glasnik, Beograd:

1 July, 1908, Jovanović, V. M., "John Bowring i srpska narodna poezija".

1 and 16 February, 1910, Jovanović, V. M., "Claude Faurel i srpska narodna poezija".

1 February, 1931, Prodanović, J., "Moralna i humana osećanja u srpskoj narodnoj poeziji".

1 April, 1931, Prodanović, J., "Psihološka opažanja i logička rasuđivanja u narodnoj poeziji".

Tait's Edinburgh Magazine for 1845, vol. XII, August, "Servia, the youngest member of the European family". (A review of A. A. Paton's book.)

Temple Bar, vol. XLVIII, September-December, 1876, "The Freeing of Servia"; also "The Poetry of Servia".

Ueber Kunst und Alterthum, von Goethe, 1824, 1825, 1826, 1827, Stuttgart.

The Westminster Review, vol. VI, No. XI, July, 1826, "Narodne Srpske Pjesme. Popular Servian Songs, collected and published by Vuk Stefanovich Karadzich" (reviewed by J. Bowring).

The Westminster and Foreign Quarterly Review, April, 1878, "The Literature of the Servians and Croats".

Zeitschrift des Vereins für Volkskunde, 19. Jahrgang, 1909, Berlin, Murko, Matthias, "Die Volksepik der bosnischen Mohamedaner".

Index

For EU product safety concerns, contact us at Calle de José Abascal, 56–1°, 28003 Madrid, Spain or eugpsr@cambridge.org.

www.ingramcontent.com/pod-product-compliance
Ingram Content Group UK Ltd.
Pitfield, Milton Keynes, MK11 3LW, UK
UKHW012329130625
459647UK00009B/169